MATE SELECTION
Across Cultures

After studying the mate selection process, we dedicate this work to Jeff Hamon and Valerie Ingoldsby, the best spouses to be found anywhere in the world.

MATE SELECTION
Across Cultures

Editors
Raeann R. Hamon • Bron B. Ingoldsby
Messiah College   Brigham Young University

SAGE Publications
International Educational and Professional Publisher
Thousand Oaks ▪ London ▪ New Delhi

For information:

Sage Publications, Inc.
2455 Teller Road
Thousand Oaks, California 91320
E-mail: order@sagepub.com

Sage Publications Ltd.
6 Bonhill Street
London EC2A 4PU
United Kingdom

Sage Publications India Pvt. Ltd.
B-42, Panchsheel Enclave
Post Box 4109
New Delhi 110 017 India

Printed in the United States of America

Library of Congress Cataloging-in-Publication Data

Mate selection across cultures / [edited by] Raeann R. Hamon,
Bron B. Ingoldsby.
    p. cm.
Includes bibliographical references and index.
ISBN 0-7619-2592-9 (Paper)
   1. Mate selection—Cross-cultural studies. 2. Courtship—Cross-cultural studies. 3. Marriage—Cross-cultural studies. I. Hamon, Raeann R. II. Ingoldsby, Bron B.
HQ801.M236 2004
646.7′7—dc21

                            2003011938

03 04 05 06 10 9 8 7 6 5 4 3 2 1

Acquisitions Editor:	Jim Brace-Thompson
Editorial Assistant:	Karen Ehrmann
Production Editor:	Sanford Robinson
Copy Editor:	D. J. Peck
Typesetter:	C&M Digitals (P) Ltd.
Indexer:	Jean Casalegno
Cover Designer:	Sandra Ng Sauvajot

Contents

Introduction

We are pleased to be able to offer this volume on mate selection to the interested reader. Our belief is that there are very few topics that would be of greater interest to more people than is the formation of this human bond. Decades of cross-cultural research establish that the family is the fundamental unit of society and that it is in fact a universal human social experience (Ingoldsby, 1995). In this collection, we attempt to increase global awareness by describing the meaningful processes, traditions, and practices associated with couple formation around the world. The reader will see numerous similarities and differences among and between the countries.

We enter our families of orientation by birth or adoption and then create our own families of procreation with adult cohabitation generally ritualized as marriage. When we consider the amount of time that we spend with spouses and the impact that these relationships have on our emotional lives, mate selection is likely one of the most important decisions that we will ever make. As it turns out, all societies have a vested interest in successful families and have values and customs that regulate the process of forming them. Exploring the similarities and differences around the globe and across our many societies is a fascinating enterprise.

This text investigates that most basic of human endeavors—couple formation—with particular attention to those relationships that lead to marriage. As the reader will see, some marriages come from agreements made between family members or arrangements negotiated by matchmakers, whereas others are the result of free choice with minimal or no apparent influence from others. Some view love as an essential precursor for marriage, whereas others hope that love will spring from a well-matched pairing. In any event, this book describes how single people and/or their families from various parts of the world negotiate the marriage market. How do individuals and/or their families filter through the pool of prospective mates to select the right partners? Which characteristics are most prized in a mate? How do variables such as personal and cultural values, religious beliefs and practices, political and historical contexts, socioeconomic standing, and interpersonal attraction affect the pairing process?

In addition to delineating the partner selection process, each chapter also examines the practices, customs, traditions, rituals, and ceremonies associated with the formalization of the relationship. As Bahn and Jaquez (2000) helped us to see in their article on Dominican bridal showers, associated rituals and traditions that are part of the marriage trajectory are very enjoyable and reveal important underlying values and information about a culture. Thus, in this text, the reader will also learn about the significance of symbolic fights between the families of the bride and groom, bride wealth negotiations, ring dances prior to the marriage, the wedding reception, *lucky days* on the Chinese lunar calendar for establishing the wedding date, the engagement party, unique foods that are prepared and shared among guests, wedding rings and related jewelry, motorcades, and marriage contracts.

Cultural diversity is so overwhelming that it is virtually impossible to do this topic justice. We have decided to highlight 14 countries from around the world. Most of them also have their own subcultural diversity. Although space limitations allow us to address in any detail only one or two of the dominant cultural patterns within each country, we are very cognizant of the tremendous diversity and variation that exist within any one country.

We have tried to represent the various geographic and cultural regions of the world. In part, each selection has been determined by our ability to identify a capable family scholar who could address that particular area. In all cases, the authors are recognized experts who have done considerable research and/or have lived in the countries about which they are writing.

We begin by examining couple formation in the United States. This provides a framework for comparison with the lesser studied groups. We then travel to the Caribbean and the people of the Bahamas. Afterward, our journey takes us from North America to South America and the Latin people of Ecuador. The republic of Trinidad and Tobago makes a logical ending point for the New World and bridge to the Old, given that this nation constitutes a blending of many peoples and cultures.

Crossing the Atlantic, our investigation takes us to Ghana in West Africa and then to Kenya in East Africa. After that, we move up into the Middle East with Islamic Egypt, Jewish Israel, and secular Turkey. Spain and the Netherlands contrast the more traditional Southern Europe with the quickly evolving North.

We continue our odyssey by moving east to the two most populous nations on earth: India and China. It is fitting to end our journey with Japan—situated in the Far East and with centuries of tradition but with a current modern Western focus.

It becomes clear that there are a number of dichotomies that emerge repeatedly in many of these cultures. The reader will find the stresses and shifts between concepts such as modernization/traditionalism, arranged marriage/free choice, love/family practicality, cohabitation/marriage, and collectivism/individualism.

Each chapter is designed to follow the same basic format. In this way, it is easier to make cross-societal comparisons and understand the flow of the mate selection process. Each chapter begins with one or two vignettes that serve as examples for how couples get together in that particular society. The vignette(s) is followed by some general background information on the country and its history. The literature on the partner selection process itself is then reviewed, culminating with an account of the ceremonies and customs that make up what we typically refer to as engagement and the wedding. Other information pertinent to the overall topic for that country may also be included. In each case, one or more relevant photos are also included to help personalize this most important and powerful human activity.

It is our hope that the reader will enjoy learning from this book as much as we enjoyed putting it together.

References

Bahn, A., & Jaquez, A. (2000). One style of Dominican bridal shower. In M. Hutter (Ed.), *The family experience* (3rd ed., pp. 121–132). Needham Heights, MA: Allyn & Bacon.

Ingoldsby, B. (1995). Family origin and universality. In B. Ingoldsby & S. Smith (Eds.), *Families in multicultural perspective* (pp. 83–96). New York: Guilford.

Acknowledgments

T his work is clearly a joint effort and would not have been possible without the expertise and assistance of a multitude of people. First and foremost, we thank our contributing authors for sharing the fascinating research they have been conducting in various countries around the world. We are grateful for their responsiveness to our feedback and their respect for deadlines. Second, we thank David M. Klein for helping us to hone our prospectus, shaping our goals and objectives for the book in response to the comments of reviewers (to whom we are also appreciative for their assistance in improving the volume). We are also very grateful to the staff at Sage Publications—Jim Brace-Thompson, Karen Ehrmann, Anna Howland, Sanford Robinson, and D. J. Peck—for answering our questions, offering support, and guiding us through the process. A special word of thanks is extended to Cherie K. Snavely, a student in family science, for her careful reading of final drafts. Finally, we are particularly indebted to Tonya L. Baker for her competent secretarial support, file management, and editorial work.

—Raeann R. Hamon
Bron B. Ingoldsby

Part I
North America

1

The Mate Selection Process in the United States

Bron B. Ingoldsby

Sarah and Joseph are members of a Hutterite colony in Montana. The Hutterites are theological cousins to the Amish, but they live communally and do allow modern technology for business purposes (Ingoldsby, 2001). There are more than 40,000 Hutterites, mostly in the Plains states and in western Canada. As is typical, Joseph is in his late 20s, but Sarah, at 20 years of age, is younger than most Hutterite brides. They have known each other for many years but have never "dated" in the sense that dating is known in the outside world. Their interactions have been mostly group activities in this or neighboring colonies as well as simple everyday interactions.

Once it was known that Sarah and Joseph desired to marry, they received the necessary permission from their parents and the church leaders, and then a date was set. Hutterite marriages are always on Sunday and usually in June or November. On the afternoon of the day before, the couple traveled to each home of the extended clan communal farm that makes up their colony, offering schnapps to each adult and receiving a blessing in return.

That evening at about 9 o'clock, everyone gathers in the dining hall for the Shivaree. There are crepe paper decorations, and in a reversal of the typical process, the men serve the refreshments. The evening consists of singing from the hymnal, usually in German but occasionally in English. The minister picks most of the songs, but sometimes the teenage girls will

3

begin a song. At around 11 o'clock, a gift (candles) is unwrapped while a colony elder tells jokes culled from Reader's Digest. *The adults then head for bed while the young people continue singing past midnight.*

The regular church service runs from 8:30 to 10:00 on Sunday morning, with the minister reading one of the standard sermons in German. Quite a few people are missing because there is a flu bug going around, and even the bride and groom are feeling a little under the weather. After a prayer, the wedding ceremony immediately begins. Joseph and Sarah are seated about halfway back, on the aisle and on separate sides. In Hutterite services, the men sit on one side and the women sit on the other, with the youngest in front. Joseph and Sarah come up to the front, holding hands and with her shoulder a little behind his.

The ceremony was written long ago and consists of questions concerning love and loyalty for the bride and groom to respond to as well as counsel. Part way through, Sarah, looking faint and nauseated, has to run out, but the preacher continues the ceremony until asked to stop. Sarah returns, and they are allowed to finish while sitting in chairs. They are declared husband and wife and then return to their regular seats in the congregation. There is no kiss or exchange of rings. After a final wedding song and blessing, they lead the group outside, where children wait with glitter and cameras.

While Joseph and Sarah rest in the afternoon, colony members visit the trailer that has been refurbished for them to look at the wedding gifts and cake that have been given to them. There is an evening dinner with more singing, and with that reception the festivities are over. The next day, Joseph and Sarah—the happy couple (happy because they are in love)— return to their normal work assignments in the community.

The wedding ceremony described above may not seem typical to the reader. However, diversity is the norm in the United States. It is the most diverse nation in the world. Nearly every race, ethnic group, and religious and political persuasion is represented. It is probably safe to say that every situation described in this text also occurs in the United States. As a result, any generalization can be an overgeneralization, and many will find that what they read in this chapter is not typical of their own experience. With that caveat in mind, in this chapter I do my best to describe the couple formation process.

Hutterite Couple on Wedding Day

Historical Context

Courtship in America began with the Colonial Puritans. European colonizers to the New World brought with them their Calvinist values on marriage, child rearing, and patriarchy. But the relative scarcity of women on the frontier increased their value and resulted in a modification of some customs. In addition to the many domestic chores, women could engage in just about any income-generating activity so long as it could be seen as helping the family (Ingoldsby & Smith, 1995).

Marriage was essential for a comfortable life, and courtships were brief. Because the Puritans were opposed to nonmarital sex, singlehood was viewed with suspicion. Single men were often forbidden by law to live alone or were taxed for the privilege. It was even forbidden for couples to ride off with sinful intent (Queen, Habenstein, & Quadagno, 1985).

In general, a young man would receive permission from the father of the woman he was interested in, and could then begin a courtship. Dating began with engagement. The woman could veto her parents' choices, but couples rarely married if the parents did not approve. It was hoped that love would develop over time, but dowries were often more important than romance. Marriage was a civil ceremony, with banns (the forerunner of today's wedding announcements) being posted about 2 weeks in advance (Ingoldsby & Smith, 1995).

Given the ban on premarital sex, the custom of *bundling* was most interesting. Fuel was expensive, so it was difficult to keep homes warm during winter nights. The suitor would often travel a considerable distance after a day's work to visit with his intended at her home during the evening. As a result, the woman could allow a favorite to get under the covers of her bed with her. The man and woman were to keep their clothes on, and a board might be placed in the middle to separate them. Church leaders opposed the practice, and parents typically stayed in the same room where the bundling occurred. The young woman controlled the practice, which allowed for a certain amount of physical closeness in an otherwise strict society. In spite of the controls and punishments (e.g., fines, public whippings), about one third of couples confessed to premarital relations during this time period (Ingoldsby, 2002).

People needed to get on with the work of adult life. Courtships, as mentioned before, were not long. In general, partners had known each other most of their lives, having met in the neighborhood or at church. The custom of chaperoning young people in their activities never developed in New England (Cate & Lloyd, 1992).

Even though the foundation of marriage was primarily economic, the ideas of love and personal fulfillment were developing as well. Men and women needed each other for simple survival and child rearing. This was especially true for the poor. However, friendship and love were beginning to be seen as increasingly important (Bulcroft, Bulcroft, Bradley, & Simpson, 2000).

Throughout most of the 1800s, men and women were divided socially into separate spheres of activity. This made it more difficult for young men and women to get to know each other. The rituals of courtship became more formal, with engagement announcements, rings, wedding ceremonies, and gifts all becoming more common (Cate & Lloyd, 1992; Murstein, 1974).

Economics continued to be the dominant force in determining mate selection. Men looked for brides who could contribute to their particular business enterprises as well as domestic tasks and child rearing (Bulcroft et al., 2000). Along with this, romantic love grew in importance. Women in particular desired stable love relationships based on communication. It was also women's responsibility to control the amount of physical affection in their relationships, and petting became less acceptable than it had been in the past (Cate & Lloyd, 1992).

Mate selection and marriage were transformed by the Industrial Revolution of the mid-1800s. Family life became more conjugal and private, and love emerged as the keystone for marriage (Bulcroft et al., 2000). The period from this point until World War I is known as the Victorian Era. During this time, men and women were even more separated by their respective spheres, and sexuality was feared and controlled (Ingoldsby & Smith, 1995).

Courtship customs for the middle and upper classes were very formal, with women receiving "callers." The man would request to visit the young woman in her home, and the rules of etiquette would let him know whether he was welcome to return. The partners' going off together to private places was frowned on, and parents kept a close eye on the couple until the relationship was close to marriage. Young people of the working class had to meet in public because their homes were not large enough to provide the necessary balance of privacy and chaperonage. By the end of this time period, the wealthy had begun to emulate the working class as they became attracted to the idea of "going out" for pleasurable activities together (Cate & Lloyd, 1992; Whyte, 1992).

Dating—relatively informal and unchaperoned activities—was the established vehicle for courtship by the 1920s (Murstein, 1974). Going to dances, movies, and "out to eat" were the staple activities. Because these occur in public and cost money, control of male-female interaction shifted from the women to the men. The automobile provided young people with unprecedented mobility and privacy and also contributed to a rise in sexual activity. Romantic love was firmly entrenched as the basis for marriage, and love and sex were promoted by the media. Although there was increasing pressure for women to provide physical pleasure to men in return for the money they spent on dates, the majority of young women had intercourse only after engagement (Cate & Lloyd, 1992; Whyte, 1992).

Willard Waller was an early and important scholar in the area of dating and courtship. Waller (1937) referred to the practices of his time as the "rating and dating complex." He found that the goal of dating among college students had shifted from love and mate selection to competition and pleasure. Men desired the most beautiful and popular women for the status that dating these women gave them among their peers, and men pushed for as much sexual interaction as was possible. Women rated their dates by things such as whether or not the men had cars, were athletic, and were popular. This short-term focus separated dating from true courtship, where it is useful to develop good communication skills and find a mate who is mature and ready for family life.

The 1930s and 1940s saw the rise of steady dating as an intermediate step between casual dating and engagement (Whyte, 1992). Rituals such as exchanging class rings and talking frequently on the phone developed as signs of mutual commitment. One result of this seems to be an earlier age of marriage. Young people not going on to college often married shortly after high school, and women in college openly planned to be married by graduation. By 1950, the average age at marriage was 20 years for women and 22 for men—the youngest average of the 20th century (Cate & Lloyd, 1992).

During the contemporary period (since 1960), marriage has continued to be an important rite of passage into adulthood. In spite of the decline in the functions that the family provides for society, marriage continues to be strongly desired by most young Americans. Weddings and honeymoons are often expensive and elaborate (Bulcroft et al., 2000).

The women's movement and improved methods of birth control contributed to more permissive attitudes regarding premarital sexual activity. First, intercourse became common while going steady rather than waiting for engagement. During the 1970s, girls began dating at 14 years of age and began going steady at 16. Dating itself has become much less formal since the 1980s, with young people just "hanging out" together. It has also become acceptable for women to do the asking and to pay for dating activities. During recent years, concerns about sexually transmitted diseases has contributed to a movement back toward more conservative practices in dating. Across time, it appears that most Americans are seriously involved with only one or two others before selecting their eventual lifetime mates. It seems that when one feels ready to marry, that person does so with the next person with whom he or she falls in love (Cate & Lloyd, 1992).

Average age at marriage had increased to 23.6 years for women and to nearly 26.0 for men by 1988 (Surra, 1990). Americans have come to depend on dating activities to provide them with the necessary decision-making information for eventual marriage. However, there is very little evidence that the process contributes to marital success in any significant way (Whyte, 1992).

Dating

In the past, we could say that young people tended to progress through a series of stages that led to marriage: casual dating, steady dating, informal commitment such as "pinning," cohabitation and/or engagement, and marriage. At each stage, fewer people were involved and the commitment was deeper. Modern dating is more fluid and informal, with the adolescents themselves, rather than society at large, in charge of the process.

Smaller communities are more likely to retain some of the formal aspects such as going to the prom and wearing the boyfriend's lettermen's jacket. In high school, the tendency is to date one's friends, so gossip and cliques can play an important role. In college, dating is the process for meeting new people, and it is more relaxed and involves fewer rules.

There are many reasons for dating in addition to mate selection. Dating can simply be for recreation or for the socializing experience of learning how to interact with members of the opposite sex. It can also play a role in one's social status.

Americans are more sexually permissive than they were in the past. The media, fashion, and music all encourage early intimacy in spite of more conservative preferences from parents and other sources. The double standard, which permitted sexual experiences for males but not for females, has been disappearing since the 1960s. Each couple now determines how intimate the man and woman will become (Cox, 2002).

About two thirds of all males and half of all females engage in sexual intercourse by 18 years of age. Females between 14 and 16 years of age are twice as likely to be sexually active today as they were just 15 years ago (Moore et al., 2000, cited in Cox, 2002). Data collected in Los Angeles (Upchurch et al., 1998, cited in Cox, 2002) indicate certain gender and ethnic differences in the timing of first intercourse. The median age for all groups is 16.9 years. The average age is 16.6 years for males and 17.2 for females. The average age is 16.6 years for Caucasians, 15.8 for African Americans, 17.0 for Hispanics, and 18.1 for Asian Americans.

The younger a person is when he or she begins to date, and especially to go steady, the more likely that person is to engage in premarital intercourse. Many young Americans begin dating by 14 years of age, and nearly 90% date before their 17th birthdays. In addition, about three fourths have been in steady relationships by 18 years of age. The earlier a person begins to date, the earlier he or she experiences steady dating, and it is in the latter category that the likelihood of sexual intimacy is high (Thornton, 1990).

Gays and lesbians are socialized in the same ways as are heterosexuals in American society. For example, men are expected to be more dominant and sexually active, whereas women are expected to focus more on nurturance and relationship development. As a result, same-sex couples are similar to cross-sex pairs in their dating approaches and expectations. Like cohabitating cross-sex couples, same-sex couples do tend to be less monogamous than heterosexual married couples. However, AIDS and the aging of the gay male population has resulted in a higher level of support for monogamous relationships (Rutter & Schwartz, 2000).

Studies indicate that 15% to 40% of men and women have been involved in some kind of dating violence. The rates are about the same for both men and women, and the perpetrators are more likely to be friends than strangers (Berkman, 1995; Cox, 2002). A woman's freshman year in college is the most dangerous time for date rape. One large survey (Sweet, 1985) concluded that 12% of college women have been rape victims and that half of the perpetrators were casual dates or romantic acquaintances.

Experience with physical violence varies by age, gender, race, and religion. More than half of those who experience courtship violence do so for the first time between 16 and 18 years of age. In one survey (Makepeace, 1987), approximately 12% of males and nearly 21% of females had experienced courtship violence of some kind. Ethnic and religious rates were as follows: Caucasian, 16.1%; African American, 28.9%; Hispanic, 23.8%; Asian American, 4.8%; Protestant, 14.5%; Catholic, 17.2%; Jewish, 5.9%, and Mormon, 16.6%. Violence rates were tied more closely to church attendance than to denomination. The rate for those who never or rarely attend services was 20.9%, whereas it was only 10.2% for those who attend more than once a week.

Levels of violence are similar for same-sex couples, but men are more likely to reciprocate violence than are women, and lesbians are more likely to leave their relationships than are heterosexual women. Jealousy plays a major role, as it does with cross-sex pairs (Renzetti, 1992).

Dating can be fraught with anxiety due to fear of rejection. As a result, many Americans are willing to present distorted images of themselves to increase the likelihood of success in getting dates. Nearly all Americans want to date people who are physically attractive, and so they attempt to make themselves more attractive so as to better compete (Buss, 1988).

In general, men will exaggerate their sincerity and commitment, as well as their income potential, whereas women will use various kinds of deceptions to enhance their physical appearance. The lying is in the direction of making oneself seem to be more similar to the desired date. Men and women do not differ in their tendency to deceive, and there is a greater likelihood for both groups to dissemble in relation to their physical appearances rather than their personalities (Rowatt, Cunningham, & Druen, 1999).

Another way of attempting to deal with the risks associated with love and dating is the use of technology in presenting oneself. Recent years have witnessed a proliferation of newspaper ads, dating services, and Internet matchmaking. In this way, people can describe themselves and what they are looking for while screening out candidates who do not appeal to them (Bulcroft et al., 2000).

An analysis of newspaper ads concludes that self-descriptions are generally positive. Men tend to stress their occupation, education, and financial status, whereas women tend to highlight their physical appearance. Women also desire men who are taller and older than themselves, whereas men desire just the opposite in potential companions (Cameron, Oskamp, & Sparks, 1977).

Mate Selection

In modern America, there are few arranged marriages. But free mate choice does not mean that a person can marry anyone. All societies have some marital regulations. There are three general rules or pressures that affect a person's ultimate marital decisions. The first is *exogamy*. This means that the individual must not marry someone within his or her own group or family. All cultures have incest taboos, and the United States follows the general Western rules that a person may not marry anyone closer than a second cousin. Some states allow marriages between first cousins in certain circumstances. Marriage to a minor (someone under 18 years of age) without parental consent is also prohibited.

Endogamy refers to the social pressure to marry someone within one's own group. There is a tendency to meet and marry people from the same racial, ethnic, religious, and social backgrounds. This is also called *homogamy,* especially when referring to research that indicates greater marital stability for those who marry individuals similar to themselves. Although it is still important to marry someone who shares one's basic values and role expectations, other aspects of endogamy have declined during recent years.

For instance, the number of interracial marriages has nearly doubled since 1980 and now accounts for about 5% of total marriages (Population Today, 1999, cited in Cox, 2002). Deviations from homogamy often indicate an exchange of economic resources on the part of the male for youth and beauty on the part of the female. Caucasians may marry black men or women who have higher educational attainment. Endogamy of religion has declined considerably during recent decades for Catholics, Protestants, and Jews (Surra, 1990).

There are about 1.5 million racially mixed marriages in the United States today. Interethnic marriages are also increasing as immigration contributes to a more diverse society. For example, about one sixth of all married Asian Americans and Latinos have spouses from different ethnic groups from their Asian and Latino backgrounds. These couples work to preserve their own traditions while merging into the shared overall identity of being Americans (Clemetson, 2000).

Another factor is *propinquity* or geographic nearness. The closer two people live to each other, the more likely they will meet and perhaps marry. For this reason, parents often send their children to selected universities so that they will interact with others who are homogamous to them in social class, education, religion, and/or other desired traits. There is a human tendency to be friends with those with whom it is convenient to interact.

There is also a tendency for women to marry "up" (hypergamy) and for men to marry "down" (hypogamy). That is, women seek mates who are a little older, better educated, and of equal or higher social status, whereas men prefer companions who are younger, shorter, and of equal or lower social status. This is referred to as the "marriage gradient." Complicating this process is the "marriage squeeze." For everyone to have a mate, there must be an equal sex ratio, but the numbers are seldom even. Although more males than females are born, by the adult years, women outnumber men. This is especially true for African Americans due to lower life expectancy rates and higher incarceration and homicide rates for African American males. This can make it difficult for a woman to find someone to marry at all, much less to marry up (Schwartz & Scott, 1994).

Not only is love by far the most important criterion for marriage, but most Americans seem to be looking for an ideal "soul mate" as well. One large recent survey indicated that 94% of young singles agree that the top priority is to marry one's soul mate. More than 80% of women indicated that it is more important for a husband to be able to communicate his deepest feelings than for him to be a good provider. However, only 42% believed that it is important to marry someone who shares one's religious beliefs (Whitehead & Popenoe, 2001).

The majority of women in college hope to meet their spouses while in school. This is becoming more difficult given that women now outnumber men in college. Perhaps more important, the noncommittal system of just "hooking up" rather than formal dating is making it more difficult for serious relationships to develop (Glenn & Marquardt, 2001).

The United States is an individualistic culture, where persons should be free to make their own decisions based on what is best for them. Romantic love and the idea of the existence of a perfect companion are promoted by the media. Many young Americans believe in the idea of living "happily ever after" (Sastry, 1999). This general mind-set is supported by research that U.S. teens, unlike those in collectivistic cultures, seek partners who are wealthy, attractive, sexy, exciting, and fun (Gibbons, Richter, Wiley, & Stiles, 1996).

Cross-cultural research (Medora, Larson, Hortacsu, & Dave, 2002) indicates that Americans score higher in romanticism than do young people in other countries such as Turkey and India. Romanticism refers to beliefs in an ideal mate and love at first sight and the belief that love can overcome all differences. Women, in particular, are becoming more romantic as time goes on.

Relationship satisfaction is consistently related to communication and self-disclosure. In addition, the particular style of love that individuals manifest is important. Passionate love (eros), friendship (storge), and altruistic love (agape) are positively related to relationship satisfaction, whereas game playing (ludus) is not (Meeks, Hendrick, & Hendrick, 1998).

Cohabitation has become a popular step in the mate selection process. There are more than 4 million unmarried-couple households in the United States today, representing a 400% increase from 1970. More than half of all first marriages are preceded by cohabitation. However, more than 40% of partners living together never marry each other, and of those who do, more than half divorce within 10 years. The divorce rate for those who do not live together first is just 30%. In spite of its high incidence, many studies confirm that cohabitation is negatively related to marital stability (Cox, 2002; Surra, 1990).

Although marriage remains very popular, it is increasingly acceptable to remain single or to postpone marriage to older ages. The stigma of being a bachelor or an "old maid" is disappearing as the media present a positive and exciting view of single life. Many remain single to avoid relationship problems and eventual divorce, especially now that women have sufficient access to economic resources to take care of themselves.

The average age of marriage today is about 25 years for women and 27 for men. The proportions of those over 35 years of age who have ever married dropped from 88.0% for men and 87.4% for women in 1960 to 68.5% and 71.2%, respectively, in 1999. The percentages are lower for African Americans than for Caucasians (Whitehead & Popenoe, 2001).

Length of courtship, as well as age, has been firmly correlated positively with marital success. Courtships of more than 2 years score consistently high as these couples have had the opportunity to experience and work out conflicts before marrying (Grover, Russell, Schumm, & Paff-Bergen, 1985). Thanks to cohabitation and elaborate wedding plans, modern Americans typically attain the age and length of courtship ideals put forth by family scholars.

Sexually conservative groups, such as Mormons, are exceptions. Age at marriage typically has been about 3 years younger than the national average, and length of courtship has been about half the national average for this religious group. For believers, marriage can be eternal if performed in one of the temples designed for special ordinances. As a result, the focus of mate selection is often on receiving a spiritual confirmation of one's choice. However, Mormons do tend to accept the romantic notions of love described earlier (Ingoldsby, 1992).

Marriage

Once a man and woman decide to marry, they become engaged. There are a number of useful reasons for an official engagement period. The two are now seen as an official couple or "item"—off limits to others. It allows others to know of their intentions and share in their excitement. Having made this formal commitment to each other, the man and woman may now see each other and their relationship in a different light. This can provide for a final, and perhaps more serious, testing of their compatibility.

There may also be a good deal of preparation that needs to be done for the up-and-coming marriage. The couple will need to begin by setting the date and selecting the location for the wedding. As with the other aspects of preparation, family members will need to be consulted because it affects them as well. Usually, female friends and family will throw one or more bridal "showers." Gathering in someone's home, they will play games and give practical gifts as well as intimate ones. The groom's friends may take him out for a final "bachelor party," which tends to be more raucous in movies than they are in real life.

Traditionally, the bride-to-be is given an engagement ring, typically a gold band with one or more diamonds. At the wedding itself, the man and woman may give each other matching wedding bands. All such customs have historical meaning (Ingoldsby & Smith, 1995), most of which has been lost to modern Americans. As a result, couples can pretty much do as they please in their observance of these practices.

There are best men, maids of honor, flower girls, ring bearers, photographers, and caterers to be selected. Usually, the bride's family pays for her gown and the groom's family covers the tuxedo expenses. The groom may also handle the details of the honeymoon. There are literally hundreds of magazines, books, and Web sites that give guidance on all the details of a proper wedding, including who is "responsible" to pay for each part.

Marie and Todd's Wedding Reception

Today, couples and their parents decide which aspects to follow and which ones to do in their own way. It has become more common for the two families to evenly divide the costs or for the bride and groom to handle most of it themselves.

The wedding itself is bigger and more expensive than it has been during most previous time periods. Close to 90% of couples have formal weddings, continuing with many of the rituals even though some of them (e.g., a white gown to symbolize virginity) have lost much of their meaning. There is a very large industry in the country to aid couples in planning their perfect weddings and honeymoons. The wedding day is seen as one of the very most important days in a person's life and, as a result, can be fairly stressful for those involved. Honeymoons can be extravagant vacations that, although rarely necessary for the initiation of physical intimacy, still have a strong symbolic value (Bulcroft et al., 2000).

Given the range of incomes among American families, it is striking how expensive modern weddings are estimated to be. One survey ("Weddings Cost Most," 2002) claimed that the average cost is about $19,000, ranging from a little more than $17,000 in southeastern and western states to nearly $32,000 in New York City.

Wedding magazines (see, e.g., *Bridal Guide*, 2002; *Elegant Bride*, 2002) are, for the most part, elaborate advertisements for beautiful gowns, jewelry, china, cakes, flowers, and related items. Along with them are a few articles on topics such as how to solve planning problems, budgeting guidance, and sexuality. Most couples will need assistance from some source to remember and plan for all of the many details that can go into a formal wedding. In general, the focus is on the bride.

Whether they are religious or not, most couples prefer to be married in a church by a minister. All that is necessary, however, is a marriage license from the county courthouse and a person authorized by the state to perform the ceremony. Each partner must show that he or she is at least 18 years of age or has parental permission and is not already married. A processing fee is required, and some kind of medical examination may be required as well.

It is not so simple for same-sex couples because only the state of Vermont recognizes any kind of civil union for them. Although religious and political opposition to gay marriages seems to be decreasing, it still remains strong. The large majority of gays and lesbians feel the same need to bond as do heterosexuals, and they prefer being in couple relationships. About 80% indicate that they would legally marry if they could (Rutter & Schwartz, 2000).

Conclusion

Over time, mate selection has moved from the hands of parents and into those of the couples themselves. As the United States has become more individualistic, marriage has come to be seen as the private responsibility of the two who are going to marry each other. Free mate choice prevails, and romantic love has become the essential—and sometimes the only—requirement.

The courtship process of dating and possible cohabitation is generally unsupervised by adults and tends to focus on recreation and pleasure, at least during its early stages. In spite of rising rates of singlehood or delayed age of marriage, being married remains an extremely important goal for most Americans. The wedding day itself is usually the most carefully prepared for and psychologically important day in a person's life, especially for the bride. Marriage is a key rite of passage into adulthood in modern society, and it provides the most important source of companionship in a busy and modern world.

References

Berkman, H. (1995, August 28). Attacks on women usually by intimates. *National Law Journal*, p. A14.

Bridal Guide. (2002, May–June). New York: Warner.

Bulcroft, R., Bulcroft, K., Bradley, K., & Simpson, C. (2000). The management and production of risk in romantic relationships: A postmodern paradox. *Journal of Family History, 25,* 63–92.

Buss, D. (1988). The evolution of human intrasexual competition: Tactics of mate attraction. *Journal of Personality and Social Psychology, 54,* 616–628.

Cameron, C., Oskamp, S., & Sparks, W. (1977, January). Courtship American style: Newspaper ads. *The Family Coordinator,* pp. 27–30.

Cate, R., & Lloyd, S. (1992). *Courtship.* Newbury Park, CA: Sage.

Clemetson, L. (2000, September 18). Love without borders. *Newsweek,* p. 62.

Cox, F. (2002). *Human intimacy: Marriage, the family, and its meaning.* Belmont, CA: Wadsworth.

Elegant Bride. (2002, Summer). New York: Pace Communications.

Gibbons, L., Richter, R., Wiley, D., & Stiles, D. (1996). Adolescents' opposite-sex ideal in four countries. *Journal of Social Psychology, 136,* 531–537.

Glenn, N., & Marquardt, E. (2001). *Hooking up, hanging out, and hoping for Mr. Right: College women on dating and mating today.* New York: Institute for American Values.

Grover, K., Russell, C., Schumm, W., & Paff-Bergen, L. (1985). Mate selection processes and marital satisfaction. *Family Relations, 34,* 383–386.

Ingoldsby, B. (1992). Mormon mate selection. *New Perspectives, 9,* 34–37.

Ingoldsby, B. (2001). The Hutterite family in transition. *Journal of Comparative Family Studies, 32,* 377–392.

Ingoldsby, B. (2002). Bundling. In *International encyclopedia of marriage and family relationships* (2nd ed., pp. 181–182). New York: Macmillan.

Ingoldsby, B., & Smith, S. (1995). *Families in multicultural perspective.* New York: Guilford.

Makepeace, J. (1987). Social factor and victim-offender differences in courtship violence. *Family Relations, 36,* 87–91.

Medora, N., Larson, J., Hortacsu, N., & Dave, P. (2002). Perceived attitudes towards romanticism: A cross-cultural study of American, Asian-Indian, and Turkish young adults. *Journal of Comparative Family Studies, 33,* 155–178.

Meeks, B., Hendrick, S., & Hendrick, C. (1998). Communication, love, and relationship satisfaction. *Journal of Social and Personal Relationships, 15,* 755–773.

Murstein, B. (1974). *Love, sex, and marriage through the ages.* New York: Springer.

Queen, S., Habenstein, R., & Quadagno, J. (1985). *The family in various cultures.* New York: Harper & Row.

Renzetti, C. (1992). *Violent betrayal: Partner abuse in lesbian relationships.* Newbury Park, CA: Sage.

Rowatt, W., Cunningham, M., & Druen, P. (1999). Lying to get a date: The effect of facial physical attractiveness on the willingness to deceive prospective dating partners. *Journal of Social and Personal Relationships, 16,* 209–223.

Rutter, V., & Schwartz, P. (2000). Gender, marriage, and diverse possibilities for cross-sex and same-sex pairs. In D. Demo, K. Allen, & M. Fine (Eds.), *Handbook of family diversity* (pp. 82–104). New York: Oxford University Press.

Sastry, J. (1999). Household structure, satisfaction, and distress in India and the United States: A comparative cultural examination. *Journal of Comparative Family Studies, 30,* 135–152.

Schwartz, M., & Scott, B. (1994). *Marriages and families: Diversity and change.* Englewood Cliffs, NJ: Prentice Hall.

Surra, C. (1990). Research and theory on mate selection and premarital relationships in the 1980s. *Journal of Marriage and the Family, 52,* 844–865.

Sweet, E. (1985, October). Date rape: The story of an epidemic and those who deny it. *Ms./Campus Times,* pp. 56–58, 84–85.

Thornton, A. (1990). The courtship process and adolescent sexuality. *Journal of Family Issues, 11,* 239–273.

Waller, W. (1937). The rating and dating complex. *American Sociological Review, 2,* 737–739.

Weddings cost most in NYC. (2002, May 3). *USA Today,* p. 1.

Whitehead, B., & Popenoe, D. (2001). *The state of our unions: The social health of marriage in America.* New Brunswick, NJ: Rutgers University, National Marriage Project.

Whyte, M. (1992, March–April). Choosing mates—the American way. *Society,* pp. 71–77.

Part II

The Caribbean and South America

2

"It's Better in the Bahamas"

From Relationship Initiation to Marriage

Raeann R. Hamon

Sherwin Sweeting, age 19 years, and Natalia Sands, 17, have known each other since primary school. They began hanging out when Natalia was 13 years old and Sherwin was 15. They saw each other a lot at school, church youth events, and the recreation center. Although they frequently gathered in groups of other young people, they often paired off to go to the beach, where they would talk and "make out." At 16 years of age, Sherwin quit high school to begin his career in crawfishing. He was fortunate to get with one of the good boats that consistently does well during fishing season. His future as a provider for his family looks bright. Over the Christmas holiday, Sherwin asked Natalia, one of the prettiest girls in her class, to marry him. They are planning a July wedding because all of the men will be home during that month. By then, Sherwin should have the couple's house built. Sherwin has been able to finance the construction of their new home from money he saved from his fishing trips and from a loan he received from old Mr. Albury, a wealthy man on the island of Spanish Wells who often lends money for such purposes. The house will be built on property that Sherwin's

AUTHOR'S NOTE: I acknowledge student research assistants Carol E. Johnson, Lauren A. Lutz, and Lori M. Kapiloff for their assistance with data collection, transcribing, and file management for this project.

21

parents gave him and will be located on the adjoining Russell Island because space on the island of Spanish Wells is at a premium.

Natalia has always been interested in Sherwin, so she is very pleased with the prospect of marrying him. She wants nothing more than to be a good wife and mother. She learned from her older cousin Bonnie's experience that it is not a good idea for a girl to leave the island and go to college if she wants to find a husband, given that all of the boys will likely be "taken" when she returns. Natalia learned from watching her mother how to take care of a husband who returns from weeks at sea. In preparation for upcoming surprise showers and the wedding, Natalia and her mother go to the stores on the island to select and set aside items the girl would like for gifts. Guests attending her shower and wedding will later purchase these items. Natalia is looking forward to her wedding but is even more excited about having children within a relatively short period of time afterward. She knows that children will keep her occupied while Sherwin is gone for long periods making a living for the benefit of the family.

The Bahamas is a coral archipelago composed of approximately 700 islands and 2,000 cays (low islands, coral reefs, or sand banks off the mainland), 18 of which are developed (Gordon, 2002). In a semi-tropical climate, the Bahamian islands cover an area of 5,382 square miles (*Background Notes*, 2000). Nassau, the capital, is located on New Providence Island and is the largest city, followed by Freeport, Grand Bahama Island. The remaining islands are referred to as the "out islands" or "family islands" and are typically less developed, more sparsely populated, and more intimate. It is not uncommon for young people on the family islands to move to urban areas in Nassau or Freeport to obtain employment, often leaving their children to be raised by their grandparents in what is deemed to be a safer, more hospitable family island environment. Located southeast of Florida, the Bahamas' proximity to North America, as well as its British colonial past, has strongly influenced lifestyles and economics since the 17th century. Whereas the Bahamian way of life once centered around piracy, slavery, bootlegging, and smuggling, today the Bahamas is heavily dependent on tourism and offshore banking, with the majority of the workforce employed in tourism, government, and financial services positions (Gordon, 2002). "It's Better in the Bahamas" is one slogan used to entice visitors to the isles of the Bahamas.

Originally inhabited by the Arawaks or Lucayans ("island peoples") and "found" by Christopher Columbus and the Spanish in 1492, the Bahamas became a refuge to a group of English and Bermudian religious dissidents, known as the Eleutheran Adventurers, in 1647. During the American War of Independence of the late 1700s, many royal loyalists and their slaves also fled to the Bahamas. The islands became a British Crown colony in 1717, attained internal self-government in 1964, and achieved its independence on July 10, 1973. Although the Bahamas continues to be part of the Commonwealth, its government is a constitutional parliamentary democracy.

The population of the Bahamas is about 304,000 people, with approximately 80% living within urban areas. Approximately 85% of the residents are of African heritage, 12% are of European heritage, and 3% are of Asian or Hispanic heritage. English is the official language, although many Haitian immigrants speak Creole. The Bahamas is described as a Christian nation, with most Bahamians being Protestants (e.g., Baptist, Methodist, Church of God, Anglican) and the remainder being Roman Catholic. Life expectancy is 71.0 years for men and 77.6 years for women (Gordon, 2002).

Research on Bahamian Couple Formation

Although there are numerous travel guides, a few books on Bahamian stories or culture (e.g., Glinton, 1994; Hamon, Hettinga, & Cobb, 1997; Turner, 1987), and multiple volumes on Bahamian history (Craton & Saunders, 1992, 1998; Saunders, 1990), very little current scholarly work is available on the contemporary Bahamian family, let alone couple formation processes in the Bahamas. In this chapter, I integrate what scholarly work does exist into a review of my own research.

During the past decade, I engaged in fieldwork in the Bahamas, focusing on Bahamian family life. Initially, I interviewed Bahamians about wives' tales and other old sayings and analyzed them for what they reveal about Bahamian family life. Several of these offered advice on preparing for marriage and prescriptions for marital success (Hamon, 1996). Most recently, I interviewed approximately 60 Bahamians, many of whom were dating or relatively newly married, about the process of couple formation from relationship initiation to marriage. Most of the interviews, consisting of a series of open-ended questions, were at least 1 hour in length and took place on the family islands of Eleuthera, Spanish Wells, and Harbour Island. Eleuthera, which means "freedom," is 110 miles long and 2 miles wide. Settlements are interspersed throughout the island and are connected by a single road, Queens Highway, which runs north and south on the island. To Eleuthera's north and accessible by boat is Spanish Wells, home to the descendants of the original Eleutheran Adventurers. The rhythm of this largely Caucasian, commercial fishing community is dictated by the crawfish (spiny lobster) season, as most residents of this cay, which is less than 2 miles long and one-fourth mile wide, make their livings from the sea and small farms. To the northeast of Eleuthera is Harbour Island, only 3 miles long by one-half mile wide and renowned for its pink sand beaches. About 1,000 people live on "Briland" and make their livings from fishing, farming, and positions related to tourism. Although there are a number of similarities among the islands, there is also a great deal of diversity among the practices and traditions of the residents of the islands.

Relationship Initiation

Given the small communities that exist on the islands, people typically know one another. Boys and girls frequently meet in school, in church, or at intersettlement activities (e.g., island festivals, church events). Some parents want their children to wait until they finish high school before they begin to go out with members of the opposite sex. More often than not, however, young people start sharing gestures (e.g., "giving you eyes," winking), calling one another on the telephone, asking friends to relay notes or messages, and meeting at community events (e.g., athletic events, dances, church activities) while they are still in school. Romantic pursuits frequently occur at younger ages on Spanish Wells. Although some—particularly those on Spanish Wells—believe that it is socially prescribed and more appropriate for females to wait for males to initiate relationships, several Eleutheran informants revealed that many girls and women have no qualms about being the aggressor. As one Eleutheran woman put it,

> We have quite a number of aggressive ladies who would [be the aggressor] if they see somebody they like. They are not going to wait for the guy to make the first call. And that goes for all age groups: teenagers, older women, and younger women. Our women know there [is] a scarcity of good men, so if they see someone interesting, they have no problem making the first move.

Marital Qualities

Although single Bahamians make their own choices in relationships, parents can and do influence their children about suitable partners. For instance, given the Christian character of the island, one young man noted, "If your parents are saved, they will pressure you to marry someone who is saved too."

One young unmarried man from a settlement on Eleuthera related,

> People are very open when it comes to expressing opinions. . . . There is no indicator like your own family. Once we start bringing individuals around . . . , there are qualities about them that they can see that you may not be able to see. . . . They would either praise you as to the good choice that you have made or advise you to proceed with caution [because] there's some shadiness about the individual's conduct or character.

Informants mentioned a number of characteristics that are of importance in looking for a partner, although distinctions were frequently made between characteristics of people they just wanted to date and have fun with and those they wished to marry. For their mates, Bahamian females desire responsible, honest, faithful, trustworthy, Christian, loving, industrious, hardworking, and family-oriented men. Most women want a husband who has a plan for his life—"not just living from day to day." For many women, it is desirable for a man to have built a house prior to marriage so that the newlyweds do not have to live with either set of parents. Many women want men who respect them and are willing to help with children and housework.

Given the incidence of Bahamian men who established extraresidential unions in the past (Otterbein, 1963), Bahamian women from all islands are emphatic about not wanting a man who is "a dawg," or "a player," that is, someone who takes advantage of women and is involved with more than one woman at a time. Such men are likely to have sweethearts (women with whom they have intimate relationships while they are also committed to a particular woman)—both before and after marriage—with whom they might also have "outside children" (children who are born to women other than their girlfriends or wives). One young Eleutheran woman noted, "Our society is based on having a main girlfriend and seeing another girl on the side. [These men] sleep around a lot." Another Eleutheran woman said that she wanted a husband who was committed to following a Christian lifestyle "because in the Bahamas we have a lot of religious people who believe in God, but their lifestyle, they don't see anything wrong with, if they are married to you, looking elsewhere for sexual satisfaction." Women on all three islands where interviews were conducted—Eleuthera, Spanish Wells, and Harbour Island—also did not want men who have drinking or drug problems, are currently married to other women, or have no life ambitions or goals. An Eleutheran man defined it this way:

Young men . . . on the islands . . . just want to live life as the days come. They're not too much really into getting married, settling down, having a family, start[ing their] own business. . . . Even if you walked around to some of our settlements . . . , under any tree you can see 10 to 12 guys just sitting down doing anything—nothing at all.

This laissez-faire approach to life is described as "anything buck up goes," meaning whatever happens happens. Some Eleutheran women, in particular, are willing to go outside their settlements and even off their islands to find a decent man.

On the other hand, Bahamian men dislike women who appear to be mostly concerned about the material resources they have to offer. Many resent the elevated status that cars, trucks, houses, and good-paying jobs give to certain individuals. A few Eleutheran men also indicated that they would prefer not to marry a woman who already has children.

Bahamian men want a wife who is physically attractive and inwardly beautiful; is from a respectable family; has a nice personality and good reputation (i.e., is not promiscuous); maintains similar likes, beliefs, and goals; would take care of her family and home; would be able to enhance her husband's identity; communicates effectively; and is industrious, independent, honest, trustworthy, responsible, dependable, well kept, stable, and supportive. One Eleutheran single man shared his mother's encouragement to marry someone from his own settlement when she would say, "Strange water is bitter, but water out of your own well is sweet." This advice highlights the importance of being able to obtain information about the partner's family of origin, whereas "if you go outside the community to marry, you don't know what you're going to pick up." Like women, men want to know as much as possible about a partner's family background.

Unlike Nassau, Eleuthera, and Harbour Island, where most of the women work to provide important family income, on Spanish Wells the general expectation is that the wife will stay home and care for her husband and children. This is particularly crucial given that there are relatively few available jobs and that the men are out smackfishing (i.e., fishing for spiny lobsters) for 4 to 6 weeks at a time. It is essential for the women to be at home to run their households and take care of their children. It is also an adaptive arrangement, given that during the 8-month crawfish season, men are home very infrequently. The lucrative incomes provided by fishing give Spanish Wells wives more financial freedom than other Bahamian wives might have so that it is not essential for the former to be employed outside the home. Thus, most men on that island want wives who will take good care of them and their children.

Intermarriage is perceived differently, depending on where one is. More than a quarter-century ago, McCartney (1976) noted that the formation of Bahamian boy-girl relationships was less likely to be based on family name, color, or social class (p. 25) than was previously the case. Today, intermarriage with people of other races is acceptable on Eleuthera. It is not unusual for black Bahamians to marry a Caucasian or foreigner. Despite this acceptance, however, it is typically intolerable to marry a Haitian. This is largely attributed to the social and cultural differences between the two groups as well as to the fact that Haitians are deemed to be "refugees" and of a "laboring class." Intermarriage with other foreigners, however, is generally accepted. Although Spanish Wells is more open than it was in the past, there is still the inclination and subtle pressure to marry within one's own race. If a person is unable to find a partner on Spanish Wells, he or she might find a match on another Bahamian island such as Abaco, where there is a larger proportion of Caucasian residents. Although marriages to foreigners (Caucasians from the United States or Europe) are acceptable, they are cause for worry because there is always the question as to whether the partners will be happy living on a small island with a different culture. For instance, a single man on Spanish Wells shared that although he dated a few American girls while in college, he would like to marry a Spanish Wells girl "because it would be [asking] a lot for another girl to come here and adapt to me being gone 3 weeks at a time [while fishing]. . . . It would be a tough adjustment."

Going Out

During previous generations, courtship was a formal affair. A young man, having consulted his own parents for their views of a particular young woman, would write a letter to the girl's parents to state his purpose and request permission to visit her (Otterbein, 1963; Saunders, 1990). Today, however, "going out" is much less formal and less supervised. As a matter of fact, whenever possible, most young people prefer to take their dates somewhere outside their own settlements so that people do not talk and make assumptions about the seriousness of their relationships.

In many ways, fewer recreational options exist on the family islands than on New Providence Island or Grand Bahama Island. For example, there is one movie theater in Governor's Harbour on Eleuthera, but it has been closed for several years. When it was open, it provided an entertaining place to go not only for Eleutherans but also for those from Harbour Island and

Spanish Wells, who would have to take a ferry across the water to the main island to attend. There are also a few dance clubs on Eleuthera and Harbour Island where couples can dance to music provided by a disc jockey or live band. Because of religious beliefs and influences, no nightclubs exist on Spanish Wells. Until recently, there was only one game room and a couple of snack shops where couples could go to talk and eat. Now, there is a large recreation facility that includes all sorts of video games, a workout room, and pool tables. The beach is also an important location for hanging out in groups or dyads. On Spanish Wells, most couples go to the beach at night to walk, talk, and "make out." Boat rides to neighboring, more secluded islands and cays also make for an enjoyable time. Although couples typically reserve going out to dinner for special occasions, there are some local restaurants that are notoriously good places to take a special someone.

Church events are very important contexts for getting together. On Spanish Wells, for instance, the three churches on the island hold their youth meetings and events on different nights of the week so that young people can attend all three churches' programs. On all three islands where interviews were conducted, church events frequently mix inhabitants of the various settlements via special services or programs.

Organized activities play an important role in going out. Athletic events (e.g., basketball games, baseball games) are a great place to meet and spend time together. Participating in sports or watching games together provides an important forum for mingling the sexes. Nearly every settlement also sponsors some sort of annual festival. These events, which last for several days, offer places for island residents to congregate and also serve as a homecoming opportunity for folks who needed to leave the island to find employment or for other reasons. For instance, the Pineapple Festival in Gregory Town, the Bay Fest in Hatchet Bay, the Heritage Fair in James Cistern, Junkanoo in Nassau, and the Regatta on Harbour Island offer important contexts for sharing unique cultural traditions and are important meeting places for sharing fun and entertainment.

More mature couples, or those with greater means, might also go off the island to nurture their relationships. Older couples, from Spanish Wells in particular, might take trips together with a group of friends to Nassau or Disney World. They might also go on a cruise or skiing trip.

Cars play an important role in going out. One young man from Spanish Wells lamented his drop in popularity when he no longer had a car: "The time I had my car, I must have went out with seven or eight girls— even more than that! Then I sold my car and nothing, no more." On Spanish Wells, even though most places are within easy walking distance, cars are necessary for "going riding" or "parking on Russell

Island." Cars offer a useful context for interaction. One young mother from Spanish Wells, herself married at 18 years of age, said, "I don't like the way we date. I hope my daughter doesn't wind up in a bush [secluded area covered with scrubby plants and trees] somewhere with a boy. . . . But it's going to happen because that is the way we date." Lack of transportation can be a problem for some, especially those who are not old enough to drive or who cannot afford a car. Not having a vehicle is particularly difficult on larger islands, such as Eleuthera, where there are great distances between settlements.

Sexual intercourse typically occurs early in relationships on the islands. More than 30 years ago, McCartney (1971) reported that sexual intercourse before marriage was "now becoming the rule rather than the exception" (p. 50). More recently, one woman from Spanish Wells said, "Sexual relationships start early because there aren't a lot of options for couples around here, so it's very difficult to abstain." There is also a lot of pressure to have sex, and even though churches discourage premarital sexual contact, most Bahamians engage in premarital intercourse. Because of the accelerated nature of couple formation on Spanish Wells in particular, most report that sexual activity begins by 14 or 15 years of age.

Privately purchasing contraceptives is also a challenge on small islands. Three young women from Spanish Wells revealed that although those working at the health clinic "can't say nothing" about who buys contraceptives, the merchants in local pharmacies or food stores "talk" about who is making such purchases. Thus, a lot of young men purchase condoms when they are visiting other islands, and some young women might use other women's prescriptions for birth control pills to avoid being the subject of others' conversations. If a young woman got pregnant prior to marriage on Spanish Wells, it would be a "hot topic." On Eleuthera and Harbour Island, children being born outside of marriage are much more common, although parents often are distraught about it.

A number of signs demarcate a more serious relationship, the most obvious of which is seeing two partners together all of the time. For instance, a resident of Spanish Wells made an important distinction: "They don't go for dates in the day here—all at night . . . unless you are a couple. [Then] you'd be together in the day." Going to the home of each partner to meet and interact more with each other's parents, meeting each other every evening, attending church together, and exchanging school rings or some other objects all are indicative of a greater level of involvement. For example, on Spanish Wells, others know that a relationship is serious when partners go out on a boat together or when a girl drives her boyfriend's motorbike around the island while he is away fishing. In addition, partners might choose to spend their money differently and change their behavior (e.g., less drinking) when they become more committed to their relationship. Also, relationships with opposite-sex friends might be curtailed so that there is no appearance of impropriety or "sweethearting."

Religious proscriptions and general public sentiments discourage couples from living together or "shacking up" prior to marriage. The churches to which many of these folks belong do not approve of cohabitation. McCartney (1976) concluded that "legal Christian marriage" is still the ideal, with "common-law arrangements" as "second-rate substitutes" (p. 27).

Engagement

A half century ago, several months after a young man began to court a young woman, he would send an engagement letter and ring to the young woman and her family. The letter was a legally binding document that represented the man's intention to marry the woman (Otterbein, 1963). Out of respect, a man in contemporary Bahamian culture may speak to a woman's parents about his desire to marry their daughter prior to formalizing and publicizing the engagement. The man typically asks the woman either in private or in front of others at a surprise engagement party. Given the smallness of the communities and the islands, it does not take long for word to spread when people get engaged.

Although not practiced on Spanish Wells, engagement parties often occur on Eleuthera. An engagement party can be planned with the prior knowledge of both the woman and the man, or it can be a surprise to the bride-to-be. In either case, family and friends are invited to share in witnessing the man's formal proposal or in hearing the couple's formal engagement announcement. A minister is invited to attend and to pray over the ring, which is then placed on the ring finger of the bride-to-be's left hand. A dinner and party ensue, with alcohol flowing freely.

A ring is usually an important symbol of an engagement and typically includes either a diamond solitaire or a band of diamonds. Rings can range in price from $500 to more than $5,000. Most rings are purchased in Nassau, on Harbour Island, in the United States (often Miami), or via a mail-order catalog. Some engagement rings are purchased as part of a wedding band set. Nonetheless, plenty of people are usually interested in seeing the ring and paying particular attention to the size of the stone.

Sharing of advice is common and expected at engagement parties. Many older, more experienced folks impress on the newly engaged that marriage is not to be taken lightly; it is a serious thing. For instance, one man from Harbour Island said that his mother-in-law impressed on him the importance of fidelity when she said, "Don't let another woman climb your guinep tree or your guineps will go sour" (Hamon, 1996). A grandmother of another man urged him to "be loyal to your wife. Let her be first." Some men are encouraged to save their money so that they can have houses when they marry. One woman was told, "Never take your business on the street. Always deal with your intimate affairs at home." "Expect turbulence in marriage," "Never go to bed angry," "Talk to each other," and "Keep the marriage interesting" are among the kinds of tidbits that women will share with each other.

Broken engagements are not uncommon and are usually the result of infidelity or major conflicts. Engagement rings may or may not be returned in such cases.

Bridal Showers

Female friends and family members often surprise a bride-to-be with one or more showers, usually as the wedding date nears. On Spanish Wells, the bride-to-be is literally showered or soaked by a hose or bucket of water on entering the party. Friends are sure to have a dry change of clothes so that the woman can enjoy the remainder of the festivities more comfortably. Lots of time and energy go into the planning of showers, and food and drinks are plentiful. Peas and rice, macaroni and cheese, cole slaw, ham, fried chicken, turkey, beef, crawfish, conch fritters, and cake are among the delectable treats that are provided by various people. Participants bring gifts, which are sometimes organized around a theme (e.g., kitchen, lingerie, linen) and which on Eleuthera are in lieu of gifts brought to the wedding. Brides across the Bahamas often register for desired items at local stores. Gifts range from lingerie to microwave ovens, to pots and pans, to bathroom towels. The bride-to-be opens the gifts in front of her guests while her maid of honor records who gave what so that thank-you cards can be mailed later.

Games provide great fun for attendees. One game requires women to pull clothes (e.g., a bikini) out of a bag and wear them or to pull vegetables or other foods (e.g., onion, pepper) out of a bag and eat them. Another game requires each woman to place a spoon, which has string tied to it, down their clothes and then pass it to the next woman in line. Another activity requires women who are unable to touch the ground with their hands to consume an alcoholic drink such as rum and soda. A guest might win a prize for having her own birthday closest to the bride's birthday, for guessing the number of candies in a jar, or for having an anniversary date

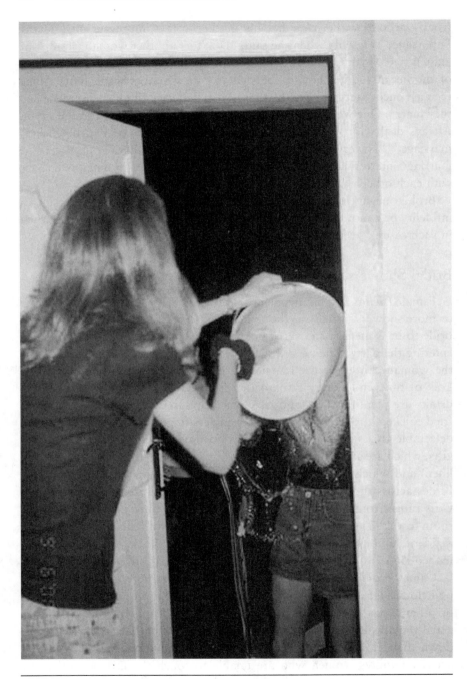

Bride-to-Be Being "Showered" at a Bridal Shower

closest to the bride's wedding date. In the settlement of James Cistern, there is a game where women had to remove an article of their clothing each time they were caught crossing their legs during the shower. During another popular activity, guests put questions into a hat, and the bride then has to answer the questions after pulling them from the hat. Many of the questions are very personal and sometimes embarrassing. Examples may include "Is [name of husband-to-be] good in bed?" and "How will you treat [husband-to-be's] child [from a previous relationship]?" Although the bride is expected to answer all inquiries honestly, she can choose not to answer. In another event, it is not unusual for guests to be asked to take some squares of toilet paper from a roll or some string from a ball of thread at the beginning of the shower. Later on in the shower, guests are asked to roll the tissue or thread around their fingers and to offer the bride advice until the tissue or thread is completely rolled.

Stag Parties or Bachelor Parties

Usually the night before the wedding, male friends and family members of the groom-to-be congregate at a home to drink (even though all drinking is discouraged on Spanish Wells) and have a good time. Food is plentiful, and guys crack jokes, talk about the changes that will come in the life of the groom-to-be, and sometimes play dominoes. Women not associated with the wedding, or possibly a stripper, might be part of some of these festivities.

Jump-in-Dance

The jump-in-dance might occur the week prior to the wedding, particularly within some more traditional black Bahamian communities that cherish cultural practices:

> People would come together and have what we call "Ring Fling." And it's a folk lore dance . . . where men and women would be in a circle and then one individual would go in the circle and dance while everyone else claps, and then you would go to a partner [usually of the opposite sex] and dance before [him or her]. And that one would come in and dance [for a short period of time and then go] to the next one. So, it's more or less like a cultural dance. . . . It's very festive with goat-skinned drums and cowbells. (as described by an informant)
> Dancing, to songs like "There's a Brown Girl in a Ring," is lively and rhythmic. (*Bahamas School Projects*, n.d.)

Pastors and priests frequently require premarital counseling for Bahamian couples planning to marry within the church, although the number of sessions, topics, and mode of delivery can vary widely. Some require only one brief session, whereas others insist on up to 6 months of guidance and instruction on topics such as finances, responsibility, compatibility, spirituality, sex, children, and family of origin. Although much of this can be performed on the family islands, sometimes couples are encouraged to participate in premarital weekend workshops in Nassau. Tourists, on the other hand, need only reside in the Commonwealth of the Bahamas for 24 hours prior to their weddings unless they expect to be married within the Catholic Church (*Bahamas Wedding Circle*, n.d.).

Wedding

Bahamian law dictates that people must be 18 years of age to marry without their parents' consent. According to the Bahamian Department of Statistics (2000), most women are 25 to 29 years of age and most men are 30 to 34 when they marry. Most informants on Eleuthera and Harbour Island suggested that people typically marry between 20 and 27 years of age. On Spanish Wells, younger marriages are the norm, with most occurring between 16 and 20 years of age. One young woman from Spanish Wells who married at 19 years of age shared a common philosophy of this island:

> Some people look at us getting married young as not a good thing, but . . . [consider] this point. When you are young, you are not set in your ways, so you [are] going to grow together and change together. . . . In marriage, you need to compromise. You can't just want it all your way. We think that is why they get married young. . . . They will stay together because they grow together.

There is a great deal of preparation for a wedding. Brides and their bridesmaids often go to Nassau or the United States (usually Florida) to purchase gowns, or they get a local seamstress to make them. They might also have their hair and makeup done in Nassau, or they might have a hair stylist come to their island. Although no blood tests are needed, a marriage license is necessary and can be purchased for $40 at the local government office on their island.

A wedding is a "big to do"—a huge social event on the island. The entire community, and sometimes the entire island population, is invited, so the church (usually the bride's) is typically full. On Spanish Wells, most weddings happen between May and July or during a lull in the crawfish season, which occurs right after the return (September through the beginning of

Bride and Groom on Eleutheran Beach

November) from the first big trip of the season so as not to interfere with the fishing season.

The couple's budget dictates how lavish the wedding will be. Although the bride's family often pays for the wedding, some families of the bride and groom share costs. In the case of a second marriage, the groom or couple typically pay for a greater portion of the expenses. In addition, it is quite common for other family members and friends to contribute major items for the wedding and reception (e.g., photographer, food or cake for the reception, music). Flowers are imported but can be purchased from a florist on the island, in Nassau, on Abaco, or in the United States. They decorate the location of the wedding (usually a church) and the reception area. The photographer takes plenty of pictures, using the church sanctuary, the beach, and beautiful gardens as backdrops.

Just as in the past when the bride was "put away" (the bride would stay with a nearby relative to ensure that the groom would not see her when he went to his future in-laws' house to inquire about the wedding plans [Otterbein, 1963]), current tradition dictates that the groom cannot see his bride on the day of the wedding until the ceremony. Another common practice on Harbour Island and Eleuthera is that the bride is almost always late—anywhere from 10 minutes to 3 hours—although this is usually attributed to last-minute things that can go wrong.

A pastor or priest most often performs the service, although certain governmental officials may also perform marriage ceremonies. Music is an integral part of the service. There might be a soloist singing musical selections, or there might be an organist, a drummer, a flutist, or another instrumentalist providing music. It is not uncommon for recordings of contemporary love songs to be played as well. On Spanish Wells, the most popular wedding hymns are O Perfect Love and The Voice That Breathed Over Eden.

The bride's friends and family sit on one side of the church, and the groom's friends and family sit on the other. Guests sign a book when they arrive and prior to being seated. The groom and his men stand in front and await the bridesmaids as they proceed down the aisle. Sometimes, they meet the bridesmaids halfway and escort them to the front. The bridal party might consist of a maid/matron of honor, bridesmaids, junior brides, petal droppers, flower girls, a best man, groomsmen, junior grooms, and a ring bearer. The petal droppers, flower girls, junior brides, and bridesmaids precede the bride down the aisle. The attendees stand as the bride enters the sanctuary and is escorted down the center aisle by her father, mother, and/or significant other. During the ceremony, the bride and groom exchange rings, hear a brief message/sermon from the pastor or priest, and exchange vows. The bride and groom sign the register, either off to the side

Bride and Groom on Spanish Wells Signing Registry With Pastor

and in front of the congregation or in a back room during the ceremony, with the maid/matron of honor and best man serving as witnesses. Immediately afterward, the bride and groom are pronounced husband and wife, and they kiss. After the ceremony is over, the newlyweds leave the church with their bridal party and ride around the island in cars, honking their horns.

Wedding Reception

Receptions are like a feast, often with more people in attendance than were at the wedding. They are held in a church fellowship hall, a community hall, a schoolhouse, or a nice restaurant. Although the meal is sometimes catered, friends and family members will frequently contribute food for the reception in an attempt to reduce costs. Dishes are likely to include peas and rice, barbecued chicken, fish, crawfish, macaroni and cheese, potato salad, and/or egg and tuna sandwiches.

Major events at the reception include eating, cutting and feeding each other cake, throwing the garter and bouquet, and toasting the bride and groom. Although drinking alcohol and dancing are commonplace at many receptions on Eleuthera and Harbour Island, nonalcoholic beverages (e.g., soda, apple cider, ginger ale) that look like champagne are served at most receptions on Spanish Wells and in a few more religiously conservative settlements on Eleuthera. On Spanish Wells, although the formal reception is "dry," a "wet reception" might take place in someone's yard after the formal reception. That way, those who disapprove of alcohol consumption are not offended at the reception.

Honeymoon

Honeymoons are not a given in the Bahamas because not everyone can afford them. If financial resources are available or a trip is given as a gift, however, a couple might get away for a week or two. Popular destinations include the United States (e.g., Miami, Orlando, Disneyland, the Poconos, Las Vegas, Atlantic City, Myrtle Beach), another Bahamian island (e.g., New Providence), or another Caribbean island (e.g., Barbados, Jamaica). Cruises are also quite popular. A main objective of the honeymoon is to just get away from everyone else for a while.

Housing

Housing for newlyweds is expensive and in short supply. Because the provision of a home has been (Otterbein, 1963), and continues to be, an expectation for the groom, there is pressure on men to plan ahead about where they will live. The ideal is that a young man will save enough to build a house prior to his wedding. On Eleuthera,

> Old people say, before a bird lays, she builds a nest to lay her eggs and adds her young ones in. The young man should learn from the bird. Today they go, get wives and children, and have no house to put them in. Don't let the bird be wiser than you. (Hamon, 1996, p. 62)

Financing the purchase of an existing home or constructing a new home can be quite a challenge. On Spanish Wells, boys quit school to begin fishing and saving for the construction of their homes. Many parents give their children some land on which to build their houses. Any additional money needed is borrowed from a bank, a family member, or a wealthy member of the community. Financing is even more problematic on Eleuthera and Harbour Island, where stable employment and collateral are issues. Given the desirability of these islands as locations for winter vacation homes for foreigners, escalating market prices are more challenging to accommodate. Difficulty in obtaining loans from the bank forces men to build their houses in stages over months or years. Many men participate in an *asue,* that is, a collective savings plan in which participants "throw" a specified amount of money each week to an "asue-keeper" for a predetermined length of time (Glinton-Meicholas, 1995, p. 16). Each asue participant, on his or her designated week, receives a "draw" or large amount of money that can be used, for example, to purchase supplies for a phase of the home construction project.

Singlehood

There is great expectation and cultural pressure to get married on Spanish Wells. One young man related, "Around here, people think that something is wrong with you if you don't get married." Unmarried people in their mid-20s describe themselves as "badgered a lot about still being single." Going to college off the island throws these young people "off-time" or out of sequence with their peers because most of those in their age cohort are married or nearly married by the time they return from college. One young woman from Spanish Wells who went off the island to obtain a college education lamented that on her return there were no eligible males available for her to marry. Such individuals are likely to go off the island or marry a foreigner.

On all three islands, there is a subtle message that something must be "wrong" if a person is not married. There is some suspicion that a single person might be a gay or lesbian. According to one man on Eleuthera, "The Bahamian society is not the society to be in if that is the case. . . . People here are not accepting." Another man said that "Bahamians do not accept open gayness" and that he did not believe gay marriage was even a remote possibility in the near future. The expression of affection in public by gay or lesbian couples is very unlikely. Most believe that Nassau would be a much more hospitable place for persons in gay relationships.

Conclusion

Finding a partner continues to be an exhilarating and sometimes heart-breaking venture in the Bahamas. Most people eventually marry partners with traits similar to their own. The engagement period serves important social and relationship-building functions. The wedding also provides an important public witness of this life-changing event. These common rituals engage the families and community in the life of the newly established couple, lending support for the partners' lives together.

References

Background Notes: The Bahamas. (2000, July). Retrieved July 19, 2002, from www.state.gove/www/background_notes/bahamas_0007_bgn.html

Bahamas Department of Statistics. (2000). *Report of 2000 Census of Population and Housing.* Nassau, Bahamas: Ministry of Economic Development.

Bahamas School Projects. (n.d.). Retrieved June 17, 2002, from www.bahamas.com/culture/school_projects/index.html

Bahamas Wedding Circle. (n.d.). Retrieved July 7, 2002, from www.bahamas-weddingcircle.com/html/the_bahamas.html

Craton, M., & Saunders, G. (1992). *Islanders in the stream: A history of the Bahamian people,* Vol. 1: *From aboriginal times to the end of slavery.* Athens, GA: University of Georgia Press.

Craton, M., & Saunders, G. (1998). *Islanders in the stream: A history of the Bahamian people,* Vol. 2: *From the ending of slavery to the twenty-first century.* Athens, GA: University of Georgia Press.

Glinton, P. (1994). *An evening in Guanima: A treasury of folktales from the Bahamas*. Nassau, Bahamas: Guanima Press.

Glinton-Meicholas, P. (1995). *More talkin' Bahamian*. Nassau, Bahamas: Guanima Press.

Gordon, L. (Ed.). (2002). *Insight guides: Bahamas*. Maspeth, NY: Langenscheidt Publishers.

Hamon, R. R. (1996). Bahamian family life as depicted by wives' tales and other old sayings. *Marriage and Family Review, 24,* 57–87.

Hamon, R. R., Hettinga, K. T., & Cobb, S. G. (1997). *"Old people say . . ."*: Tales *from Eleuthera*. Grantham, PA: Messiah College Reprographics.

McCartney, T. O. (1971). *Neuroses in the sun*. Nassau, Bahamas: Executive Ideas of the Bahamas.

McCartney, T. O. (1976). *Bahamian sexuality*. Nassau, Bahamas: Timpaul Publishing.

Otterbein, K. F. (1963). *The family organization of the Andros islanders: A case study of the mating system and household composition of a community in the Bahama Islands*. Pittsburgh, PA: University of Pittsburgh Press.

Saunders, G. (1990). *Bahamian society after emancipation: Essays in nineteenth and early twentieth century Bahamian history*. Nassau, Bahamas: D. Gail Saunders.

Turner, T. (1987). *Woman take two*. New York: Vantage.

3

Mate Selection Preferences and Practices in Ecuador and Latin America

Paul L. Schvaneveldt

Juan, age 25 years, and Maria, 23, both are residents of Guayaquil, the largest city in Ecuador. Juan is a recent graduate of a university and is employed by a bank as an assistant manager. Maria is a senior majoring in accounting at a local university, where she and Juan met more than a year ago. Juan and Maria share a common group of friends who gather often to discuss work, school, music, boyfriends/girlfriends, politics, careers, and other activities. Juan and Maria get to know each other better as the group of friends attend movies together, go dancing, and attend parties at others' homes. Juan and Maria gradually see each other more often and do things together informally. Eventually, their relationship develops into a serious and committed romance, with both dating each other exclusively. Notions of romance tend to dominate their relationship at this stage. For example, they write romantic poems, sing songs, and offer gifts as tokens of their love and affection. Eventually, these romantic feelings become so strong that Juan and Maria decide to marry. This is a private decision that is made by the couple, with Juan asking Maria to marry him, as is usually the case in Ecuador (personal interview, J. Andrade, superintendent of schools,

Cuenca, Ecuador, 2002). (urban middle/upper socioeconomic status couple in Ecuador)

Pedro is 19 years old and works for a local construction company as a laborer. He had to drop out of school at 14 years of age to help support his family financially. Monica is 17 years old and also left school early to help support her family. She spends most of her time working with her family doing household chores, caring for younger siblings, and attending to livestock (e.g., a milk cow, chickens, sheep). Pedro and Monica live in the same rural village and have known each other throughout their childhood. Pedro and Monica begin to date informally and do things together with their group of friends. Eventually, they develop strong romantic feelings for each other and become known as an exclusive couple. Eventually, Pedro and Monica become sexually intimate and Monica becomes pregnant unexpectedly. Neither family can afford a formal wedding ceremony, so Pedro and Monica decide to live together (personal interview, M. Martinez, parish priest, Village of Turi, Ecuador, 2000). (rural/lower socioeconomic status couple in Ecuador)

The social stratification that is evident in the above examples illustrates the differences in mate selection practices in Ecuador. This chapter provides an overview of the historical influences, demographic characteristics, theoretical perspectives, and practices and preferences of couple formation in Ecuador and Latin America.

History

Latin America has some features in common with North America. Latin America had an indigenous people who were conquered by colonialist Europeans. There were slaves imported from Africa and a plantation economy. Colonial status was eventually overcome, but the historical legacy was a mixture of races, ethnicities, and socioeconomic status (SES) groups. The colonizers in Latin America were from Spain and Portugal and were strongly influenced by Catholic and Moorish ideologies. Thus, modern Latin America is predominantly Catholic, speaks mostly Spanish or Portuguese, and has stark divisions in wealth and economic opportunity (De Vos, 2000).

Historically in South America, the European colonists were mostly men, with a men/women ratio of perhaps 6 to 1. Many of these men had sexual relationships with members of indigenous populations; consequently, much of the population in Latin America is Mestizo, meaning a mixture of European and native blood. In addition, plantation owners often imported slaves from Africa and would have sexual relations with female slaves, with their offspring sometimes being referred to as Mulatto or Zambo. Thus, people in contemporary Latin America may be white (European descent), Mestizo, Mulatto, indigenous (Indian), or black, with Mestizo as the most common racial category. Little scientific information is available on race relations in Latin America in regard to family life.

The feudal system of the colonists significantly influenced marriage and fertility practices. Because many of the indigenous people and slaves were treated as property, many were not legally married to their partners, and a tradition of having sexual relations with one's partner without legal marriage emerged. This practice and custom is still prevalent in Latin America in the form of cohabitation or *Union Libre*. Some of the native populations practiced Union Libre prior to colonization by Europeans. Price (1965) described "trial marriages" as an important first step toward marriage in Andean cultures since the days of the Incas. Premarital sexual relations were common and socially approved of in the highlands of Peru during pre-Columbian times. References to the custom of trial marriage are found as early as 1539, which was only a few years after the arrival of Pizarro. A trial marriage generally precedes a Catholic wedding among the contemporary Quechua, a group of indigenous people from the Andes mountain region. In the community of Vicos in the Andes Mountains of Peru, courtship behaviors include considerable sexual freedom, playful fighting, and gift exchanges. There is free mate choice, but the Quechua are very endogamous and virtually all of them marry partners within 10 miles of the community. The period of cohabitation is called *Watanaki*, which means "having a year together." The young man generally just informs his parents that he wishes to enter into Watanaki with a particular young woman. The parents give their approval and then visit the woman's parents, who usually feign surprise and indignation before giving their consent. Only about 7% of contemporary marriages in Vicos are not preceded by this trial.

Demographics of Marriage and Mate Selection in Latin America

The average age at first marriage in Latin America is 22 years for women and 26 for men. The proportion of men or women ever married by age

50 years is 90% to 91%, very similar to that in the United States. The age at first marriage is an important indicator of women's employment status, education level, fertility, and general SES. Women who marry at later ages (late 20s or early 30s) tend to have higher education levels, higher SES, and lower fertility rates. The union type (legally married vs. cohabiting) also is related to education, SES, and fertility. Those who have lived together in a consensual union were found to have higher fertility rates, lower levels of education, and lower SES (De Vos, 2000).

Most research conducted in Latin America has focused on fertility and health practices. The 1987 Demographic and Health Survey of Ecuador is one of the few large-scale and representative studies that also examined marital and family issues (Institute for Resource Development/ Westinghouse, 1988). A randomly selected sample of all women in Ecuador, ages 15 to 49 years, participated in the study. The vast majority (95%) of all the eligible women in Ecuador participated in this study for a final sample size of 4,976. Nearly 60% of the respondents lived in urban areas, and the remaining 40% lived in rural regions. The educational levels of the respondents were as follows: no education, 7.8%; primary education, 47.5%; secondary education, 35.5%; and higher education, 9.2%. Regarding respondents' marital status, 31% reported that they had never been married, 42% were married at the time of the interview, 21% lived in Union Libre, 1.5% were widowed, 4% were living in commuter marriages, and relatively very few (0.5%) reported being divorced. It should be noted that many persons in this study (22.1% of the sample) were under 20 years of age at the time of the interview and would likely form intimate unions later in their lives. Furthermore, many in the Union Libre or single category were separated but not legally divorced from their spouses. The vast majority of the women (88.5%) reported that they had only one union or no union in their lifetimes. The average age at first marriage for those who were married at the time of the interview was 19 years, indicating a relatively young age at marriage.

For those survey respondents who reported being parents, the average age at birth of a first child was 20 years. Sexual activity began at 18 years of age, and the average number of children ever born to a respondent was 2.5 for women of all ages. When examining only women age 40 years or over ($n = 687$), when women have most likely completed childbearing, the average number of children born to the respondents was 5.67. Women reported that the ideal number of children was 3. Comparisons were made between rural and urban women in the survey. In general, rural women reported more children, a younger age at marriage, a younger age at first sexual intercourse, lower levels of education, a greater number of desired children, and a younger age at first childbirth than did women from urban settings.

Gender Role Shifts

Changes in gender roles occurred in Latin America, as they did in many areas of the world, and probably have affected couple formation practices. Although no studies are available from Ecuador, Rosenberg (1983) studied the impact of female employment on couple formation in Bogotá, Colombia. Interviews with employed women and their housewife neighbors revealed that working women married on average 2 years later (age 22 instead of 20) and subsequently had fewer children across their life courses. In a related study, Heaton and Forste (1998) examined survey data of large samples from Colombia, Peru, and Bolivia for changes in marriage and fertility patterns. The results indicated that the greater the education level of a woman, the later the age at marriage (two thirds of uneducated women are married by 20 years of age) and the fewer the number of children coupled with increased contraceptive use. These findings further illustrate how SES and region influence mate selection practices in Latin America. As mentioned previously, a common practice of couple formation in Latin America is cohabitation before a formal wedding ceremony. This practice of Union Libre means "free union," inferring fewer obligations and commitments than with a formal marriage.

Union Libre

In general, there is ambivalence regarding consensual unions in Latin America. Most do not see such unions as a violation of social mores. In Ecuador, the differences in cohabitation rates by region are very dramatic. Only 10% live in Union Libre in the sierra or mountain areas, whereas more than half of the people live in consensual unions in the coastal areas. In general, people in Latin America tend to be in Union Libre if they live in rural settings, have lower levels of education, and are younger (De Vos, 2000). Interestingly, pregnancy does not increase the likelihood of a couple legalizing their consensual unions. There is very little use of birth control in these samples, and it is probable that those who are worried about the legitimacy of their children form legal marriages from the beginning (Goldman & Pebley, 1986).

Many consensual unions do become formalized later in life. In Colombia, more than 41% of the women in relationships, ages 20 to 24 years, were living in Union Libre. By ages 45 to 49 years, only 20% of women were cohabitating. In Peru, these numbers were 40% and 15%, respectively (De Vos, 2000). Approximately two thirds of all consensual unions eventually become legal marriages.

Why is living together without being legally married so common in Ecuador and throughout Latin America? Divorce historically has been very difficult to attain in Latin America, so some people may choose to live together prior to formalizing their relationships, and many might not legally marry until later in life. Furthermore, some people might not have the financial resources to pay for the legal documents and religious ceremonies that accompany a marriage. Another motivating factor for consensual unions involves the formation of a couple after the separation of a previous marriage. Because of the Catholic Church's negative view toward divorce, many may be legally married to their former partners but are unable to legally divorce and so will live in Union Libre with their new partners. Because of the prevalence of informal unions, there tends to be an ambivalent attitude toward formalizing and dissolving the union.

Mate Selection

The choice of a mate in Latin America is nearly entirely of free choice, meaning that people choose their partners without obligation from family or other community organizations. The theoretical perspective explaining the process of selecting a mate is discussed in this section.

Homogamy and Exchange

Homogamy is the principle explaining that people tend to form unions (formally or informally) with those who are similar to themselves in regard to age, race, religion, SES, education level, and physical attributes. Very closely related to this principle is the idea of exchange theory. In a free choice society, people are motivated to find partners with the greatest number of positive attributes as possible (e.g., good looks, stable personality, earning potential, nurturing, potential fertility) and to avoid those with negative characteristics (e.g., criminal behavior, drug use, health problems, infidelity).

One way in which to illustrate the importance of similarity in couple formation is to look at education level. Data gathered circa 1980 show that the correlation between partners' education levels was relatively large and significant. It was .33 in Paraguay, .61 in Panama, .53 in Chile, and .71 in Ecuador for those in formal marriages. This means that those in formal marriages have very similar levels of education (De Vos, 2000).

A group of studies addressed the particular traits that Latinos look for in potential mates (Gibbons, Richter, Wiley, & Stiles, 1996; Stiles,

Ecuadorian Couple Engaged to Be Married

Gibbons, & Schnellmann, 1990). Teens in Guatemala, Mexico, Iceland, and the United States were asked to rank in importance 10 qualities of the ideal person of the opposite sex. It was hypothesized that rankings would reflect the collectivistic or individualistic values of the particular cultures. The U.S.

sample demonstrated individualistic traits by valuing qualities such as having lots of money, being fun and sexy, and being physically attractive. Guatemalan adolescents showed collectivistic values by ranking liking children as important and being physically attractive as less important. Those from Iceland and Mexico had mixed results, with Mexican teens valuing intelligence, kindness, and honesty but also physical attractiveness.

Young (1989) conducted an exhaustive review of the exchange theory literature on marital worth in the United States and came to the following basic conclusions. First, homogamy or similarity in terms of race, religion, and family background will contribute to a person's value on the marriage market. Second, social class is important in the mate selection process, and people tend to marry within their own class level. Third, there are gender differences in that males prefer younger and physically attractive mates, whereas females seek older, financially stable companions who possess certain attractive inner qualities. Fourth, those who are divorced or have children from previous unions are viewed as less desirable as marriage partners. Fifth, the use of alcohol, tobacco, or drugs lowers a person's worth on the marriage market. Sixth, chronic illness and sexually transmitted diseases negatively affect worth as a potential companion. Seventh, extensive sexual history, including having many partners, being bisexual or homosexual, and/or being a rapist, will have a strong negative influence on a person's perceived marital worth. Each of these conclusions was substantiated in Young's own research with college students in various parts of the United States. This study was replicated in Ecuador to explore mate selection preferences and practices.

Methods

The goals of the study were to identify those characteristics viewed as positive or negative in a potential marriage partner and to identify general couple formation practices in a sample of individuals from Ecuador (Ingoldsby & Schvaneveldt, 2003). Participants indicated their marital status as single (38.0%), married (33.9%), cohabiting (16.5%), or divorced/separated or remarried (11.6%). The age range of respondents was 17 to 63 years, with a median age of 27. Nearly 62% of the respondents identified their racial background as Mestizo (mixed race), 33% identified theirs as white, and the remainder reported themselves to be black (4%) or Indian (1%). The most common occupations for women were maid, housewife, and secretary; whereas for men they were businessperson and construction worker.

Mate Selection Practices Results

The married respondents reported that they met their partners in their neighborhoods (30%), in their workplaces (24%), at school (24%), via mutual friends (9%), or by other means (13%). These results illustrate that principles of propinquity operate in a similar manner in Ecuador as in the United States. *Propinquity* is a term that refers to meeting one's partner in a shared environment such as school, work, neighborhood, or religious organization. It is interesting to note that some changes have occurred between younger and older generations. The respondents were asked to indicate how their parents met each other, and the responses differed slightly from the younger generation. The parents were reported to have met in their neighborhoods (47%), by other means (16%), via mutual friends (15%), in their workplaces (14%), or at school (8%), indicating that members of the younger generation are more likely to meet at work or in school than in their neighborhood settings.

Respondents were asked to indicate the two major reasons for marriage. The majority of respondents indicated that the primary motivating factor for marriage would be love (63.3%), followed by pregnancy (26.3%), desire for emancipation (3.9%), family obligation (2.6%), fear of being alone (1.3%), and rebellion (1.3%). The secondary motivating factors for marriage were: love (32.6%), emancipation (23.3%), family obligation (14.0%), fear of being alone (16.3%), pregnancy (4.7%), and other (4.7%).

Mate Selection Preferences Results

Using a 5-point Likert scale, respondents indicated whether they would be willing to marry someone with a particular characteristic (1 = *absolutely no*, 2 = *probably no*, 3 = *does not matter*, 4 = *probably yes*, 5 = *absolutely yes*). Table 3.1 contains the outcomes, listed in order from most to least desirable. As can be seen, the list focuses on traits that might be considered to be attractive mate characteristics or drawbacks in terms of value on the marriage market. The biggest deal breakers, where more than 90% of respondents indicated that they would not marry someone with this particular trait, were in the areas of sexuality and drug use. Someone who has AIDS or another sexually transmitted disease, is a rapist, is bisexual or homosexual, uses illicit drugs, drinks daily, or has mental health problems would not be considered marriage material. Other traits where two thirds or more of the sample gave negative responses involved someone who

Table 3.1   Percentages of Respondents Willing to Marry Someone With a Particular Characteristic

Item	Absolutely No	Probably No	Does Not Matter	Probably Yes	Absolutely Yes
Is homosexual	94.2	4.1	1.7	0.0	0.0
Drinks alcohol daily	89.3	9.9	0.8	0.0	0.0
Is bisexual	86.8	9.1	3.3	0.8	0.0
Has a sexually transmitted disease	85.1	11.6	1.7	1.7	0.0
Has a history of health problems	75.8	20.0	2.5	0.8	0.8
Has been exposed to AIDS	81.0	14.9	0.8	3.3	0.0
Has raped someone else	80.8	11.7	2.5	3.3	1.7
Takes illicit drugs	79.3	11.6	3.3	5.0	0.8
Has an extremely bad temper	74.4	14.9	5.8	3.3	1.7
Has no desire to have children	67.8	9.1	8.3	8.3	6.6
Is not interested in sex	67.8	16.5	6.6	5.8	3.3
Expects you to earn the money	62.5	14.2	10.0	8.3	5.0
Has been divorced more than once	59.5	18.2	9.9	9.9	2.5
Is considered to be a lazy person	58.7	27.3	11.6	2.5	0.0
Has been in prison	56.2	24.0	10.7	8.3	0.8
Thinks work is more important than family	54.5	26.4	7.4	8.3	3.3
Has chronic health problems	54.5	23.1	9.1	12.4	0.8
Has a bad reputation	50.4	26.4	10.7	9.9	2.5
Has many sexual partners	48.8	14.9	16.5	16.5	3.3
Is very fat (obese)	45.5	26.4	18.2	8.3	1.7
Has serious acne	42.5	19.2	20.8	11.7	5.8
Gets angry often	42.1	26.4	15.7	8.3	7.4
Was previously married with children	42.1	24.8	10.7	13.2	9.1
Has been raped	39.2	20.0	19.2	15.8	5.8
Does not practice any religion	38.0	15.7	29.8	6.6	9.9
Cannot have children	36.4	18.2	14.0	21.5	9.9
Smokes tobacco	34.7	21.5	24.0	11.6	8.3
Thinks the man should be in charge	30.6	21.5	10.7	14.9	22.3

Item	Absolutely No	Probably No	Does Not Matter	Probably Yes	Absolutely Yes
Is at least 10 years older than you but wealthy	30.6	18.2	15.7	21.5	14.0
Is nervous and worries a lot	29.4	26.1	18.5	18.5	7.6
Is 5 to 10 years younger than you	28.1	15.7	18.2	17.4	20.7
Was previously married with no children	26.1	14.3	16.0	29.4	14.3
Was divorced one time only	24.8	19.0	21.5	22.3	12.4
Is not Catholic	24.0	10.7	41.3	11.6	12.4
Does not like to dance	22.5	22.5	39.2	7.5	8.3
Is 30 to 40 centimeters shorter than you	22.5	17.5	24.2	18.3	17.5
Drinks alcohol once in a while	20.7	12.4	27.3	28.1	11.6
Is considered good looking by most	16.7	7.5	37.5	23.3	15.0
Has experienced premarital sex	15.8	10.8	30.0	23.3	20.0
Is very skinny	14.9	17.4	38.8	14.0	14.0
Is not physically attractive	14.2	18.3	32.5	19.2	15.8
Is a different race from you	10.7	12.4	32.2	26.4	18.2
Is not a university graduate	10.7	9.1	42.1	10.7	27.3
Is 30 to 40 centimeters taller than you	10.0	10.8	28.3	20.8	30.0
Is of your religious faith but not active	6.8	7.6	33.1	23.7	28.8
Is of a different social class from you	6.6	19.0	39.7	19.0	15.7

does not want children, has been previously married with children, is not interested in sex, has chronic health problems, has a bad reputation, has been in prison, expects the spouse to earn the money, has a bad or very bad temper, is very overweight, has had many sexual experiences and partners, has been divorced more than once, is lazy, and feels that work is more important than family.

Interestingly, religion does not seem to be very important. It does not seem to matter whether one's potential spouse is Catholic or even active in one's religious faith so long as the potential spouse has a religious affiliation. Respondents were not impressed with wealth or physical attractiveness (although acne was a concern regarding the latter), unlike the case in U.S. samples. Being a smoker or having been raped does not help one on the marriage market, but then neither does not liking to dance. Comparisons were made on demographic variables to illustrate any potential differences among groups of people.

Sex Differences

Men were much less willing to marry a person who is very obese than were women, indicating that men tended to place greater importance on physical characteristics than did women. In addition, men were less willing to marry a person who has been previously married than were women. Possibly reflecting the gender role expectations for men and women in Ecuadorian culture, men were less willing to marry someone who has chronic health problems than were women. Traditional gender role expectations are still a major influence on Latin American society and may influence women to be more nurturing than men (De Vos, 2000).

Education Differences

People with at least some university education were more inclined to marry a person who has a sexually transmitted disease than were people with no university education. It is likely that those with more education are more aware of the treatment and risks associated with a sexually transmitted disease than are those with limited educational opportunities. As would be expected, people with no university education showed a greater acceptance of a person who is not a university graduate than did those with at least some university educational experience.

Age Differences

Older people were more willing to marry a person who cannot have children than were younger people. It is likely that older individuals already were parents and saw less need to marry a person who could have children. As would be expected, older persons were more accepting of a partner who has been previously married than were younger people.

SES Differences

Interestingly, those from higher SES backgrounds were more willing to marry someone who expects them to earn the money than were those from lower SES backgrounds. Perhaps this represents greater egalitarian gender roles, where both men and women are expected to be engaged in the paid workforce. As modernity theory explains, changes in gender role attitudes are most likely to occur first among higher SES individuals (Inkeles, 1996). This notion is further reflected in that individuals from higher SES backgrounds reported less inclination to marry someone who thinks that the man should be in charge of the marriage than were those from lower SES backgrounds.

Religious Affiliation

Persons with no reported religious affiliation showed a greater willingness to marry someone who does not desire to have children than did persons who were Catholic. This likely reflects the pronatalist values associated with Catholicism.

Marital Status

Both married and single persons were asked whether they would, hypothetically, consider marrying a person with a particular characteristic. Single people were more inclined to marry a person who drinks once in a while than were people who were already married. Perhaps married people are more aware of the risks and challenges of alcoholism to a marriage than are single people. Single individuals reported a greater acceptance of marrying a person who expects them to earn the money in the relationship than did those who were already married. The relative naïveté of single people likely explains these differences in that married people are probably more aware of the financial struggles associated with family life and see the need for both partners to enhance family income. Surprisingly, no significant differences were identified between people who have cohabited previously and those who have never cohabited.

Summary

Goode (1963) concluded that much of the world is experiencing a drift toward Western culture and that this change has occurred as a result of a variety of economic, political, and technological revolutions over the past centuries. The specific question that guided the current study was the following: Do Latin American cultures reflect this same Western drift, and is there evidence that a social exchange orientation reflects couple formation preferences and practices? The answer seems to be yes.

In general, the respondents from Ecuador in this study responded very similarly to respondents in studies using similar instruments in North America (Buss, Shackelford, Kirkpatrick, & Larsen, 2001; Young, 1989). The results of this study support the notion that most young people marry for love. It was the major reason for marriage reported in this study, and it is within this context that people select partners who can provide the greatest value on the marriage market. Ecuadorian people expressed a preference for selecting partners who are physically attractive, wealthy, healthy, emotionally stable, and religious. Respondents also expressed that many traits and characteristics were very negative in terms of marital worth, including sexual promiscuity, bisexuality or homosexuality, a lack of interest in sexual relationships, laziness, bad temper, having been in prison, nervousness, worrisome, mental health problems, illicit drug use, alcoholism, smoking, and exposure to sexually transmitted diseases.

The literature of Latin American couple formation practices indicates that cohabitation before marriage is common and culturally accepted. Latin American couples tend to be more endogamous and to marry at younger ages than U.S. couples. Women are on average about 2 years younger than men at marriage, similar to the pattern in North America. Better educated women also tend to marry later and have fewer children. In contrast to studies on U.S. samples, some Latin Americans rank inner qualities and personality traits higher than they do physical or individualistic traits in terms of attractive characteristics of potential mates.

Engagement and Wedding

At the beginning of this chapter, two stories were presented to illustrate how men and women meet each other and how the relationships develop. This final section discusses how couples establish more permanent partnerships. As the reader may recall, Juan and Maria, the partners who met at the local university, have decided to marry. They inform their parents of their decision to marry. On learning of the couple's decision, the parents of Juan accompany him to the house of Maria to visit with her parents. During this visit, Juan's parents inform Maria's parents that their son is deeply in love with their daughter and that they wish to marry. The prospective groom's father asks permission from the bride's father for the marriage to take place.

Latin American Couple on Wedding Day

If permission is granted, a wedding date is set at this time. Also present at this initial meeting between parents is a Catholic priest who blesses the engagement ring that is placed on Maria's hand by Juan. This begins the period of engagement or *Noviazgo* that can last from 3 months (if the prospective bride is pregnant) to several years, with a 1-year engagement being most common. Juan and Maria decide to marry in 12 months, when she will have completed her university education. They plan to marry at the local Catholic church, and just prior to the formal wedding ceremony, they obtain legal marriage documents from local government agencies. The formal wedding ceremony takes place in the Catholic church and is performed by the Catholic priest. Following the wedding ceremony, Juan and Maria have a large wedding reception with music, dancing, drinking, and partying for several hours. Invited guests include family members and friends. At the conclusion of the wedding party, Juan and Maria leave for a honeymoon, where they vacation together for a few days before returning to their home, work, and life together (personal interview, J. Andrade, 2002).

Pedro and Monica, the couple from a poor rural village in Ecuador, have established themselves as an exclusive dating couple. Eventually, Pedro and Monica become sexually intimate and Monica becomes pregnant unexpectedly. Given the limited economic resources of both families, Pedro and Monica do not have a formal engagement. Furthermore, they cannot afford a formal wedding ceremony, so the partners decide to live together in Union Libre. They choose to reside near their families in the same village (personal interview, M. Martinez, parish priest, Village of Turi, Ecuador, 2000).

Conclusion

These examples illustrate the influence of social class and residency (urban vs. rural) on couple formation practices in Ecuador and Latin America. Middle- and upper-class persons from urban areas tend to have longer periods of dating, formal engagements, and formal wedding ceremonies prior to establishing shared residencies. Persons from lower SES backgrounds and rural areas tend to form relationships at younger ages (late teens), form domestic partnerships without formal wedding ceremonies (although many legally formalize their marriages later in life), and experience unintended pregnancies. Social class and residence (rural vs. urban) are distinguishing factors in couple formation practices in Ecuador as in much of Latin America. Future research needs to explore the process that leads to partners' forming a relationship and how that varies within Latino culture (e.g., dating practices, engagement rituals, extended family reactions). Couple formation practices in Latin America are explained by a social exchange perspective and are similar to practices and preferences of individuals throughout much of the Western world.

References

Buss, D. M., Shackelford, T. K., Kirkpatrick, L. A., & Larsen, R. J. (2001). A half-century of mate preferences: The cultural evolution of values. *Journal of Marriage and Family, 63,* 491–503.

De Vos, S. (2000). Nuptiality in Latin America: The view of a sociologist and family demographer. In S. L. Browing & R. R. Miller (Eds.), *Till death do us part: A multicultural anthology on marriage*. Greenwich, CT: JAI.

Gibbons, J., Richter, R., Wiley, D., & Stiles, D. (1996). Adolescents' opposite-sex ideal in four countries. *Journal of Social Psychology, 136,* 531–537.

Goldman, N., & Pebley, A. (1986). Legalization of consensual unions in Latin America. *Social Biology, 28,* 49–61.

Goode, W. J. (1963). *World revolution and family patterns*. New York: Free Press.

Heaton, T., & Forste, R. (1998). Education as policy: The impact of education on marriage, contraception, and fertility in Colombia, Peru, and Bolivia. *Social Biology, 45,* 194–213.

Ingoldsby, B., & Schvaneveldt, P. L. (2003). Perceptions of acceptable mate attributes in Ecuador. *Journal of Comparative Family Studies, 34* (2).

Inkeles, A. (1996). Making men modern: On the causes and consequences of individual change in six developing countries. In A. Inkeles & M. Sasaki (Eds.), *Comparing nations and cultures: Readings in a cross-disciplinary perspective*. Englewood Cliffs, NJ: Prentice Hall.

Institute for Resource Development/Westinghouse. (1988). *Encuesta demogràfica y de salud familiar* (Demographic survey of family health). Quito, Ecuador: Iñaquito y Joaquin Auz.

Price, R. (1965). Trial marriage in the Andes. *Ethnology, 4,* 310–322.

Rosenberg, T. (1983). Employment and family formation among working-class women in Bogotá, Colombia. *Journal of Comparative Family Studies, 14,* 333–345.

Stiles, D., Gibbons, J., & Schnellmann, J. (1990). Opposite-sex ideal in the U.S.A. and Mexico as perceived by young adolescents. *Journal of Cross-Cultural Psychology, 21,* 180–199.

Young, M. (1989). *Mate selection in contemporary America: An exchange theory perspective*. Unpublished master's thesis, Utah State University.

4

Mate Selection in Trinidad and Tobago

A Multireligious, Multicultural Perspective

Winston Seegobin

Kristen M. Tarquin

"When I was 17 years old and still in school, my father told me that he had chosen a wife for me. I realized that I did not have a choice and decided to go along with his decision. My father made all the arrangements for the wedding. We were poor, and I remember that I wore shoes for the first time on my wedding day. During the ceremony, I saw my bride's fingers were of a fair complexion, which assured me that she was a good woman. So, my love life began by seeing my wife's fingers. I saw my wife for the first time after our wedding ceremony. She was 14 years old." (Scenario 1)

"God can give specific direction in selecting a marriage partner if you would ask Him. This may be surprising to many, but He does give guidance as clearly as we are speaking now. This was my experience during the late 1970s. It was difficult to talk about mixed marriages in my family. The idea of marrying someone of another race caused great tension and anxiety. There were many deep cultural issues that I couldn't challenge without causing pain and hurt to others. The situation really led me to prayer to seek the Lord's advice on the choice that confronted me. At that time, there

were several girls from whom I could have easily chosen. But the Lord told me very distinctly, after months of contemplation, that this was the girl He wanted me to marry. I did not hesitate. The next day, I told her about it, and that settled the matter for us. Of course, since then, we've had problems—but no regrets." (Scenario 2)

T rinidad and Tobago are the two southernmost islands of the Caribbean, located just off the coast of Venezuela. This twin-island state has been described as "one of the most economically developed and possibly the most ethnically diverse and religiously heterogeneous Caribbean territory" (Yelvington, 1993, p. 1). As a result, there are a variety of ways in which mates are selected. This chapter begins with a short history of the islands, discussing how the various ethnic groups came to the islands. The cultural contexts and demographic data are then presented. Mate selection is discussed from a variety of religious perspectives, including Hindu, Muslim, and Christian. Unique features of these relationships, as well as similarities to other cultures, are highlighted. Common law relationships, parental and community involvement, and perspectives on singleness and homosexuality are discussed. Examples from interviews conducted are used to illustrate the various aspects of mate selection.

A Short History

The republic of Trinidad and Tobago was initially inhabited by the Arawak and Carib Indians who migrated from South America. The Arawaks were peaceful, whereas the Caribs were fierce and aggressive. In 1498, Christopher Columbus came to Trinidad and named the island after three mountain peaks. The Spaniards enslaved the Arawaks and Caribs and put them to work in the mines. As a result of brutalization and diseases, the Arawaks died rapidly. The Caribs tried to resist enslavement by the Spaniards but were eventually overcome, and most of them died. Trinidad remained under Spanish rule until it was captured by the British in 1797. In 1802, it became the first British Crown colony. During the 17th and 18th centuries, Tobago was ruled by the Dutch, French, and British and changed ruling powers a number of times (Williams, 1942).

Under British rule, slaves from West Africa were brought to Trinidad and Tobago to work on the sugar, cocoa, and coffee plantations.

Yelvington (1993) noted, "The Africans were of varied ethnic, cultural, linguistic, and religious groups" (p. 5). With the abolition of slavery in 1834, Chinese from the Whampoa and Namoa (Cantonese ports), as well as Portuguese from Madeira, were invited to come as indentured laborers but were found to be unsuitable for work on the plantations. Consequently, they became involved as traders. Later, after World War I, Syrians and Lebanese joined the Chinese and Portuguese as "trading minorities" (Yelvington, 1993). Indentured laborers from India were then brought to work on the plantations (Gopaul-McNicol, 1993). Between 1845 and 1917, 144,000 Indians from Calcutta and Madras came to Trinidad and Tobago, bringing with them their cultures, religious traditions, and languages. Yelvington (1993) noted, "While Hinduism and Islam were 'allowed' to be practiced—certainly more so than Africans were allowed to practice their religious traditions under slavery—it is probably correct to say that these religions were not encouraged by the power elite" (p. 7).

During the middle of the 19th century, there was a clear division of labor along ethnic lines. The whites owned the plantations, the Chinese and Portuguese were traders, the blacks and coloreds were employed in the skilled manual occupations and moving into professional positions, and the Indians were primarily in agriculture. Blacks and Indians also lived in different geographic areas, with blacks living in the urban areas in the north of Trinidad and Indians living in the country areas in the central and south of Trinidad. Blacks were the primary group in Tobago. Marriage between the races did not occur, as is evident by this quote from Brereton (1979), who reported that the protector of immigrants in 1871 wrote that "there is not probably at this moment a single instance of an indentured immigrant . . . who cohabits with one of the negro race" (cited in Yelvington, 1993, p. 8).

Cultural Contexts

The republic of Trinidad and Tobago has a population of 1,274,799. Males make up 49.9% and females make up 50.1% of the population. In terms of ethnic background, 40.3% of the population reported being from an Indian background, 39.6% are from an African background, 18.4% are from a mixed background, 0.6% are from a white background, 0.4% are from a Chinese background, and 0.2% are from an "other" background (0.4% did not indicate their background). In terms of religious background, 29.4% reported being Roman Catholic, 23.8% are Hindu, 10.9% are Anglican,

5.8% are Islamic, 3.4% are Presbyterian, and 25.7% are "other" (1.0% did not state their religious background) (Ministry of Finance, Planning, and Development, 1998). In general, people from an African background identify with Christian and Muslim religions, whereas people from an Indian background identify with Hindu, Muslim, and Christian religions. The Chinese usually identify with Christian religions, even though some continue to practice ancestor worship and some forms of Buddhism.

The total number of marriages in 1997 was 7,418, which was a 4.2% increase from 1996. Regarding age groups of the brides, 2.0% were under 15 years of age, 12.9% were 15 to 19, 30.0% were 20 to 24, 24.1% were 25 to 29, and 14.6% were 30 to 35. Regarding age groups of the grooms, nearly 2.0% were 15 to 19, 19.7% were 20 to 24, 29.2% were 25 to 29, and 20.1% were 30 to 34. In terms of religious background, 54.1% of the marriages were Christian, 20.4% were Hindu, 6.3% were Muslim, and 19.2% were civil (performed by the state) (Ministry of Finance, Planning, and Development, 2000).

The total number of divorces in 1997 was 1,278, which represented a decrease of 12.3% from the 1996 figure. The highest percentage of divorces (25.9%) occurred among individuals married for 10 to –14 years (Ministry of Finance, Planning, and Development, 2000).

As a result of the history of Trinidad and Tobago, there are a variety of cultural heritages and backgrounds, with the most prominent being the African and Indian cultures. However, Trinidad and Tobago can truly be described as multicultural because of the mixing of the cultures that can be described as "Caribbean culture." Even though distinctions in the cultures continue, cultural integration also occurs, as is quite evident by some of the food, music, and festivals. These distinctive and integrative practices are also present in the mate selection process and in marriages. For many years, marriages occurred primarily within ethnic groups. Interracial or mixed marriages were frowned on and despised. Most marriages still occur within the ethnic/cultural groups. However, there has been a small rise in mixed marriages over the past 20 years. Although most of these marriages occur with individuals from African and Indian backgrounds, the Chinese also participate. Acceptance of mixed marriages is slow, and some groups have shown a strong resistance. For instance, a local newspaper reported the dissatisfaction of a Hindu priest with the finding that the mixed (interracial) group had the largest population increase (13%) between 1980 and 1990, implying an increase in interracial marriages:

> Hindu women who do not marry their own are diluting themselves and their sisters, pundit Ramesh Tiwari, president and spiritual founder of the

Edinburgh Hindu temple, has said. To maintain her lineage, the Hindu woman must marry her own; to marry outside of her religion is "sad, very sad." "Our scripture teaches us to maintain our identity. Only the finger of the Hindu male should apply *seindoor* on the forehead of a Hindu woman." Seindoor, a red powder mixed with ghee (cattle butter), is applied to the forehead of a Hindu woman to indicate she is married. (Chouti, 1996, p. 3)

On the other hand, a recent study by St. Bernard (1999) reported that parents seem to have considerable openness to interracial relationships. He found from his sample of 3,931 cases that 64.9% of the Indians, 93.4% of the Africans, 85.7% of the Chinese, 89.5% of the whites, and 93.8% of the mixed groups indicated that they had no objection to their children marrying someone of a different race. It appears that the phenomenon of interracial marriages is becoming more popular and acceptable. One of my interviewees from a Chinese background reported that his parents did not have any objections to his marriage to an Indian woman.

Mate Selection: A Religious Perspective

Hindu Marriages

Marriage is an integral part of the Hindu culture. Barrow (1996) noted, "The family as an institution and the close and enduring bonds are at the centre of East Indian culture. The conjugal union is the focal point of the family, and marriage is the norm for all East Indians" (p. 341).

Although a majority of the Hindu marriages were arranged, most of the marriages now occur by choice; that is, individuals choose their own mates. Two types of arranged marriages and marriage by choice are discussed in this section. In some of the early arranged marriages, the individuals did not see each other before the marriage ceremonies. All of the arrangements were done by the parents, and there was no contact between the marriage partners. An 81-year-old man who has been married for 64 years explained,

Well, what really happened, as a young man I did not want to get married. We begin from there. Because I was 17 [years of age] and my father was a family man, he decided that he must have somebody home to help the old lady. And he really made all the arrangements. I did not know even after the arrangements were made, who it was made with and where it was made. So, this is how our marriage began. My wife had a similar problem; we spoke about it after we got married. She did not know me, she did not know who she was going to get married with, but her mother was old and she decided before she passed away [that] she wanted to see her daughter married. So, this is where the whole thing began.

In another form of arranged marriages, the prospective bride and groom see each other briefly and then a decision is made, but no dating or courtship occurs before the wedding. One of my brothers was married in this manner. He, along with an uncle and other male relatives, visited the home of the potential bride. While they were seated in the living room, the potential bride served them drinks and left the room. That was the only contact, and a decision about the marriage was made after leaving the home. Most of the arranged marriages are done in this manner. At times, arranged marriages are done for legal purposes, as the following story of a man from India illustrates:

> I knew that if I had to stay here [in Trinidad], I had to get married, so I was looking for a girl who could stay with me and stay with me for the rest of my life. . . . The person I was visiting was a friend of mine; he is a jeweler. He used to go by my mother-in-law to sell jewelry and other things from house to house; he knew them too. So, one day he took me there, and I saw my wife, and we decided to get married.

However, the majority of marriages involve free choice, and some include dating. In the free choice marriages, the individuals meet each other at work or at a social event. They discuss their attraction to each other, and if the attraction is mutual, they begin dating. Sometimes, parents are consulted when the relationship gets serious. Some of the factors that are given serious consideration in these marriages are character, educational level, and employment of the spouse, in particular, the husband. Caste is no longer considered an important element. Nevadomsky (1982–1983) noted that in a rural village called Amity,

> Arranged marriages used to be the norm. Today, most marriages are based on free personal choice. In the village, 66% of the married women under 35 years of age chose their own spouses in contrast to 17% of the married women over 35. Personal choice is to be expected where emphasis is placed on the affective bond between spouses, and young people have considerable freedom of movement in and out of the community. (p. 192)

The Wedding Ceremony

The Hindu wedding ceremony takes place over a 3-day weekend and involves many ceremonies and rituals as well as much symbolism. There are similar occurrences at the homes of both the bride and the groom. The bride is referred to as the *dulahin* and the groom as the *dulaha*. The Hindu priest, referred to as the *pundit*, is very involved in the proceedings. During early times, the pundit, by looking at the astronomical signs of the bride and groom, determined the date and time of the wedding. Many weddings took place during the night. However, during recent times, most weddings take place over a weekend, with the main ceremony on a Sunday.

The wedding begins on Friday night with the *muti kurwa* (digging dirt) ceremony, which takes place at the homes of both the bride and the groom. It begins with a ceremonial dance led by older women accompanied by tassa drumming. They go to a designated spot and dig dirt, which is taken home and used in the building of the *bedi*. The bedi is a small mound, built with dirt from the homes of the bride and groom, that signifies the joining of not only two people or two families but also two villages or communities. A *marrow* or tent erected from bamboo stands above the bedi, and the wedding ceremony takes place under that tent around the bedi. At the homes of both the bride and the groom, a ceremony is performed where saffron powder mixed with coconut oil is applied as a beauty treatment. Five girls who are under 10 years of age apply the saffron mixture to the feet, knees, shoulders, heads, and hearts of the bride and groom. Usually, there is some Indian singing that takes place during the night.

On Saturday night, usually called the "farewell night," the patching of the *laawa* (rice) occurs, and the marrow is completed with decorations. There is usually special singing by an Indian musical band, and professional dancing is performed. A meal is offered to guests and relatives.

Sunday is the most important day in the wedding. There are final saffron applications. The groom has a special bath with herbs and spices, and he is dressed in a *jorajamma* (a brightly colored gown). A headpiece called a "crown" is placed on his head. The significance of the crown is that the groom is "king for a day." After getting dressed, he is transported by car with several cars following (called a *baraat*), with the lead car playing Indian music through loudspeakers. Those in the wedding party from the groom travel to the home of the bride. When they get there, they are received by the relatives of the bride. As they meet, the bride's father offers a *lota* (brass cup) of water with five coins and a single flower, a symbol of welcome to the groom's father and his wedding party. They embrace and exchange greetings. The groom is then greeted by the bride's mother and other female relatives and is welcomed by the bride's younger brother. The bride's father and the groom are then involved in *puja* (audible Hindu prayers).

The next part of the ceremony, referred to as the *Neychoo* and *Emli Ghotaai*, is performed by the bride's mother and her maternal uncle. Five mango leaves are used. Each leaf is circled over the heads of the mother and bride and then given to the bride to bite the tip of the stem and keep it in her mouth. After this is completed with the five leaves, the bride is given some water. She then puts the stems and the water in the right hand of her mother, who swallows all of it. The bride is then honored by puja and receives gifts from the groom's older brother. At this point, she leaves to get dressed in a *sari* (a special gown that is usually red).

The bride's father welcomes the groom again and gives him a taste of honey, a symbol of love's sweetness. The groom, with clasped hands, touches various parts of the bride's father's body. The bride returns, and both the bride and groom are worshiped by the bride's parents. The bride then sits opposite the groom around the bedi. At this point, the partners repeat their wedding vows together, saying,

> In the presence of God and man, we both declare that we are accepting each other as husband and wife out of our own sweet will and without compulsion of any kind. Our hearts are one, and we would bear each other in the best possible manner, and carry out our household duties to the best of our abilities. I do promise I will not let go of this hand as long as I shall live.

The feet of the groom are then washed, and there is an offering of *aareti* (a brass plate with lighted *canfer* [similar to a candle]) in the middle, flowers, and gifts of a *lota* (brass cup) and *tharia* (brass plate) by the relatives of the bride. The bride and groom then make oblations into the fire in the middle of the bedi of *ghee* (cattle butter), *googool* (Indian incense), rice, sugar, and *laawa* (patched rice). Then they take seven steps together—representing vigor, vitality, prosperity, happiness, wealth, seasons, and friendship—and walk seven times around the bedi, with the bride leading the first four times. They throw some laawa into the sacred fire in the middle of the bedi each time.

The bride and groom are then covered with a piece of cloth, and the groom applies seindoor to the parted hair of the bride. Wearing of the seindoor in the middle of the head is a symbol of the wedded state. The bride and groom then exchange rings. The groom's father presents to the groom the Mangal Sutra necklace, which is worn only by Hindu married women. He places it around the neck of the bride. The bride and groom, accompanied by the marriage party, then leave for the groom's home, where they are welcomed by the mother of the groom and rice is thrown. The bride usually goes to her parents' home 2 days after the wedding and returns to her new husband's home 5 days later. Often, the newlyweds then go on a honeymoon to another Caribbean island or the United States.

The Bride, Groom, and Priest at a Hindu Wedding in Trinidad

Muslim Marriages

Muslim marriages are based on the Koran, the Muslim holy scriptures. Most Muslims choose their own mates. A man and woman may meet each other at a regular Muslim meeting, or they may meet through an introduction by a friend or relative. They exchange phone numbers and continue their conversation over the phone. If the woman is interested in the man, she gets to know him better through phone conversations and also talks with other people about him. If her interest continues, she tells her parents about him and then invites him to her home to meet her parents. He usually comes by himself, but he may bring a friend or relative. At this meeting, the man is introduced to the woman's parents and is offered a meal. This is followed by a time of mutual talking and sharing. If the woman's parents approve of the relationship, they invite the man to continue visiting their home to spend time with their daughter. She can also go out with him accompanied by a chaperone such as a relative or close friend who has the parents' approval. When the man invites his parents to meet hers, it means that the relationship is serious and that they are planning to get married—a "seal." Formal arrangements for the wedding then begin.

However, there are some exceptions to the procedure just described. Parents will allow their daughter to date, meaning to go out without a chaperone, if they trust their daughter not to have any physical contact with the prospective mate. On the other hand, some people date secretly due to these strict procedures. Parents usually become very angry when they find out about such secret dating, and they may ask that the relationship be terminated. Sometimes, this results in the two young people "running away" or eloping. At times, it may even end with the two committing suicide. However, this occurrence is rare.

Arranged marriages also occur with Muslims, as the following comments by a Muslim priest illustrate:

> But with the Indians, Indian Muslims, at the beginning there was a question of arranged marriages, and you will appreciate now more than ever nobody threw away their child. If my daughter was supposed to get married to you, I have to find out what kind of man you are and so on and look at your background. It was not a question of wealth; it was a question of character. So, it meant I was not throwing away my daughter. So, these arranged marriages went on for quite a long while. A little bit of the caste system came into play because of the caste system they came from. So, you will find that they will look at the upbringing.

The Muslim wedding ceremony (referred to as the *neeka*) is divided into four parts: affirmation, consent, dowry, and sermon. The affirmation is taken from the Koran and states, "There is no God but God. He is alone and has no partner, and Mohammed is his messenger." The consent is done in two ways. The first occurs with the bride and groom together in the mosque (Muslim church), where they repeat their vows in each other's presence. In the second type of consent, the bride and groom are in separate rooms. They do not see each other during the ceremony, but a messenger (called a *wakeel*) and two witnesses are sent back and forth with the vows. The wakeel is the representative of the girl. He asks the girl whether she will accept him to carry the message on her behalf and whether she agrees to get married to the man. She gives consent three times. Then, he decides with her on the prearranged dowry, which is a very important part of the ceremony. The groom pays the dowry from his earnings. It is paid during the ceremony or at a future time. The bride then joins the groom in the room where all the guests and relatives are gathered. At this time, the repetition of vows, the exchange of rings, the sharing of a drink, and the signing of the legal documents occur. The sermon, which is the last part of the ceremony, is the same in all weddings.

A Muslim priest reported that the Koran teaches that a man or woman is only "half a person" until he or she is married. Thus, it appears that singleness is not encouraged. He also mentioned that a man is allowed to marry more than one wife, quoting from the Koran: "If you fear that you shall not be able to deal justly with the other, marry a woman of your choice: two or three or four." A local newspaper highlighted the story of a Muslim priest with four wives. Two of the wives who were interviewed expressed that they were satisfied with their marriages. One of the wives expressed that such a marriage allowed her to feel like both a single woman and a married woman at the same time (Cambridge, 2002; Clarke, 2002).

Christian Marriages

People from a Christian background make up the majority of the population. In fact, Christian marriages made up 54.1% of all marriages in 1997. Of those marriages, 20.0% were Roman Catholic, 9.3% were Baptist, 8.6% were Seventh Day Adventist, 7.6% were Anglican, 3.8% were Presbyterian, 2.3% were Methodist, and 48.4% were other Christian denominations (Ministry of Finance, Planning, and Development, 2000). There is some variation on how mate selection takes place. The majority of cases involve free choice. However, for some people, spirituality plays a major role in their choice of a partner. One pastor recounted that he chose his mate as a direct result of the leading of God. He mentioned that he was not searching for a mate but that God brought a woman to his mind and told him to marry her. He wanted it to be confirmed with a sign. The sign was that he would see her standing at the side of the street while he was driving to work the next day, that he would ask her to travel with him in his car, and that she would consent to his marriage proposal. The situation occurred as he desired. She accepted his proposal, and the two were later married. The pastor did not go on any dates with the woman, did not spend any time with her alone, and did not kiss her until the wedding day.

Marriages also occur as a result of family or personal pressure. A woman reported that she was having some difficulties at home with her parents, and so she got married to move out of her parents' home. Another person reported that he got married because his partner was pregnant. He had grown up without a father in his own home, and he did not want his child to grow up without a father. However, he mentioned that the marriage lasted only a few years.

Most Christian marriages do not occur in these ways. Most people choose partners who they deem attractive, they date and court each other, and they usually get engaged when they decide that they want to get married. In contrast to the custom in the United States, a ring is usually not presented to the woman at the time when the proposal occurs. Rather, the ring is given at a formal engagement party, where relatives and friends are gathered to celebrate the occasion. The pastor or minister may be present to bless the ring, and dinner is served. The proposal is still traditional and is initiated by the man.

Christian wedding ceremonies are in many ways similar to those in the United States. The groom wears a tuxedo, and the bride wears a white wedding gown. The bride and groom meet at the church, where the pastor/minister officiates. There are bridesmaids and groomsmen, a page boy and a flower girl, and the exchange of vows and rings. A wedding reception follows at the bride's home, a restaurant, or a public meeting hall. There are speeches and toasts to the wedding party, lots of food, and (often) dancing. The newlyweds usually leave for a honeymoon immediately following the reception. It is customary to take a lot of pictures or even to videotape the ceremony.

Common Law Relationships

Some people choose to live together before they get married. Although it is becoming more common, this is still not seen as an acceptable practice and is not approved by the community. Living together, commonly referred to as "shacking up," occurs for a variety of reasons, including financial, convenience, and intentional. One interviewee reported that he visited his girlfriend at her parents' home and often found himself spending the night on the couch in the living room. After doing that for a while, he eventually moved into his girlfriend's bedroom, and they started living together. A woman reported that she "shacked up" with her boyfriend because she wanted to be with him but was not ready to get married. She indicated that her parents had lived together before they got married. In 1998, legislation was passed by an act of parliament in Trinidad and Tobago granting persons in "common law relationships" (meaning cohabiting couples) equal rights to possessions and property as persons in legal marriages (*Trinidad and Tobago Gazette*, 1998).

The Role of Parental and Community Involvement

The consent and approval of parents is an important aspect of mate selection. It is not unusual for individuals to take their prospective spouses home to

A Bride and Groom From an African Background in a Christian Wedding

meet their parents before the decision is made to get married. In particular, the approval of the mother is important. Many interviewees reported that they routinely took their potential spouses home to meet their parents as part of the courting process.

In some cases, parental approval can affect future family relations, as is evident by the account of an 18-year-old Muslim female who reported that her parents told her the following:

> If you love us and believe that we know what's best for you, we will always help you make the right choice. And if you really love us, you will not interact or get married to someone without our consent. If you do not listen to us, and you go ahead and get married without our consent, you are cut off from the family, and we will no longer have anything to do with you.

For some individuals, the community involvement in the mate selection process and the approval of the community are important. The perceptions of the community are also considered when dating and marital decisions are made. One woman recounted that she realized that she did not want to get married to her partner 2 months before the wedding, but she believed that it would have been an embarrassment to the family to call off the wedding because all of the preparations had already been made. Therefore, she went through with the wedding. The marriage lasted 7½ years, and she is now divorced.

Community support is also an important aspect of the wedding. It is customary in many weddings for all of the food to be cooked by friends and relatives. In addition, the community helps in paying for the expenses of the wedding. One interviewee recounted that his wedding cost only $100 (U.S. $17) because all of his friends and relatives pitched in to help with the expenses.

The Perception of
Singleness and Homosexuality

Marriage is still the expectation in Trinidad and Tobago. Consequently, singleness is perceived as unusual. It is generally believed that there is a fundamental flaw with any person who chooses to be single. In addition, there is more of a stigma attached to single women than to single men. People remain single for a variety of reasons, including devotion to their careers, negative experiences in dating relationships, not meeting the right person, and responsibilities at home such as caring for aging or sick parents.

Homosexuality is seen as taboo. Homosexual behavior is perceived as wrong and abnormal. Consequently, homosexual relationships are not sanctioned by the community. Homosexual marriages are not permitted.

Conclusion

Mate selection occurs in a variety of ways in Trinidad and Tobago because of the multireligious and multicultural nature of the country. The history and origins of the people have significantly affected the structure of marriage and the family. Although some cultural and racial integration has occurred, there continue to be distinctive traditions and practices that accompany both mate selection and marriages in the various religious and ethnic groups. A local dish made from spinach, coconut, crab, and spices—called callaloo, meaning a mixture of various ingredients—is a good metaphor for the diversity and unity of the twin-island state.

References

Barrow, C. (Ed.). (1996). *Family in the Caribbean: Themes and perspectives.* Kingston, Jamaica: Ian Randle.

Brereton, B. (1979). *Race relations in colonial Trinidad 1870–1900.* Cambridge, UK: Cambridge University Press.

Cambridge, U. (2002, October 20). He knows how to treat a woman. *Trinidad Express,* pp. 4–5.

Chouti, S. (1996, October 26). Pundit knocks mixed marriages. *Trinidad Express,* p. 3.

Clarke, S. (2002, October 20). Liberated by Islam and polygamy. *Trinidad Express,* pp. 5–6.

Gopaul-McNicol, S. (1993). *Working with West Indian families.* New York: Guilford.

Ministry of Finance, Planning, and Development. (1998). *Statistics at a glance.* Port of Spain, Trinidad: Ministry of Finance, Planning, and Development, Central Statistical Office.

Ministry of Finance, Planning, and Development. (2000). *Population and vital statistics 1997 report.* Port of Spain, Trinidad: Ministry of Finance, Planning, and Development, Central Statistical Office.

Nevadomsky, J. (1982–1983). Changing conceptions of family regulation among the Hindu East Indians in rural Trinidad. *Anthropological Quarterly, 55,* 189–198.

St. Bernard, G. (1999). Ethnicity and attitudes toward interracial marriages in a multiracial society: The case of Trinidad and Tobago. In R. R. Premdas (Ed.), *Identity, ethnicity, and culture in the Caribbean* (pp. 157–184). St. Augustine, Trinidad: University of the West Indies, School of Continuing Studies.

Trinidad and Tobago Gazette. (1998, November 25). [Legal supplement, Part A], p. 16.

Williams, E. (1942). *History of the people of Trinidad and Tobago.* New York: A & B Books.

Yelvington, K. (Ed.). (1993). *Trinidad ethnicity.* London: Macmillan.

Part III

Africa

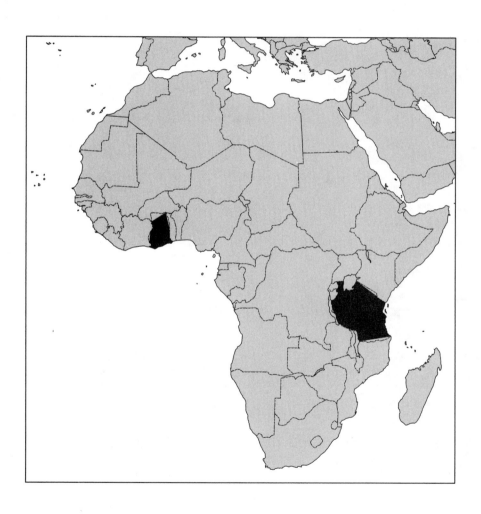

5

Tradition and Change in Family and Marital Processes

Selecting a Marital Partner in Modern Ghana

Baffour K. Takyi

Akwasi: For marriage matter, na me I no go do the things wanna my parents do ooo!

Akosua: For this wanna modern world, who go go marry somebody wey e no dey like am? For me, I dey go marry the person wey I like.

This exchange between Akwasi (a young Ghanaian man) and Akosua (a young woman) in their typical West African pidgin or broken English (e.g., Creole) exemplifies some of the ongoing transformations in modern Ghana. Translated into "proper" English, Akwasi's argument is that he will not adopt the outdated method of courtship that was popular with his parents' generation. Agreeing with Akwasi, Akosua emphasizes that nobody during these modern times should marry another person who he or she did not personally court.

AUTHOR'S NOTE: I am indebted to Nancy B. Miller and Ferdinand Yomoah for their helpful comments on an earlier draft of this chapter.

D eeply ingrained in the psyche of many Westerners is an image of the typical African marriage in which the influence of kin and family members is paramount. Equally important in this discourse is the notion that parents, with little input by the key stakeholders, arrange the marriage. The implication is that African marriages may lack romantic attraction and love that are often associated with Western (modern) marriages and their strong emphasis on individual choices and actions. This image has been shaped, in large part, by news media reports about what prevails among some of the few remaining nomadic groups as well as by early 20th-century, small-scale ethnographic studies on family processes in Africa (see, e.g., Caldwell, 1982; Fortes, 1950; Goody, 1976; Radcliffe-Brown & Forde, 1950).

As attested to by the exchange between Akwasi and Akosua in the vignette above, this received image needs to be modified in light of the transformations that have occurred in Africa. These transitions are, in large part, the result of Africa's encounters with the outside world and the subsequent changes that have resulted from these contacts. Indeed, as a result of the imposition of European colonial rule, the development of cash-based economies, and Western forms of schooling and religion (especially Christian and Islamic theologies), family and marital processes in Africa have been affected in many ways, including how Africans select their partners (Bledsoe; Bledsoe & Pison, 1990, 1994; Hetherington, 2001; Locoh, 1990; Oppong, 1983; Takyi, 2001). Also, the recent rate of urbanization in the region may have accentuated these changes even more given that sociologists often associate urban residence with a nontraditional way of life and behavior. This may be the case with Ghana, where the percentage of its population living in urban areas nearly doubled from 12.8% in 1948 to 23.0% in 1960 and had risen to approximately 40% by 2000 (Ghana Statistical Services, 1984; Population Reference Bureau, 2001).

Despite the reported changes in family processes in the sub-Saharan African region, most scholarship on families during the past 40 years has been dominated by studies examining the reproductive behavior of Africans (for some exceptions, see Meekers, 1995; Smith 2001). This undue interest in reproductive behavior research has been influenced, to a large extent, by concerns in the research community over Africa's rapid population growth since the mid-1950s and the consequences of such a development for socioeconomic growth and processes in the region. Furthermore, although national surveys on reproductive behavior in Africa have become commonplace during the past three decades, there have been no questions asked about mate selection, making it difficult to investigate contemporary trends and patterns regarding partner selection and practices.

The task of examining contemporary patterns of partner selection has been made easier by the availability of data from a recent survey, the Ghana Female Autonomy Micro Study (GFAMS), which asked questions about mate selection. GFAMS, conducted during 1992 and 1993, was aimed at providing current information on family dynamics in Ghana (Oheneba-Sakyi, Awusabo-Asare, Gbortsu, & Aryee, 1995). In all, 909 dyads from several urban and rural communities were interviewed. During the interviews, the respondents were asked questions about household decision making and their attitudes toward gender roles, marital rights, and mate selection practices. The questions on mate selection inquired about how the dyads chose their current marital partners and on what bases the choices were made. Because one of the goals of the survey was to identify recent changes in marital behavior in Ghana, those surveyed were asked to indicate how they chose their current partners as well as whether the selections were made independently of family members, whether the decisions were made with the help of others, whether consent was received from family members, or whether the unions were arranged. This chapter uses responses to these questions to provide insight into recent patterns of mate selection in Ghana. Before reporting the findings, I provide a brief overview of customary or traditional patterns of mate selection as reported in earlier discourse.

Family Formation, Forms, and Patterns of Mate Selection in Ghana

Social anthropologists, sociologists, and social demographers during the past 50 years in Africa have reported that Africans put much emphasis on family and married life. This emphasis reflects the important role assigned to this institution in Africa. Indeed, in many African countries, because the government's role in the provision of social services and support is minimal, family members usually are the primary providers of support for the young and the aged. In addition, the low level of socioeconomic development in Africa and the fact that official sources of assistance are limited to the very few who work in the formal sectors of the economy means that it makes economic sense for one to be married and also have children who could provide what Caldwell (1982) called a "flow of wealth" from the young to the old. Not only is the family the source of social and economic support, the Ghanaian family is also the main agent of social control, serving in most cases as the center of most religious activities, not to mention childbearing, in a country where being unmarried and childless is viewed as both a liability and a curse (Ebin, 1982; Takyi, 2001; Takyi & Oheneba-Sakyi, 1994). In a context where the family puts so much pressure on women to bear children, where governmental support in sickness and old age is nearly nonexistent, and where children are viewed as the main breadwinners during times of need and old age, it is simply suicidal and irrational for a couple to be childless. Moreover, because men in several African societies want children as much as do women, they are often warned against marrying women who cannot bear children (irrespective of the reason behind the infertility). Bledsoe (1990) reported that some men require proof of fertility before marriage.

Due in large part to the fact that marriage and family life are the backbone of African social organizations, it is not surprising that existing studies find that few Africans remain unmarried throughout their life courses (Caldwell & Caldwell, 1987; Lesthaeghe, 1989; Nukunya, 1992). Although it is true that the proportion of women marrying by 20 years of age is declining rapidly in some countries in Africa, Singh and Samara (1996) and Cohen (1998) have reported that by 20 years of age, most women in Africa are married. Although most Africans ultimately marry, how marriages are contracted in Ghana is somewhat different from what occurs in the industrialized Western nations. Unlike the pattern in the Western world where a marriage is viewed as an event, African marriages generally involve a number of practices and processes, as suggested by previous studies (see, e.g., Aryee, 1985; Awusabo-Asare, 1988; Meekers, 1992; Radcliffe-Brown & Forde, 1950). Often, a multitude of processes and ceremonies accompany these marital transitions before the husband-to-be can officially claim the bride as his wife. Because marriage under the traditional system is best seen as a formal relationship between families rather than as an individual endeavor, every effort is made to involve the larger extended family members in the selection process and marriage ceremonies. This view is exemplified by the belief of the Akans of southern Ghana that marriage is so important that it should not be left in the hands of people deemed too young to make prudent and rational decisions.

The Marriage Process: In Search of a Partner

Although indigenous and customary practices involving marriages in Ghana vary from one ethnic group to another, Nukunya (1978) observed that three essential attributes are common to most marriages. The first deals with the issue of marriage payment (often referred to as "bride wealth"). The second focuses on the formal handing over of the bride by her parents

Bride Exchanging Vows With Groom, With Extended Family Members in Background

to the groom and his parents. The third centers on the marriage ceremony before the actual marriage. Among the Akans of southern Ghana (Goode, 1963) and the Tallensi of northern Ghana (Fiawoo, 1978), a system of marriage involving betrothals (*asiwa*) is used as one way of locating marriage partners even before the marriageable age is attained. In general, traditional betrothals are relied on when parents, especially fathers, desire their daughters to be connected with desirable families. Under such circumstances, the parents of the bride-to-be could accept money or token gifts with the understanding that, in the future, their daughter would become the wife of the man with whom the alliance is sought.

The Role of the Family and Collective Responsibility

Another unique feature about indigenous Ghanaian marriages is that the relationships are often governed by a series of social norms and expectations. In societies where childbearing is viewed as an important part of the marriage process, it is not uncommon for family members to demand proof of fecundity before the conclusion of the marriage contract (Ghana

Statistical Services, 1989). As noted earlier, individual choices are often subordinated to those of the family group when it comes to selecting partners, a practice that Lesthaeghe (1989) noted may be due to the economic and social functions of marriage in the context of Africa. Not surprisingly, Nukunya (1992) reported that in selecting potential spouses in Ghana, certain qualities and conditions have to be met. For example, it is the duty of the family of each party to make sure that their potential in-laws do not come from a family with any known serious diseases (including lunacy and epilepsy), are not known criminals or witches, do not engage in quarreling, and are hardworking and respectful.

The involvement of family and kin members serves another purpose: to ensure that the couples are compatible in their values, expectations, and lifestyles before marrying (Takyi & Oheneba-Sakyi, 1994). According to conventional wisdom, the similarities in backgrounds would create a congenial environment for the stability of the relationship, thereby reducing the possibility of any disruptions. Despite all of the efforts at preserving the future relationship, some studies have cast doubt on the stability of African marriages (Caldwell & Caldwell, 1987). Some studies have suggested that divorce rates may be rising in the region (Amoateng & Heaton, 1989; Bruce, Lloyd & Leonard, 1995; Hutchinson, 1990; Lloyd & Gage-Brandon, 1993; Takyi, 2001). Nukunya (1978) and other scholars have also argued that the involvement of the prospective in-laws in the marriage has the added effect of establishing the needed networks that are expected of couples as they participate in family activities, including funerals, weddings, and other social gatherings. Moreover, the use of family members has helped in identifying whom one could traditionally marry, based in large part on the various marriage prohibitions that are found among some ethnic groups in the country.

Although the reliance on family and kin members in the courtship and marital process appears old-fashioned to Westerners, this practice is consistent with the African belief that marriage is an alliance between families rather than between individuals. As such, family members position themselves in such a way as to maximize their gains and reduce their losses in the marriage market. Consistent with the expectation of parental involvement, it is expected that the wishes of the extended family would be paramount, often overriding individual concepts of romantic love and individuation that serve as the basis of mate selection in Western societies. In that sense, the processes associated with courtship and marriage in traditional Africa should be viewed as part of the negotiations—ideals that are not that different from the assumptions of social exchange theory about marriage.

Courtship, Engagement, and the Marriage Contract

Although customs differ from one area to the other, the search for a marriageable partner in Ghana is often regarded as the responsibility of the man. Given this expectation, which is rooted in large part in traditional practices of socialization, it has been considered unthinkable and a disgrace for a woman to openly express her interest in a man. The unintended consequence of this practice is that a woman is often put at a disadvantage because she has to wait for the man to make the first move. In the absence of such a move, a marriageable woman could find herself marrying someone else for whom she may have very little affection.

In cases where a man has expressed an interest in a woman, tradition has dictated that the family members make the initial inquiries on behalf of the man. In indigenous Ghana, a marriage usually begins with a visit to the parents of the bride-to-be, where the groom-to-be's parents request permission and consent for their son to marry the daughter. By tradition, a marriageable girl is viewed as one who has undergone the important rites of passage, usually performed just after the onset of menarche, where a girl is believed to be ready to receive suitors. As noted by ethnographers, African teenagers undergo a variety of initiation rituals prior to entering the adult world. For the most part, these initiation rites provide individuals, especially young girls who are socialized into their future roles as mothers and wives, with instruction about what will be expected of them during the next phase of their lives. After the teenagers undergo these rites, it is the duty of family members to arrange the terms and conditions of the bride wealth to be paid.

Depending on the ethnicity of the parties involved and the socioeconomic status of the parties, a transfer of some wealth or traditionally accepted commodity (bride wealth) usually occurs between the groom's parents and the bride's family before the marriage is consummated. Indeed, the bride wealth can take many forms, as specified by the normative practices of the particular area. For example, among the Akans of southern Ghana, the bride wealth involves the payment of a token amount that includes, in most cases, some money to the bride's family and drinks such as gin and schnapps. In the northern and upper regions of Ghana, these transactions involve the exchange of goods and services and/or cattle. According to Assimeng (1981), these transactions give public recognition to the marriage, especially one consummated under customary law. Moreover, the act signifies the legal transfer of the rights of parents in their daughter to the groom and his family. As a result, the bride wealth is often shared by the bride's entire family. At the same time, the payment confers to the groom the productive and reproductive services of the bride while guaranteeing the bride some rights of protection (Assimeng, 1981).

On the day of the marriage, both parties meet at the house of the bride, where the groom's parents will officially ask permission from the bride's family members on behalf of their son. Coincidentally, although the negotiations may have been done between the two families over the period that may be akin to an engagement in Western societies, on the day of the marriage it is common for the bride's parents to ask their daughter whether she actually wants to be married to her future husband. If the answer is negative, the marriage ceremony is deemed over. In reality, this does not normally happen given the initial input by the family members throughout the engagement period. It is this involvement of family members that the ethnographic literature alludes to as the undue influence of kin in choosing a mate in Africa.

The influence of family members is more evident regarding marriages consummated under customary law. In Ghana, three types of marriages are recognized under the existing rules and regulations: customary law marriages (the most flexible), marriage under the Ordinance (civil) or Church rules, and marriage contracted under Islamic religious beliefs and regulations. Consistent with Islamic regulations that are the source of legitimization for such unions, marriages contracted under Islamic laws could be either monogamous or polygamous. According to Takyi and Oheneba-Sakyi (1994), most Ghanaians (more than 80%) marry under the provisions of customary law. In general, marriages under customary law practices are considered the most flexible and tend to be based on existing rules and regulations found in the particular locality. Moreover, and in contrast to marriages under the Ordinance that are similar to civil marriages and forbid plural unions, marriages under the customary law could be either monogamous or polygamous. Indeed, although the majority of marriages in Ghana are monogamous, the available data also indicate that about a quarter of them are polygamous (Timæus & Reynar, 1998).

Changing Patterns of Mate Selection: Increasing Self-Selection

In the most recent year for which data are available, it is apparent that individualistic ties, as opposed to communal ties, are becoming the norm when it comes to mate selection. As shown in Figure 5.1, a sizable proportion of men and women who were surveyed in southern Ghana reported selecting

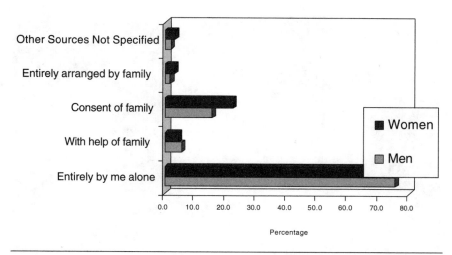

Figure 5.1   How Married Men and Women Selected Their Current Partners: Southern Ghana, 1992–1993

their own partners, a finding that is at odds with earlier ethnographic evidence. Among those sampled, 75.9% of the men and 69.0% of the women reported selecting their current partners by themselves. Such a development is consistent with some recent reports to the effect that, in urban areas in particular, it has even become common for couples to be married without informing their respective parents at all ("FIDA Holds," 1999).

Figure 5.1 also shows that although most of the respondents reported that they selected their current partners entirely by themselves, a closer inspection of the data indicates that gender plays a role in the decision-making process. In comparison with the men, the number of women respondents who sought the consent of their family members was somewhat higher. Given the different socialization patterns of men and women, coupled with the fact that the male-dominated African family structure tends to establish acceptable norms that influence male-female relationships, this variation in mate selection by gender should come as no surprise. Indeed, scholars who have examined gender relations in Africa have reported that men tend to make the decisions that affect women's lives. In some cases, the women are not consulted but only informed about the decisions (Dodoo, 1998). Also, it has been suggested that in many parts of Africa, male activities are always recognized as predominantly important (as opposed to female activities), with the cultural systems giving more authority and value to the roles and activities of men (Dodoo, 1998). Under

Bride and Groom With Extended Family Members of the Groom

such a system, it appears that the degree of personal selection varies by the gender of the person making the choice.

Even though Ghanaian men and women may be selecting their own partners, the data also show that the influence of family and kin members has not been ignored completely. Indeed, a closer examination of Figure 5.1 shows that about 15.5% of the men and 22.1% of the women sought the consent of their family members in choosing their partners. The involvement of family members in various supportive capacities when it comes to selecting a potential mate implies that people might not be abandoning the old order completely. Rather, as has been pointed out by scholars who have examined nuptial patterns in contemporary Africa, people might be blending the two, creating unique structures and processes that may be different from practices found in other parts of the world (Lesthaeghe, 1989; Meekers, 1995; Smith, 2001). In the case of Ghana, for example, some have pointed out that it is common for married people to perform the required traditional rites, such as the payment of bride wealth, and then to rush to the many Christian churches found throughout the country to have their marriages blessed by a priest or Imam. Others combine aspects of a Western-style wedding with the traditional practices. Similarly, the

Table 5.1   Age Cohorts and Patterns of Mate Selection Among Men and Women: Southern Ghana, 1992-1993 (percentages)

	Men			Women		
	18 to 38 Years	39 + Years	All	16 to 33 Years	34 + Years	All
Choice of partner						
Entirely by me alone	79.4	70.3	75.4	73.9	57.9	66.8
With help of family	3.6	7.9	5.5	3.4	6.2	4.6
Consent of family	14.1	17.3	15.5	17.2	28.2	22.1
Entirely arranged	1.4	2.2	1.8	2.4	4.0	3.1
Other sources (not specified)	1.6	2.2	1.9	3.2	3.7	3.4
n	505	404	909	519	390	909

NOTE: Both models were significant at the .001 level.

existence of polygamous as well as monogamous unions in contemporary Ghana is viewed as indicative of the existence of traditional and modern influences in African family relationships.

Although the findings in Figure 5.1 provide some useful insights into contemporary mate selection patterns in southern Ghana, they tell us nothing about the possible generational influence on the process. Given the likelihood that the younger age cohorts may have been affected more by social changes than were the older Ghanaians, the extent to which recent marital behavior is influenced by age was investigated. Using the mean age of the respondents as cutoffs (men were coded into two age groups [18 to 38 and over 38 years], and women were coded into two age groups [16 to 33 and over 33 years]), their patterns of mate selection were analyzed (Table 5.1).

In comparison with the older respondents, the younger age cohorts were more likely to have selected their own partners (79% of men ages 18 to 38 years vs. 70% of men over 39), a finding that is true for both men and women. Among the women, the difference between the younger and older age groups was even higher (74% vs. 58%). The variation in mate selection by age cohort in Ghana is consistent with studies from other parts of Africa. In a recent study of young Igbo men and women in Nigeria, Smith (2001) found that the younger generations were more likely than their parents and grandparents to insist on choosing their marriage partners. Although the generational changes are evident regarding mate selection, the extent to which factors such as ethnicity, religion, and socioeconomic position affect men and women of different generations is not addressed in this chapter. It is important to consider these issues, however, so as to paint a realistic picture of some of the changes that are occurring in marital processes in Ghana. In further analyses that investigated the forces that affect mate selection, urban residence, education, and age were found to be closely related to the likelihood that respondents would select their own partners.

Conclusion

The available evidence shows that contemporary Ghanaian marriages are increasingly becoming less traditional regarding the selection process. Indeed, the popular image of African marriages as devoid of individual choices contrasts sharply with what has been reported in Western societies. As has been alluded to in earlier anthropological work from the region, a consideration of African marriages would not be complete without refer- ence to the role played by family members, both in the selection of poten- tial mates and in the ceremonies that accompany the process. Under such a scenario, it has been suggested that the actions of kin and family members in large part dictate who family members can and cannot marry. Despite these earlier reports, few recent studies have examined courtship and pat- terns of mate selection, making it difficult to assess any shifts in behavior. The study reported here was designed to fill this knowledge gap in part.

Overall, data from southern Ghana indicate that the traditional patterns of mate selection may be changing. For the most part, and in contrast to ear- lier periods in which the influence of family members was more pronounced, the current analysis shows that personal and individual choices appear to guide the way in which Ghanaians are now selecting their partners. Although the consent of parents and family members continues to be sought by some people, the trend toward self-selection is not unique to any partic- ular group, as both men and women report self-selecting their partners.

The observation that mate selection practices in Ghana are changing and becoming an individualized affair is consistent with the predictions made dur- ing the 1960s that family processes throughout the world would converge over time (Goode, 1963; Inkeles, 1980). Also, the increasing trend toward self-selection of marital partners reported in Ghana is not a unique phenom- enon. A number of scholars have observed a similar development throughout the sub-Saharan region, including Nigeria (Smith, 2001), Kenya (Hetherington, 2001), and Togo (Meekers, 1995). More important, these studies also point to the increasing notions of romantic love, intimacy, and attraction as fueling this growing trend. Although young people are no longer compelled to live by the norms and mores that guided their parents' generation and marital choices, the trend toward self-selection, as opposed to reliance on kin and family, should not be viewed as a recent development. Indeed, it may be accurate to suggest that these developments are actually a continuation of trends that were set in motion as a result of Africa's incorporation into the global economy (see, e.g., Kaufmann & Meekers, 1998; Oppong, 1981, 1983). Given the increasing trend toward globalization and interdependence of the world, this trend is likely to continue.

This chapter's initial observations about recent Ghanaian marriages also highlight the contradictions between agencies of modernization and agencies of traditionalism in postcolonial Africa. Rather than wholeheartedly changing their behavior to mirror that found in Western societies, many Africans might not be completely abandoning their traditional ways of doing things. This is evident in the dynamics behind the courtship, dating, and accompanying rites that are part of the marital processes in Ghana. Even in the context where many people are choosing their own partners, it is increasingly becoming clear that the input of family members is not fading. As Meekers (1995), Pool (1972), and many other scholars have suggested, what is happening in "modern" Africa can be considered as the amalgamation of traditional and modern values about marriage where traditional religious practices and foreign religion forms (e.g., Christianity, Islam) can coexist. For example, Aryee (1985) noted that in Ghana, Catholics and Protestants can live with customary marriage practices, such as polygamy, that are unacceptable in Euro-American teachings based on the concept of individuation and romantic attraction.

Another example of the coexistence of the two practices can be gleaned from a recent report that appeared in one of the local Ghanaian newspapers ("Don't Rush," 1999). In the report, the author pointed out that the timely intervention by the police and officials of the Department of Social Welfare at Elmina in the central region saved a 16-year-old girl from being forcibly offered for marriage by her parents. Although the parents of the young girl reportedly were originally from the country of Mali in West Africa, they were residents of southern Ghana. Unfortunately for the parents, while the parents were discussing how to go about the forced marriage formalities, the girl heard the plan and quickly wrote to inform the Girls' Education Unit of the Ghana Education Service, which then took action to prevent the marriage ("Don't Rush," 1999).

One of the challenges facing contemporary Ghanaians, and for that matter many Africans, is how best the people can balance age-old tensions between romantic passion and family stability. Indeed, the coexistence of tradition and modernity can create a great deal of tension in the family. Thus, during a time of rapid changes, families and individuals need to compromise if they are to achieve their common goals of survival and independence. Some researchers have suggested that what we may be seeing in African marriages is based on compromises between strict family arrangements and the independent choices of couples. In the ongoing amalgamation of the old and the new, it is common for some to argue that the homogenization that Goode (1963) foresaw has not occurred, nor has the impact of Westernization on African marriages been quite as pronounced as Goode anticipated. As many earlier scholars pointed out, Africans may have adopted aspects of Western culture into their own systems, thereby creating hybrid institutions that are neither African nor Western. Moreover, as a result of recent migratory patterns (both internal and international), increasing women's education and changing socioeconomic status may continue to have an impact on family and marital relationships throughout the region. In Ghana, the growth of Pentecostal, Evangelical, and charismatic religious groups (especially those originating in Africa) are changing the religious landscape in the country and might also affect future marital processes. Indeed, anecdotal evidence suggests that some of these Christian denominations are more likely to require their members to date, court among themselves, or marry according to civil/religious prescriptions, which in Ghana tend to involve an official wedding. Given current trends, one would expect significant changes to occur in family and marital processes, thereby undercutting the existing traditional arrangements.

References

Amoateng, Y., & Heaton, T. (1989). The socio-demographic correlates of the timing of divorce in Ghana. *Journal of Comparative Family Studies, 20,* 79–96.

Aryee, F. (1985). Nuptiality patterns in Ghana. In S. Singh, J. Y. Owusu, & I. H. Shah (Eds.), *Demographic patterns in Ghana: Evidence from the Ghana Fertility Survey 1979–80* (pp. 17–48). Voorburg, Netherlands: International Statistical Institute.

Assimeng, M. (1981). *Social structure of Ghana: A study in persistence and change.* Tema, Ghana: Ghana Publishing.

Awusabo-Asare, K. (1988). Interpretations and demographic concepts: The case of Ghana. *Population and Development Review, 14,* 675–687.

Bledsoe, C. (1990). Transformations in sub-Saharan African marriage and fertility. *Annals of the American Academy of Political and Social Science, 510,* 115–125.

Bledsoe, C., & Pison, G. (Eds.). (1994). *Nuptiality in sub-Saharan Africa*. Oxford, UK: Clarendon.

Bruce, J., Lloyd, C., & Leonard, A. (1995). *Families in focus: New perspectives on mothers, fathers, and children*. New York: Population Council.

Caldwell, J. (1982). *A theory of fertility decline*. Canberra, Australia: ANU Press.

Caldwell, J., & Caldwell, P. (1987). The cultural context of high fertility in sub-Saharan Africa. *Population and Development Review, 13,* 409–438.

Cohen, B. (1998). The emerging fertility transition in sub-Saharan Africa. *World Development, 26,* 1431–1461.

Dodoo, F. N. A. (1998). Marriage type and reproductive decisions: A comparative study in sub-Saharan Africa. *Journal of Marriage and the Family, 60,* 232–242.

Don't rush to say I do—Priest. (1999, April 13). *Ghana Review International.* [Online]. Retrieved October 13, 2002, from www.ghanaweb.com/ghanahomepage/newsarchive/

Ebin, V. (1982). Interpretation of infertility: The Aowin of south-west Ghana. In C. MacCormarck (Ed.), *Ethnography of fertility and birth* (pp. 141–159). New York: Academic Press.

Fiawoo, D. (1978). Women and customs in Ghana. In *Background papers to the Seminar on Ghanaian Women in Development*. Accra, Ghana: National Council on Women and Development.

FIDA holds on marriage laws and Constitution. (1999). *Ghana Review International.* [Online]. Retrieved October 13, 2002, from www.ghanaweb.com/ghanahomepage/newsarchive

Fortes, M. (1950). Kinship and marriage among the Ashanti. In A. Radcliffe-Brown & D. Forde (Eds.), *African systems of kinship and marriage* (pp. 252–284). London: Oxford University Press.

Ghana Statistical Services. (1984). *Census reports*. Accra, Ghana: Author.

Ghana Statistical Services. (1989). *Ghana demographic and health survey, 1988*. Accra, Ghana: Author.

Goode, W. (1963). *World revolution and family patterns*. London: Free Press.

Goody, J. (1976). *Production and reproduction: A comparative study of the domestic domain*. Cambridge, UK: Cambridge University Press.

Hetherington, P. (2001). Generational changes in marriage patterns in central province of Kenya, 1930–1990. *Journal of Asian and African Studies, 36,* 157–180.

Hutchinson, S. (1990). Rising divorce among the Nuer, 1936–83. *Man, 25,* 393–411.

Inkeles, A. (1980). Modernization and family patterns: A test of convergence theory. *Conspectus of History, 1,* 31–62.

Kaufmann, G., & Meekers, D. (1998). The impact of women's socioeconomic position on marriage patterns in sub-Saharan Africa. *Journal of Comparative Family Studies, 29,* 101–114.

Lesthaeghe, R. (Ed.). (1989). *Reproduction and social organization in sub-Saharan Africa*. Berkeley: University of California Press.

Locoh, T. (1990). Family trends and demographic transition in Africa. *International Social Studies Journal, 26,* 476–482.

Lloyd, C., & Gage-Brandon, A. (1993). Women's role in maintaining households: Family welfare and sexual inequality in Ghana. *Population Studies, 47,* 115–131.

Meekers, D. (1992). The process of marriage in African societies: A multiple indicator approach. *Population and Development Review, 18,* 61–78.

Meekers, D. (1995). Freedom of partner choice in Togo. *Journal of Comparative Family Studies, 26,* 163–179.

Nukunya, G. (1978). Women and marriage. In *Background papers to the Seminar on Ghanaian Women in Development.* Accra, Ghana: National Council on Women and Development.

Nukunya, G. (1992). *Tradition and change in Ghana: An introduction to sociology.* Accra: Ghana Universities Press.

Oheneba-Sakyi, Y., Awusabo-Asare, K., Gbortsu, E., & Aryee, F. (1995). *Female autonomy, decision making, and demographic behavior among couples in Ghana.* Final report of the Ghana Female Autonomy Micro Study (GFAMS), Ethnic Studies Program, California State University, Fresno.

Oppong, C. (1981). *Middle class African marriage.* London: Allen & Unwin.

Oppong, C. (1983). *Female and male in West Africa.* London: Allen & Unwin.

Pool, J. (1972). A cross-comparative study of aspects of conjugal behavior among women of three West African countries. *Canadian Journal of African Studies, 6,* 233–259.

Population Reference Bureau. (2001). *World data sheets.* Washington, DC: Author.

Radcliffe-Brown, A., & Forde, D. (Eds.). (1950). *African systems of kinship and marriage.* London: Oxford University Press.

Singh, S., & Samara, R. (1996). Early marriage among women in developing countries. *International Family Planning Perspectives, 22,* 148–157.

Smith, D. (2001). Romance, parenthood, and gender in a modern African society. *Ethnology, 40,* 129–151.

Takyi, B. K. (2001). Marital stability in an African society: Exploring the factors that influence divorce processes in Ghana. *Sociological Focus, 34,* 77–96.

Takyi, B. K., & Oheneba-Sakyi, Y. (1994). Customs and practices about marriages and family Life in Ghana. *Family Perspectives, 28,* 257–281.

Timæus, I., & Reynar, A. (1998). Polygynists and their wives in sub-Saharan Africa: An analysis of five demographic and health surveys. *Population Studies, 52,* 145–162.

6

Connecting Generations

Kamba and Maasai Paths to Marriage in Kenya

Stephan M. Wilson

Lucy W. Ngige

Linda J. Trollinger

As my sisters and I went about doing our daily chores, we choked on the dust stirred up by the herd of cattle and goats that had just arrived in our compound. I was surprised when I found out that these animals were my bride wealth, negotiated by my parents and the family of the man who had been chosen as my husband. His name is Simayia ole Mootian, and he is 27 years old. I have never met him. Because I have recently been circumcised, I am considered to be a woman. So, I am ready to marry, have children, and assume adult privileges and responsibilities. My name is Telelia ole Mariani. I am 14 years old.

Here, life is difficult, and I wonder how this will change my life. I wonder whether he already has other wives. I wonder how we will live. Will we live together, or will he live away from the family to work in the city? Does he have a job? I probably will not continue in school or have a job. Instead, I will be having and taking care of children.

Many people are infected with HIV/AIDS. That is changing the way children, parents, and grandparents take care of each other. I wonder whether he could have HIV/AIDS. If I become infected, who will care for our children? Will they have it? My mind is in a whirl of questions; I am excited, happy, nervous, and concerned. (Maasai—traditional/rural)

The bustle of city life interrupts my thoughts of Mueni wa Musili. She is 21 years old, smart, fun, and beautiful. I am Wambua wa Mutia, a high school graduate. I am now 24 years old. Mueni and I love each other and want to get married, and we have chosen each other for marriage. Our parents say that to be respectful of tradition, our families should be involved in the choice and arrangements for bride wealth. We both want further education, but because so few people are allowed to go to the public universities, and because the cost of the private universities is so far beyond the means of the average Kenyan, we are hoping to at least get some additional technical postsecondary training. Her family thinks that further training is unnecessary for a woman, and my family thinks that she is too old and not worth the bride price that her family expects. We want to make our own decisions, yet we do not want to be disrespectful of our elders', parents', and families' wishes.

With all the worry over jobs and unemployment, increasing rates of HIV/AIDS, and other changes in our communities, this family tension increases the difficulty and stress in our lives. We feel torn between the old ways and the new practices that are taking place in society. It is not that we want to reject tradition, but we want to be able to choose what we feel is best for us. (Kamba—modern/urban)

The basis for establishing marriages varies by culture. For example, Western cultures place great emphasis on romantic love, whereas in other parts of the world the reasons for coupling and/or marriage vary across groups, cultures, and situations. People marry for economic reasons, for sheer survival, and/or to enhance their personal or familial economic position or status. People also marry for sexual, social, and/or emotional convenience. Additional bases for marriages may be avenues for building family or political alliances, religious reasons, and societal expectations. Thus, to understand couple formation, it is necessary to look at the culture, economy, and social geography in which marriage occurs.

The republic of Kenya is a place of great beauty and diversity, straddling the equator on the eastern coast of Africa. It is about the size of Texas or France and has a population of more than 30 million people. Much of the country is semi-arid or desert that cannot support human settlement; nearly

80% of Kenyans live on 20% of the land and mostly in rural regions. Religious affiliations include Christian (70%), Islam (6%), Hindu (1%), and indigenous religions (23%). There are more than 70 ethnic groups, with the largest being Kikuyu, Luhya, Luo, Kalenjin, and Kamba (*Population*, 2000).

Most Kenyans, regardless of ethnicity, share a pattern of social life that is organized around strong clan and extended family ties. These links are described by both obligations to and privileges from those who are a part of the lineage, whether by birth or marriage (Kayongo-Male & Onyango, 1984). Today, however, these links are being stretched by urban migration, adoption of elements of other (Western) lifestyles, and both the lure of and pressures for young adults to embrace "modern" ways of life, represented by dress, language, diet, pop culture, and religious and political ideas.

Most Kenyan young adults are faced with severely limited economic resources (the annual per capita income is U.S. $340), a shortened life expectancy due to AIDS (which may affect as many as one of six young adults), a moderate literacy rate (79%), and a very high (and likely greatly underestimated) unemployment rate (35%) (*Embassy of the Republic of Kenya*, n.d.). The infant mortality rate in Kenya is estimated at 59 per 1,000 live births, with a life expectancy of 47 years for males and 49 years for females (*Marriage*, 2001; *Population*, 2001). In comparison, the United States has a per capita income of $34,199 (equivalent to the wealth of more than 100 average Kenyans), a 99% literacy rate, a 5% unemployment rate, an infant mortality rate of 28 per 1,000 live births, and an overall life expectancy of 77 years (74 for men and 79 for women) (*World Desk Reference*, 2002a, 2002b).

It is useful to examine the context of Kenyan marriage from a social exchange framework, which posits that individuals evaluate reciprocal relationships through a ratio of rewards to costs. People seek to maximize rewards and minimize costs by comparing what they receive in a relationship with what they have to give up in the relationship, constantly evaluating whether or not there is a better alternative (Winton, 1995). For example, a husband may receive benefits of family alliances, status, sexual exchanges, labor, and continuation of his family-of-origin lineage, whereas a wife may receive economic resources, her adult status as wife and mother, and protection. Extended family members also gain rewards such as family alliances, continuing their lineage through the children of the union, and caregiving for elders. In addition, the wife's family may receive economic gain from the bride wealth. The exchange network includes persons, goods, labor, money, advice, affection, and other material and nonmaterial goods. Exchanges are based on an unwritten "intergenerational contract" that is derived from values, habits, and behaviors of reciprocity (Cattell, 1997) shared in that culture. In a good Kenyan marriage, both the marrying children (man and woman) and their families (husband's and wife's parents and extended families) will evaluate the marriage as a favorable exchange.

Marriage and kinship in Kenya is a complex web of financial, social, and spiritual worlds that cannot be separated. From an East African perspective, marriage establishes and reinforces family alliances and connects all generations of a community—past, present, and future (Kayongo-Male & Onyango, 1984; Mbiti, 1970). Marriage and the social interactions leading to marriage involve a lengthy process, marked with negotiation and ritual. Being allowed to marry signifies community recognition that a person occupies a position of maturity and responsibility.

Familially, individuals are tied to each other and are bonded by blood and marriage. Kinship, based on a clan system, is the strongest force in East African societies. Kin are bound by specific expectations that govern group behaviors and ensure a social cohesion, assistance in times of need, and a sense of belonging. In East Africa, the concept of kinship, which is grounded in collectivism, includes not only those who are living (*sasa*) and their ancestors but also all those who were known by some persons still alive (also part of the sasa) as well as those dead ancestors who are not remembered personally by anyone alive in this time (*zamani*). Kin also extend into the future to those yet to be born. Thus, marriage and birth are connecting points for all generations. Past generations continue to live through current and future generations (Mbiti, 1970). Marriage provides for the continuation and unity of family through procreation and alliances (Jackline, 2001; Kayongo-Male & Onyango, 1984).

Socially, marriage is a symbol of status and an avenue through which individuals gain further acceptance and respect within the community (Nthaka & Kirima, 2001). Traditionally, marriage, which was considered to be a duty to family and society (Dyson-Hudson & Meekers, 1996), was restricted to only those who had been initiated. The initiation process, which is deeply rooted in East African cultures, is an important rite of passage for both male and female youth (i.e., circumcision for males, clitoridectomy for females) that entitles the initiated to adult privileges and responsibilities. During recent decades, female circumcision and some other related rituals have greatly decreased. Nonetheless, the initiation process, which is deeply rooted in East African cultures, symbolizes the end of childhood and an entry into adulthood that entitles the initiated to full adult privileges (e.g., to initiate sexual relationships) as well as adult responsibilities to the community (Mbiti, 1970). Among some groups, beauty scars, changes in name or dress, or other outward symbols give witness to the change in status.

Because family members are linked by strong reciprocal aid relationships that involve complex rights and responsibilities, older family members have a legitimate say in the marriages of younger relatives (Harrell-Bonds, 1976; Kayongo-Male & Onyango, 1984). Thus, in addition to social exchange, marriage demonstrates the complexity of multidirectional interactions that take place within the extended family. In many communities, celibacy during adulthood is suspect both because it seems to be a rejection of widely expected adult responsibilities and because it appears to refute loyalty to one's family. Marriage is socially preferred over singlehood by the majority of Kenyans (Mbaya, 1999).

Financially, the attainment of marriage is a determining factor for inheritance. Grounded in the fear that wealth may be lost if there are no descendants, in some communities single men could not inherit family wealth (Nthaka & Kirima, 2001). The giving of bride wealth is a substantial commitment from the groom and his family to the family of the bride in appreciation for the opportunity of marriage and as a demonstration of the valuing of the young woman. Whether in the form of livestock, food, goods, money, or a combination of these, it significantly affects the families of both partners while affirming the value (in a real way) of the woman, both as a person and as a wife (*Marriage,* 2001; Nasimiyu, 1997). Accumulation of the bride wealth usually involves assistance from all family members, who have an "investment" in making the marriage work. The bride's family is obligated to return the bride wealth if the marriage fails. The economics of marriage reach beyond the married couple and can have a dramatic impact on the families of both partners. From the social exchange perspective, each family has a stake in the success of the marriage as a result of multidirectional exchanges, which confirm attainment of adult status and privilege, induce formation of family alliances, and undergird economic transactions.

Legally, Kenyan marriages are informal or formal. Informal (customary) marriages are those that follow traditional customs relating to couple formation and lack a formal government recording. Formal (civil) marriages, which are often expensive, stem from the increase of organized religion and provide a recorded marriage certificate. This certificate makes it possible for the wife to claim her husband's property for herself and her children in the event of his death (Hetherington, 2001). The legality of marriage has a bearing on the validity of the marriage, inheritance, child custody, dissolution (Kayongo-Male & Onyango, 1984), and even burials of family members (Cohen & Odhiambo, 1992). Christian and Islamic marriages are recognized by law (Kayongo-Male & Onyango, 1984).

Spiritually, marriage and procreation are sacred and are acts that bring together all members of the community across time—the departed, the living, and those yet to be born. Marriage and procreation maintain the "rhythm of life," and everyone is expected to participate (Mbiti, 1970).

Fertility

Fertility is central to how Kenyan marriages are understood and is one criterion for being seen as a responsible and productive adult member of one's clan. Having children not only gives evidence of the productivity of the couple but also provides the link across time to past and future generations. Pregnancy is seen as the ultimate seal for a marriage. Because of the importance placed on childbearing, the failure to produce a child carries serious implications, such as humiliation and shame, and sometimes serves as a justification for a man to take subsequent wives when there is no progeny produced by a sexual union.

Polygyny

Polygyny, the practice of having multiple wives, is practiced in many families in Kenya. By tradition, having multiple wives was a sign of wealth and was seen as evidence of higher social status of the family (Kagunge, Serah, Angela, & Moeni, 2001). Another reason for this practice stems from the importance placed on having children. If a woman was infertile, it was common for the husband to take another wife to fulfill reproductive expectations (Harrell-Bonds, 1976; *Marriage,* 2001). An infertile woman may herself "take a wife" toward the same goal (as discussed later in this chapter).

Polygyny is also an alternative to divorce and so contributes to greater family stability (of one kind) and long marital durations (Timæus, 1998). Having multiple wives contributes to continuing family existence and continuing availability of assistance. The extent of polygyny is affected by four main factors: economic status of the man, region of residence, level of education of the initial wife, and death/inheritance. Because marriage is a connection to a particular lineage, levirate and sororate marriages may occur. In some groups (especially in western Kenya), when a husband dies, one of his brothers (or another close male relative) commonly inherits the wife or wives of the deceased (levirate marriage), yet children born to that union are considered to belong to the deceased man. In cases where the wife dies, the widower often takes his wife's unmarried sister or paternal cousin as a wife (sororate marriage) (Kayongo-Male & Onyango, 1984).

In addition, certain practicalities about polygyny are assumed. The presence of additional wives and mothers provides assistance with necessary tasks and child care if one mother becomes ill or dies (*Marriage,* 2001). It provides additional alliances as well as social and economic advantages to co-wives. An increased number of children provide a larger workforce to accomplish needs and tasks as well as to provide support during old age (Hertrich & Pilon, 1998). A strong element of social exchange is reflected in the interactions of child care, household tasks, crop labor, status, fertility, and elder care among co-wife, husband-wife, and extended family dynamics.

The rate of polygynous marriages in Kenya is declining. The 1998 figures reported that 16% of married Kenyan women were in polygamous marriages, with the higher proportions being among older women and in the Nyanza Province of western Kenya (24% of married women in this region). In comparison, the polygyny rate for Kenyan women in 1977 was 30% (Mbaya, 1999). During the early 1990s, a study of Kikuyu men indicated that 17% were in, or planned to be in, polygynous marriages, whereas 28% of their fathers were in polygynous marriages (Adams, 1994). This decline is influenced by changes taking place in Kenyan society such as transitions in gender role expectations, the mate selection process, education levels (especially for women), and religion. Christianity seems to be a factor in both later age of marriage and the decline in polygyny (Kaufmann & Meekers, 1998).

Premarital Negotiations: Bride Wealth

Premarital negotiations involve the determination of the bride wealth, which is an important institution in East African society (*Marriage,* 2001). The basic premise of bride wealth is the offering of significant exchange (e.g., livestock, food, goods, money, other valuable commodities) as compensation for and recognition of a woman's labor contributions to her parents' family (Nasimiyu, 1997). Although some Westerners may view this as "buying" a wife, according to African beliefs, it is not like that at all. Rather, it legitimizes not only the woman's value but also the marriage contract (Mbiti, 1970). The size of the bride wealth depends on the economic status of the groom and his family; no man should be rejected solely on grounds that he could not raise the bride wealth. Raising the bride wealth is a demonstration that the man is ready to care for a wife and children and that he will invest in the marriage. The solidarity with family, the efforts to raise the bride wealth, and the public and shared decision tie the bride and groom not only to each other but also to their extended families.

Cattle as Bride Wealth

On the marriage of a woman, her family experiences a significant loss of resources. Thus, bride wealth is an expression of commitment to the woman by the groom's family and shows respect to her and her family (Cole, 1998; *Marriage*, 2001). Often, the bride wealth is never fully paid; the fun and teasing are a kind of family resource created by the give and take of negotiations and public discussions.[1] The average amount of bride wealth has been decreasing in response to factors such as decreased access to land, scarcity of livestock, and increased value placed on education as well as social changes such as gender norm modification and Christian disapproval (Ensminger & Knight, 1997; Hetherington, 2001). Despite the widespread practice and economic implications for African families, the bride wealth practice has drawn criticism from outsiders as being patriarchal and an important factor in promoting the status quo of male social dominance (Bell & Song, 1994; Gitahi, 2002).

Mate Selection

No one custom of mate selection can be generalized to all Kenyans. There are ethnic, socioeconomic, religious, and regional differences. Traditionally, a girl was betrothed at an early age (e.g., before 10 years), and by puberty (12 to 14 years) she was married to a young man in his 20s, if it was a first marriage, or to an older man if she was being given as a second or later wife. In contrast, a woman's husband was considerably older, an age difference that was often necessary for him to gather the bride wealth for the girl's family (Dyson-Hudson & Meekers, 1996) and to attain appropriate status (Mbiti, 1970). Today, the age gap between Kenyan women and men at marriage is closing, with women now marrying at a later age (United Nations Children's Fund, 2001). Currently, the median age for first marriage in Kenya is 19 years for women and 25 years for men. Rural women tend to marry 2 years earlier than do urban women.

Choosing a Mate: Qualities and Approach

One common responsibility of a family and the larger clan is to regulate sexual and reproductive behaviors through marriage to an outsider. An inappropriate mate might be someone who is too close a relative, is from a lower social class, or has incompatible values (e.g., being a witch, having a close relative who practices or subscribes to witchcraft).

Certain attributes or characteristics are considered to be virtues of a suitable wife. Among those traits considered valuable are absence of witchcraft in the family, hardworking, a good example or role model, respectful, attractive, strong, humble, patient, and obedient (Chesaina, 1997) as well as talkative, courageous, and from a family with a good reputation (Kagunge et al., 2001). Lazy, aged, and/or irresponsible women are the last to be selected as mates (Nthaka & Kirima, 2001). Maturity among men is highly regarded. Bravery, confidence, good character, and hardworking, as well as adequate economic status, are preferred qualities in potential husbands (Jackline, 2001). Emphasis is placed on knowing one's duties and role expectations as a mature person and on having the ability and willingness to work hard (Abbott, 1997). Among some communities, the right to marry is affected by birth order, with the elder siblings being expected to marry first (Nthaka & Kirima, 2001). The most important qualities in a prospective mate are good character, hard work, respect for elders, and potency in men and fertility in women (which would be confirmed at marriage). The groom's family must have wealth in the form of cattle, which is used to pay the bride's family.

Traditionally, the process of selecting a woman took place in one of three ways. Either (a) the father of the groom would choose an appropriate wife, negotiate with the woman's family, and then inform the son; (b) the father of the groom would select a woman, inform the son of this choice, and if the son approved, then negotiations with her family would begin; or (c) the son would select a female in whom he was interested and inform his father, who would then begin negotiations with her family (Kagunge et al., 2001). Many years ago, the choice and arrangements were made while the children were still very young—before they were old enough to marry. Today, especially among urban and educated families, the choice of partners is solely or increasingly a decision of the young adults themselves.

Once the suitable prospective wife has been identified, preliminary discussions about marriage take place between those representing the bride and those representing the groom—not simply between the bride and groom themselves (Jackline, 2001). A representative of the man's family approaches the father of the woman's family and engages in protracted and often metaphoric conversation about topics such as availability of water or stones for a fire, asking questions in ways that would suggest whether the man's daughter is available for marriage and whether the family is open to the match (Mbiti, 1970; Nthaka & Kirima, 2001). For example, if a man has a daughter eligible for marriage, an inquiry might go as follows:

> "We are very thirsty, and someone told us that if we came this way, we might get some water or have someone direct us in the direction of the river. Are we in the right place? Do you have water, or can you kindly show us the river?" A negative response from the woman's father would be expressed in a similar fashion: "This place has neither water nor [a] river. I suggest you pass along, and you might be successful, because someone else came along earlier and drank what water there was." This indicated that the girl was already engaged. (Nthaka & Kirima, 2001, p. 5)

Once the marriage negotiation is accepted and finalized, it is customary for the families to share ceremonial beer. Although there is not a specific rite or exchange between the bride and groom to mark the engagement, there can be an exchange between the families to mark the forthcoming marriage; this practice is seen as symbolic of friendship and acceptability (Mbiti, 1970). Often, a small amount of the beer is poured on the ground, perhaps near a ceremonial spot or tree, in remembrance of and deference to departed family members as well as in deference to as yet unborn members of the clan. In some instances, couples have ignored the traditional selection processes and have eloped, bringing about serious consequences. In the Meru society, for example, an eloping couple could face excommunication and banishment from the community (Nthaka & Kirima, 2001).

Formalization of the Couple

There is no one wedding practice that is common to all Kenyans. Ceremonies, rites, and wedding practices vary according to ethnicity (i.e., tribal or ethnic group) and regions, by social and economic status or education levels, as well as to religious affiliations. Some consist of many days of rituals, others celebrate 1 day or with a series of rituals, and still others include a symbolic fight between the families of the bride and groom (Jackline, 2001; Mbiti, 1970). Because of the complexity of rites of passage and the emphasis on progressing through these social markers, marriage is often constituted over time through a series of events, rites, and exchanges that occur at increasingly formalized levels rather than with a specific one-time ceremony as is done in most Western cultures (Harrell-Bonds, 1976; Karp, 1987).

Comparison of Maasai and Kamba

To provide insight into the similarities and differences across Kenyan ethnic groups, two ethnic groups, the Maasai and the Kamba (in the language of the Kamba, or *Kikamba,* the Kamba people are Akamba), are used as examples. The Maasai are perhaps more familiar in the West due to dramatic depictions of Maasai life—striking warriors, pastoralists, and lion hunters. The Kamba were selected as representative of the majority Bantu traditions. The Kamba are farmers and herders, have adapted to urban cash economies, yet have retained many of the traditions that have sustained their communities for centuries.

Maasai Mate Selection

Maasai life is centered on a number of ceremonies and rituals. For females, initiations are focused on circumcision and marriage. For males, age sets move them toward adulthood and are marked by transitions around events such as precircumcision (*enkipaata*), circumcision (*emuratta*), marriage (*enkiama*), warrior graduation (*eunoto*), and the junior elder ceremony (*orngesherr*). At orngesherr, a man gains full responsibility for his own family and is free to move from his father's homestead (Hamisi, 2002). In Maasai society, division of labor is gender based. Female responsibilities include raising children, building houses, getting water and firewood, making clothing, slaughtering cattle, and distributing milk (*Maasai*

Maasai Bride and Groom

Culture, 2001) as well as performing traditional beadwork. Maasai men care for the herds, build enclosures, find water sources, provide protection for the group, sell cattle, purchase beads, and make weapons and tools (e.g., spears, shields, clubs, machetes). Women are heads of their households, whereas men are considered to be the heads of their families.

As with other African societies, marriage is an important part of Maasai life. Marriage (enkiama) not only brings families together but also controls the distribution of cattle. Cattle, the chief item of wealth, play a significant role in marriage as a part of the bride wealth negotiations. Marriage dictates the ownership of cattle (*Maasai Culture,* 2001).

Maasai men may marry when they achieve elder status, whereas women may marry once they have been initiated. For this reason, wives are often much younger than their husbands. Mate selection among the Maasai involves negotiations between representatives of both the bride (*esainoti*) and the groom (*olayamisho*). In other instances, the man may choose his own wife by declaring his interest through gifts of livestock. If his offer is rejected, however, the livestock must be returned (*Maasai Culture,* 2001). These gifts are parallel to the Western custom of an engagement ring for a promise of marriage.

Kenyan Bride and Relatives

The bridal costume consists of a dress and many ornaments. Because the bride's work is community based and focuses on giving and receiving, her dressing becomes a community responsibility rather than a personal selection. Sets of necklaces (the bridal costume) are consistent with the colors of the particular clan. The common name for these necklaces is *masaa* (Hamisi, 2002). The marriage ceremony itself consists of a blessing, the woman having her head shaved, adornment of beads, and a toast of honey beer. After the ceremony, there is a symbolic shedding of tears to express sadness of the bride's leaving her own family as the bride's mother and sisters accompany the couple to the groom's home. On the bride's arrival to her new husband's home, she receives gifts from his family members (*Maasai Culture*, 2001).

Divorce is uncommon in Maasai life because marriage is seen as a union of families rather than of two individuals and so has more and further reaching implications. If problems arise within a marriage, a council of elders is summoned to assist in resolving the differences (*Maasai Culture*, 2001).

Traditional Kamba Mate Selection

In the traditional Kamba culture, the rite of passage from childhood to adulthood for both boys and girls was circumcision, which was also a prerequisite for marriage. What follows is largely a description of rituals and mores of several decades ago. However, vestiges or major parts of many of these remain in some form even today.

Traditional mate selection was exclusively parental choice by male elders of similar socioeconomic classes. It was the responsibility of a father to search for a bride for his son among his friends of similar status. A wealthy man would normally select his son's prospective in-laws from among his associates who had marriageable daughters. In other words, the choice of the family from which his son would get a bride came first, and the choice of the actual bride came second. Neither bride nor groom was consulted in the matter. It was a purely parent-arranged mate selection process directed toward marriage (*imutwaano*).

The elders conduct premarital negotiations. Once an elder has selected his prospective daughter-in-law's family, he and his clan approach the girl's father and his clan for bride wealth negotiations. The traditional basic bride wealth required to seal a marriage is three goats (one male and two female), or some other odd number of goats such as five, seven, or nine, which are referred to as *mbui sya ntheo*. The male goat is slaughtered to shed the blood that seals the marriage contract. According to Kamba tradition, without shedding of this blood, the marriage is not recognized as customarily binding. Additional forms of bride wealth include traditional beer (*uki* or *kithembe*), sugarcane, livestock (including cows, sheep, chickens, and goats), honey, bananas, sweet potatoes, and/or other items depending on the wealth of the groom's family and the bride wealth demanded by the bride's family.

On the night of the presentation of mbui sya ntheo, the girl's parents perform a sexual intercourse ritual with each other. Their sexual intercourse associated with the negotiations for marriage of their daughter symbolizes the coming together of a man and a woman, the coming together of his family and her family, and the impending joining of the child of their union with another family. Marriage, as well as sexual intercourse leading to conception, connects people from current and past generations, people from existing and newly created family lines, and people who may embrace or resist the new union.

On the following day, the strap that had tied the slaughtered goat is returned to the boy's parents as a sign of acceptance. The suitor's father (or elder male relative) sends two calabashes of beer to the girl's parents, accompanied by three elders who act as witnesses. On arrival at the girl's family compound, one calabash is placed at her mother's sleeping place. The elders then gather and drink the beer in the other calabash. Beer in the mother's calabash is first served by the girl's mother to her husband and then to the boy's father. Sharing the mother's gift beer is a sign of consent for the marriage. When the beer is finished, both fathers bless the young couple.

A few weeks after the mbui sya ntheo ceremony, the bride wealth is fixed during another beer-drinking ceremony. During mbui sya ntheo, the suitor's father supplies a bull, a goat, and a sheep for slaughter. Gifts are taken to the girl's mother from the boy's mother and her women friends (e.g., sugar cane, sweet potatoes). The final beer, *uki wa ntheo* (beer for walking to the homestead), is brewed by the boy's father, who invites the girl's party to come to his home to meet the suitor's family, friends, and neighbors. Similar to the mbui sya nthe, the boy's mother serves beer from a calabash.

It should be noted that it is the clan's responsibility to raise the bride wealth required and not necessarily the responsibility of groom's father alone. Bride wealth is regarded as a communal responsibility rather than an individual one. In other words, even a relatively poor man from a wealthy clan gains the wealth status from his extended family wealth. The Kamba are well known for their generosity in settling matters concerning the extended family system.

Once the bride wealth has been paid or payments have begun, the suitor's father brews beer called *uki wa waaya* (beer for claiming the bride).

On this occasion, the girl is not allowed to go with her fiancé. Sometime after this ceremonial meeting, the young man goes to her home with two elderly women relatives. They carry more beer (gifts) for the girl's parents to be used to bless the bride and groom. While the elders are taking this beer, the girl quietly leaves. The groom and his women relatives arrive back at his home with the bride and announce her arrival.

The groom's mother greets and accepts her new daughter-in-law by covering the young woman's neck with *ghee* (a rare commodity). This is a symbol that the bride is precious and now acceptable as a new member of that family. The bride proceeds to the groom's hut, but no sexual intercourse is allowed on the first night of their marriage. The bride moves to her groom's family home and is installed in her mother-in-law's hearth (although the bride has her own matrimonial hut) for training in the roles of a wife, mother, and daughter-in-law. This could take several years, depending on the age of the bride, her ability to have several children, and the duration it takes to have those children. It is the mother-in-law's prerogative to install her daughter-in-law in her own hearth when she considers her ready to assume full responsibility for her conjugal household. This provides further demonstration that marriage is not a purely couple affair but rather an extended family matter.[2]

Contemporary Kamba Mate Selection

In contrast, many young men and women themselves initiate contemporary educated Kamba mate choice. They believe in individual choice and love as the basis for marriage. Young people meet in social institutions such as schools, colleges, workplaces, and church and other religious forums; through social networks and at social events; and through friends and acquaintances. A cross section of newly married Kamba found that spouses reported "falling in love at first sight." Once their love and mutual friendship mature for marriage, they approach their parents to introduce their chosen mates and to ask for their parents' approval and blessings. Today, family arrangements of marriage are strongly resented by the young, who insist on personal choice of marriage partners. At the same time, however, they do value their parents' consent and advice on marriage. Once parents of both parties approve of their children's mate choices, they follow the traditional practices and rituals pertaining to Kamba customary marriage (without further reference to their children). The parents, in a way, relive their own experiences in performing the customary marriage in the same way as it was performed on their behalf by their own parents—intergenerational linkages among the past, the present, and the future.

Bride wealth is negotiated in the same way as in the traditional marriage. The basic bride wealth requirement of three goats must be met in all recognized Kamba customary marriages. Additional wealth may be required, and instead of the traditional cattle form, the equivalent in monetary terms is acceptable. Once the parents fulfill the customary marriage rituals, the bride and groom are given "permission" to contract the wedding ceremony of their choice with the support of their parents. The majority of educated Christian couples choose a Christian wedding ceremony, whereas others opt for statutory marriage.

Among the similarities between traditional and modern marriages are that, in both cases, bride wealth is given to the bride's family by the groom's family. In addition, the traditional marriage rituals, such as slaughtering the male goat (*senge*) to seal the Kamba customary marriage, are performed. Libation that symbolizes the union of the past, present, and future generations united by this marriage contract is also performed. Customary marriage is considered as the primary form of marriage legally recognized in Kenya, not only by the Kamba but by all ethnic groups in Kenya as well. The Western Christian wedding ceremony is considered as secondary to fulfill other requirements such as acquiring a legal marriage certificate or adhering to one's faith in solemnizing a holy matrimony.

Exchange of gifts is a sign of goodwill between in-laws. The bride is considered the greatest gift a family can give to another. Therefore, the groom's family gives gifts to the bride's family. Such gifts include bedding (blankets and bed sheets), *kanga* (a cotton cloth used for clothing, carrying, and covering), and baskets and ropes for the bride's parents and grandparents. The bride herself receives household goods such as furniture (bed and beddings), kitchen equipment and utensils, and a shopping basket (*kyondo*). Modern brides and grooms might receive gifts such as washing machines and microwave ovens as well as basic household equipment and furniture.

Traditionally, divorce was a rare occurrence but was considered necessary when a marriage failed. When a couple had serious disagreements, separation was considered as a stopgap measure. If many reconciliation efforts between the couple and families were found to be fruitless, however, divorce was considered as a last resort. In the traditional marriage, a man divorced his wife and not vice versa. A wife could be divorced on the grounds that she was a habitual adulterer or witch or due to bad character on her part. Customary divorce was said to have taken place when the wife's family returned the bride wealth paid to her family at the time of contracting the marriage. The returned bride wealth is referred to as the *mbui sya maleo,* which translates literally to the "goats of rejection" of the daughter.

In all cases where bride wealth was returned to the groom's family, the mother became the custodian of the children born of the union, and this further meant that her offspring were rejected as well. The divorced woman was free to remain single or to remarry. In the exceptional cases where the wife was separated and the husband kept custody of their children, the bride wealth was not returned to the husband's family. This was regarded as separation, whether the husband and wife were reunited or not.[3]

Woman-to-Woman Marriages

Marriages in Kenya take many forms, including monogamy, polygyny, and woman-to-woman marriages (which do not involve lesbianism as found in Western societies). Currently, there are no statistics about woman-to-woman marriages because this form of marriage is not recognized under Kenyan law. However, it is an acceptable form of customary marriage in many communities in Kenya, and it has existed throughout the history of humankind.

The main reason for contracting woman-to-woman marriages is desperation and turmoil experienced at both the individual and social-cultural levels by the so-called major women (those who initiate these marriages). Those who contract this type of marriage generally are middle-aged, childless, or in polygynous marriages or have had their property rights threatened. Fertility is so central to the understanding of Kenyan marriage that infertility provides a rationale for woman-to-woman marriages among childless women.

In a woman-to-woman marriage, the so-called minor woman has the reproductive capacity and physical energy that the major woman seeks. The major woman pays a bride wealth to the family of the minor woman, and she thereby "culturally marries" the minor woman and adopts any illegitimate children she may already have. The major woman assumes the dual role of husband to the minor woman and father to her children. Although the children call her "grandmother," the wider community refers to the major woman as the "husband and father." There is no stigma attached to this new status acquired after the marriage.

If the minor woman is single and without children, the major woman identifies one of her male relatives whose duty is to sire children for her through the minor woman. The male relative has no other contractual or legal obligation to the minor woman apart from sexual union. The choice of the man is unilaterally that of the major woman; the minor woman has no say in the matter, nor is she permitted to have sexual union with any other males. The identified male is usually a married man with his own wife or wives and with children of his own. The children born of the union with the minor woman belong to the major woman together with any children she may have adopted from the minor woman during the time of their marriage. When the man succeeds in siring a child with the minor woman, the major woman rewards him with a gift of cattle (much like bride wealth).

Among communities that practice woman-to-woman marriages, a major woman who contracts this form of marriage redeems her status of valuable womanhood but can own and inherit her deceased husband's property, and she commands respect from both men and women in her community. She continues to live with her male spouse but practices sexual abstinence. Furthermore, her male spouse does not have a sexual relationship with the minor woman; such sexual contact is taboo. The minor woman and her children can own and inherit property through her female husband (the major woman). In some communities such as the Nandi, the major woman is given a special identity as a male elder. She is given male jewels such as copper earrings, and she gives away her feminine beaded earrings to the minor woman. Male elders treat the major woman as one of their own kind. She attends their meetings and ceremonies, and special blessings are conferred on her eldership. If she is wealthy and can afford multiple bride wealth, she can marry many wives (polygynous). Woman-to-woman marriage is a culturally sanctioned form of marriage prevalent among many communities in Kenya.[4]

Contemporary Kenyan Families in Transition

Contemporary Kenyan families are faced with changes brought about by economic need, migration, population and family structure, war and conflict, education and technology, changing attitudes and behaviors, religious beliefs, and devastating diseases such as AIDS. Some of these changes are negative and contribute to an erosion of solidarity with tradition and the family unit. Other changes are positive and contribute to a forward progression, to improvements, and to new opportunities. Regardless, changes are inevitable and some adaptation is required.

Young people in Kenya find themselves faced with difficult choices—holding onto and preserving traditional practices and views, adopting new mores and values, and finding some way in which to mesh the two views together. Decisions regarding preservation versus incorporation are necessary. Although such decisions are not easy, they will most likely continue to generate widening and different responses and choices between young adult children and their elders.

As Kenya becomes more involved in the global society, roles, practices, and realities of Kenyans will continue to change. With a move toward a more nuclear family structure within some societies, contemporary families are drifting from social organization around extended family and community child rearing to a more nuclear institution. Single parenthood, divorce, and changing attitudes about sex are on the rise (Omungala, 1989). Kaufmann and Meekers (1998) argued that changes in marriage patterns have been brought about by migration for employment, education of women, and changes in the status of women rather than by Western influence and regional differences. Hetherington (2001), however, pointed to the intersection of Christianity, capitalism, Western influence, and education of women as significant factors of change in marital patterns over the past three generations that have led to declines in polygyny, bride wealth, and circumcision and to increases in individual choice of mate selection. Marriage stages are becoming less distinct than in previous generations as a result of uprooting and social transition (Frederiksen, 2000) as well as changes in values and gender norms, the decreasing availability of land, and diminishing livestock herds (Mountain Voices, 2001).

Conclusion and Implications for the Future

Kenyan couple formation and marriage are the result of a diverse and variegated process reflective of ethnicity, generation, clan, religion, and social influences such as urban-rural differences, levels of education, and gender attitudes. These are strongly steeped in family, tradition, and spirituality that merge past, present, and future family members into a lineage ensured by marriage and fertility. While some hold tightly to traditions and others let go of most traditions, Kenyans are faced with changing roles, rights, and responsibilities surrounding marriage and partner selection. Most young adults are creating patterns that meld traditional and contemporary expectations, and although great emphasis is still placed on fertility, during recent decades there have been decreases in the practice of polygyny, the marriage age gap, bride wealth, family size, and female circumcision. At the same time, the average age at first marriage and the education levels for women are increasing, as are the rates of premarital sex, nonmarital childbearing, and individual partner choice. Marriages range from the traditional to the contemporary, and many couples try to mesh the two into new traditions. Nevertheless, it would appear that marriage and family remain at the center of Kenyan society.

Because of transitions within Kenya, there are many areas of incomplete information about Kenyan family dynamics, thereby providing extensive opportunities for future investigation. Among the questions for scholars to research and families to respond to are the following. To what extent will young adults move to an individual choice-driven process of mate selection? How do religious, educational, and gender changes affect Kenyan families and the long-term stability of marriages? How will these change the way in which marriage is viewed? How much, and in what ways, does the concern about AIDS influence marriage choice? How might changes in the couple formation process bring about changes in family policy? How might the quality of life for urban and rural families be improved regarding obstacles they encounter and opportunities they can access? As families in Kenya, like others around the world, face changes in traditions, attitudes, and behaviors, it will be interesting to watch how they adapt to the new demands and meshing of intergenerational values.

Notes

1. We thank Michael N. Mbito, a Kenyan doctoral student in the Department of Child and Family Studies at the University of Tennessee, Knoxville, for his review and valuable comments, including this one insight about the emotional bonds reinforced by teasing about bride wealth. We also express our appreciation for Kathleen A. Wilson's review and comments based on her 3 years of living and working in Kenya as a U.S. Peace Corps teacher in Nzambani Location in Kitui and later as an Augustana College administrator while her spouse was a Fulbright fellow.

2. We express appreciation here to Patricia Kamene Musembei (head teacher at Kavisi Primary School near Wikililye), Benjamin Kithome (pastor at the Presbyterian Church of East Africa in Kitui), and Catherine Mumo (head teacher at Mulango Girls High School). These colleagues consulted with many Kamba elders and contributed cultural information from reference books, conversations with local professionals, and corroborated information that Stephan Wilson and Lucy Ngige had gathered by interviews and other means.

3. Lucy Ngige collected Kamba information through a focus group discussion in Donyo Sabuk, Machakos District. The participants were Gabriel Mutiso, age 70 years; Anne Mutavi, 58; Martha Mulinge, 46; John Kioko, 30; and Victoria Kalile, 27. Stephan Wilson collected additional Kamba information through interviews with Sammy Musili (a Roman Catholic priest in the Kitui Diocese) and several Kamba (who asked that their names not be used).

4. We acknowledge the following contributors through in-depth interviews conducted by Lucy Ngige with Daniel Ole Simoto on the Maasai customary marriages: Mzee Kioko on the Kamba woman-to-woman marriages, Mama Jedida Githui (deceased) on the Kikuyu customary marriages, Mzee Raphael Tiroko on the Nandi woman-to-woman marriages, and Alice Akanga on the Kisii woman-to-woman marriages.

References

Abbott, S. (1997). Gender, status, and values among Kikuyu and Appalachian adolescents. In T. S. Weisner, C. Bradley, & P. L. Kilbride (Eds.), *African families and the crisis of social change* (pp. 86–105). Westport, CT: Bergin & Garvey.

Adams, B. N. (1994). Kikuyu bride wealth and polygyny today. *Journal of Comparative Family Studies, 25,* 159–166.

Bell, D., & Song, S. (1994). Explaining the level of bride wealth. *Current Anthropology, 35,* 311–316.

Cattell, M. G. (1997). The discourse of neglect: Family support for the elderly in Samia. In T. S. Weisner, C. Bradley, & P. L. Kilbride (Eds.), *African families and the crisis of social change* (pp. 157–183). Westport, CT: Bergin & Garvey.

Chesaina, C. (1997). *Oral literature of the Embu and Mbeere.* Nairobi, Kenya: East African Educational Publishers.

Cohen, D. W., & Odhiambo, E. S. A. (1992). *Burying SM: The politics of knowledge and the sociology of power in Africa.* Portsmouth, NH: Heinemann.

Cole, H. (1998, Spring). What is lobola? *Signature Bride.* [Online]. Retrieved December 12, 2001, from http://melanet.com/awg/history/lobola.html

Dyson-Hudson, R., & Meekers, D. (1996, Fall). The universality of African marriage reconsidered: Evidence from Turkana males. *Ethnology, 35,* 301–320.

Embassy of the Republic of Kenya. (n.d.). Retrieved April 3, 2002, from www. kenyaembassy.com

Ensminger, J., & Knight, J. (1997). Changing social norms: Common property, bride wealth, and clan exogamy. *Current Anthropology, 38,* 1–49.

Frederiksen, B. F. (2000). Popular culture, gender relations, and the democratization of everyday life in Kenya. *Journal of Southern African Studies, 26,* 209–222.

Gitahi, C. (2002, May 13–19). Using bride price as excuses for violence. *East African Standard.* [Online]. Retrieved May 15, 2002, from www.eastandard. net/issue/issue13052002006.htm

Hamisi, K. (2002). *Maasai and agents of change.* [Online]. Retrieved May 22, 2002, from http://maasai-infoline.org

Harrell-Bonds, B. E. (1976). Stereotypes of Western and African patterns of marriage and family life. *Journal of Marriage and Family, 38,* 387–396.

Hertrich, V., & Pilon, M. (1998). African polygyny: What's new? *Cento de Pesquisas e Desenvolvimento News* (French Centre on Population and Development). [Online]. Retrieved October, 30, 2001, from www.ceped.ined.fr/cepedweb/activate/publi/chr04an.html

Hetherington, P. (2001). Generational changes in marriage patterns in the central province of Kenya, 1930–1990. *Journal of Asian and African Studies, 36,* 157–180.

Jackline, N. K. (2001). *Aembu cultural marriage.* Unpublished manuscript, Kenyatta University, Nairobi, Kenya.

Kagunge, M. G., Serah, K., Angela, K. T., & Moeni, M. S. (2001). *Marriage among the Kamba community.* Unpublished manuscript, Kenyatta University, Nairobi, Kenya.

Karp, I. (1987). Laughter at marriage: Subversion in performance. In D. Parkin & D. Nyamwaya (Eds.), *Transformations of African marriages* (pp. 137–154). Manchester, UK: Manchester University Press.

Kaufmann, G. L., & Meekers, D. (1998, Spring). The impact of women's socioeconomic position on marriage patterns in sub-Saharan Africa. *Journal of Comparative Family Studies, 29,* 101–115.

Kayongo-Male, D., & Onyango, P. (1984). *The sociology of the African family.* Essex, UK: Longman.

Marriage. (2001). Retrieved October 13, 2001, from www.kenyaweb.com/history/religions/marriage.html

Maasai Culture. (2001). Family. [Online]. Retrieved October 31, 2001, from www.african-soul.com/tribes/maasai/familymain.htm

Mbaya, M. (1999). Other proximate determinants of fertility. In *Kenya Demographic and Health Survey, 1998* (pp. 67–78). Calverton, MD: Macro International.

Mbiti, J. S. (1970). *African religions and philosophy.* Garden City, NY: Doubleday.

Mountain Voices. (2001). Oral testimonies from Mount Elgon, Kenya. [Online]. Retrieved April 3, 2002, from www.mountainvoices.org

Nasimiyu, R. (1997). Changing women's rights over property in western Kenya. In T. S. Weisner, C. Bradley, & P. L. Kilbride (Eds.), *African families and the crisis of social change* (pp. 283–298). Westport, CT: Bergin & Garvey.

Nthaka, N. L., & Kirima, M. D. (2001). *Marriage in the cultural Meru society.* Unpublished manuscript, Kenyatta University, Nairobi, Kenya.

Omungala, R. O. (1989, March). A changing society. *World Health,* pp. 11–12.

Population. (2000). Retrieved November 1, 2001, from www.kenyalogy.com/eng/info/pobla.htm

Population. (2001). Kenyaology: Population and culture. [Online]. Retrieved November 6, 2001, from www.kenyaology.com/eng/info/pobla.html

Timæus, I. (1998). *Polygyny in the sub-Saharan Africa* (Center for Population Studies, No. 37). London: London School of Hygiene and Tropical Medicine. Retrieved October 18, 2001, from www.lshtm.ac.uk/eps/cps/dfid/37.htm

United Nations Children's Fund. (2001). Early marriage: Child spouses. *Innocenti Digest, 7.* (Florence, Italy: UNICEF Innocenti Research Centre).

Winton, C. A. (1995). *Frameworks for studying families.* Guilford, CT: Dushkin.

World Desk Reference. (2002a). Kenya. Retrieved June 7, 2002, from www.travel.
    dk.com/wdr/KE/mKE.htm

World Desk Reference. (2002b). United States. [Online]. Retrieved June 7, 2002,
    from www.travel.dk.com/wdr/us/mus_intr.htm

Part IV
The Middle East

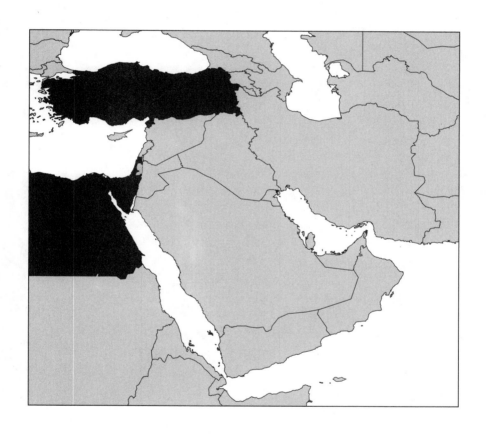

7

Love, Courtship, and Marriage From a Cross-Cultural Perspective

The Upper Middle Class Egyptian Example

Bahira Sherif-Trask

Said is in his early 20s, and even though he is very content with his life, his father is encouraging him to marry. His father's advice is that marriage "saves a man from foolish actions." After some hesitancy, Said agrees to an arranged marriage with a distant cousin. As the date of the impending marriage approaches, Said is filled with trepidation because he has never met his bride and is unclear about what to expect. Said is a merchant and partner in a trading firm. One afternoon, he spontaneously visits one of his partners, a distant cousin, at his home to take care of a business deal. As he and his partner are working out their business arrangements, they are served tea by a young girl who flits in and out of the room. By the time Said has returned to his own home, he has made a decision. He approaches his father, asks him to break off the formal engagement, and—to everyone's great surprise—insists on marrying the young girl who served him tea and who happens to be the youngest sister of his partner. As a reason for the

AUTHOR'S NOTE: This article is based on fieldwork conducted in Egypt by the author during the 1990s and is part of a larger study on upper middle class families in an Islamic context.

marriage, Said formally announces that this union will cement the business dealings in his firm. However, Said secretly admits to his younger brother, Anwar, that he is in love because the young girl, Fatima, is the loveliest girl he has ever seen. He describes her as being 15 years old and having gray-green eyes, long black hair, and very white skin. After a short engagement of 4 weeks, Said and Fatima are married. The year is 1925.

Amina and Tarek are newlyweds. Amina is tall, attractive, and gregarious and likes to wear jeans or overalls. In contrast, Tarek is relatively short and tends to be soft-spoken. Amina and Tarek met at Cairo University, where they both studied psychology. They have known each other for 10 years. Initially, Amina and Tarek were drawn to one another by common interests and friends at the university. Neither one dared to tell his or her parents about their relationship, even though the two secretly formed an attachment after about 2 years. Amina is convinced that if her father had suspected that she had a boyfriend, he would have pulled her out of the university and forced her to marry one of her distant cousins. During the couple's final year at the university, however, Tarek started to visit Amina's home, and after several visits, he asked her father for permission to marry her. Amina's father had no particular objections to this match given that Tarek came from a reputable family similar to his own in terms of wealth, education, and reputation. Furthermore, after graduation, Tarek had found a good job at a small international import/export company. Amina and Tarek became engaged 4 years before actually marrying. They waited because they wanted to find just the "right kind of apartment" and to furnish it completely in just the "right style" before moving in. Their apartment is very modern and light, decorated with round white Japanese paper lamps and expensive Persian rugs. Amina and Tarek are particularly proud of their white kitchen, with its white cabinets trimmed in red. They constantly talk about how much happiness their apartment brings them, and it is the object of envy among their friends. Amina has even commented that she "would have waited another 2 years in order to get the apartment to be perfect." Amina and Tarek's parents and friends greatly admire the couple and always cite them as "the example of a love match in contemporary Egypt." The year is 1998, and Tarek is Said's grandson.

In the contemporary Western context, little is known about courtship, love, and marriage in the Middle East—and in other parts of the Islamic world in general. Stereotypes persist that tradition and religion are the pervasive factors influencing marriage arrangements. Implied in this idea is that, fundamentally, the mate selection process and marriage are unchanging institutions. Nonetheless, fieldwork on this topic illustrates that these conceptions are misleading. The narrative above illustrates that, even in the course of two generations, the issues and conflicts encountered by young Muslim Egyptian couples require very different responses as a result of changes in time, place, and/or circumstances. In addition, the story from 1925 demonstrates that it cannot be assumed that couples from earlier generations adhered more closely to tradition, as is sometimes presumed (see, e.g., Altorki, 1986, p. 124). Each couple's story must be considered in its own context, which includes social, economic, and familial factors that are negotiated against the ever-present background of Islamic law and social tradition. As described later, some of the young couples in this study entered contractual arranged marriages along very traditional lines, basing their decisions solely on familial considerations and advice. Others, while seeking ways in which to operate within accepted practice, moved further from tradition as they tried to balance the demands of economic, social, and ideological considerations. Nor are the issues and conflicts limited to only the marital process. Contacts with young Muslim couples suggest that as upper middle class women move increasingly into the workplace, issues such as the crossover between social levels and the need for women to travel on their own create an increasing need for selective choice and negotiation of the accepted social and Islamic practices and tenets when it comes to courtship and marriage.

Literature on Islamic Marriage and Families

Until very recently, research on Islamic marriage and family formation was extremely sparse except for the occasional ethnographic monograph that included a brief description of marriage rites (see, e.g., Altorki, 1986; Ammar, 1954; Rugh, 1984). More recently, several studies have focused either on the historical contexts of Islamic marriages (Shatzmiller, 1996; Tucker, 1988), on age at first marriage in various Islamic societies (Heaton, 1996), or on the comparative legal aspects of Islamic marriages (Mir-Hosseini, 1993). Nevertheless, studies focusing specifically on contemporary issues of marriage and family in the Islamic world are virtually nonexistent. The paucity of scholarly research in this area is particularly striking given the dramatic increase of Muslims throughout the world (Aswad & Bilge, 1996). This lack of research has led to misunderstandings and prejudices that can be rectified only through greater knowledge.

The Marriage Market

In Egypt, as throughout the Islamic world, marriage is at the heart of social and religious life (Baron, 1991; Mir-Hosseini, 1993; Tucker, 1991). Every young woman and every young man expects to marry, and the fulfillment of the marital union is seen to be in the resulting children. Few Egyptians (of any class) do not marry, and a single adult is usually the subject of a great deal of matrimonial interest on the part of his or her extended family, neighbors, and colleagues. Cultural norms negate the possibility of living alone, so both men and women live at home until marriage. Therefore, marriage becomes the point at which a child formally becomes an adult by setting up his or her own household. From an early age, upper middle class Egyptian women and men are made aware of their obligations and duties to their families and of their responsibility to make a good marriage, have children, and uphold the reputations of their families by being faithful in marriage.

Even as recently as two generations ago, most marriages were arranged by the potential bride's or groom's family, with little input on the part of the individuals who were to be married. In contrast, in contemporary Cairo, the young people in my study prided themselves on participating in "love matches" with people they met either at work or at school. Thus, contemporary conditions place parents in the awkward position of enforcing traditional norms within a context that encourages and promotes "Western" styles of love and marriage. On the one hand, parents allow their offspring to make their own marriage choices. On the other hand, parents resort to traditional forms of evaluating and researching the potential brides or grooms and their families' backgrounds and reputations. Furthermore, it must be noted that "choices" refers to marriage and does not entail the Western concept of dating and "getting to know one another" in an intimate manner.

Social Position

A surprising number of marriages among the middle class Egyptians in this study continued to be arranged, or at least orchestrated, by parents and relatives. Families take such an intense interest in the various matches because of the implications that this arrangement will have, not just for the two individuals but for the two families as well. Even today, marriage is viewed by both parents and children as the joining of two families. Therefore, it is considered of the utmost importance that both families have as much knowledge as possible about one another before a marriage. As Amina (from the earlier vignette) described,

My father was very concerned about my marrying Tarek. He said that he liked him, that he was polite and a hard worker. But I heard my parents talking right before the engagement, and it turns out that my father had made several phone calls that week inquiring about Tarek. I was very surprised because my mother knows their family. But my father has a friend who worked with Tarek's father. He wanted to check if there might be something we don't know about Tarek's family. Sometimes here in Egypt, people hide their problems like insanity or divorce. My father says that some men still beat their wives. I was not worried. I have known Tarek for a long time, and I believe in his word. My father thinks that I am naive, but I also know that he was anxious since I was the first of his daughters to marry. Both sets of our parents now visit regularly. They are very much like us.

For many Egyptians, Amina and Tarek represent a modern couple that makes independent decisions. Nonetheless, Amina's description about the period right before her engagement reflects a common familial strategy on the part of many Egyptian parents. On the one hand, they allow their offspring to make their own marriage choices. On the other, they resort to traditional forms of evaluating and researching the potential brides or grooms. Children are warned from an early age of the dangers of ignoring social position and are restricted from playing with other "inappropriate" children. This preoccupation with social status carries great importance at the time of courtship, for if this issue is ignored, a marriage may be marked by difficulty or even failure.

Among the families in my studies, one woman in particular recounted her marital experiences with a partner who came from a lower status family. Shirin is a young woman, now in her early 30s, who recounted that her marriage to Mustafa failed after approximately 8 years. Although she never specifically addressed the issue of Mustafa's family origins and lack of wealth in her conversations, she did describe many fights originating from Mustafa's sense that Shirin's family "was constantly visiting" and that "they usually ignored him during conversations." In contrast, Mustafa, also in his early 30s, complained that during the course of their marriage, Shirin constantly criticized his actions and condemned him because he originally came from a village in the Nile delta and lacked an urban upbringing like her own. In response, Shirin angrily complained that Mustafa attempted to limit all of her movements, including her interactions with close friends:

Mustafa and I were always fighting. He did not like my friends because he felt that they introduced me to liberal ideas such as going to the swimming pool without him and [because] they encouraged me to spend his hard-earned money on the newest fashions when we needed his salary for our household expenses. This was, of course, not true. My father is a very generous man. He always let me buy what I needed. Mustafa just did not see things in the right way. He is a peasant, you see, and they think differently. Mustafa did not grow up in Cairo. He did not understand that it is important to go to the club. This is the problem when you marry someone who is from a different type of family. I warn my younger sister all the time.

Shirin also stated,

Mustafa never treated me with respect. He did not understand that I am a Cairene, that I studied at a French school, [and] that I should not spend all of my time doing housework. Mustafa only wanted to have everything around the house done in the same manner as his mother.

Today, Shirin is married to a Cairene, Ali, who spends much of his time working in Saudi Arabia as an engineer. As a result, she now has a great deal of freedom to move about with her friends, movement that consists primarily of visiting other women's houses or the local club. In our conversations, Shirin acknowledged that one reason for the success of her second marriage was her husband's regular absence from the house. Nonetheless, she did point out that, due to his background and education, he trusted her to stay in Cairo with their baby and her family instead of forcing her to move to Saudi Arabia with him.

Affirmation of the importance of equality in social standing is found in the concept *al-kafa'a,* which is one of the basic requirements to validate a marriage contract (al-Misri, 1994). Al-kafa'a is interpreted to mean equality in religion and social standing between the proposed husband and wife; in terms of social status, the wife should be equal to or inferior to the husband, but never the reverse (Fluehr-Lobban, 1987). Al-kafa'a is defined as "a suitable match," not as "a recommendation for whom to marry," and it is thought to protect a woman's interests when the father or grandfather of a young woman wishes to marry her to someone without her consent (al-Misri, 1994). Suitability is defined as equivalence in lineage, religiousness, and profession and in being free of defects that would permit annulling the marriage contract, with color and race not playing a role within this consideration (al-Misri, 1994). The concept of equality ensures that certain basic criteria are met so as to make the marriage partners a "good match" for one another.

Nowadays in Cairo, level of education and employment opportunities often may outweigh other factors in determining the rank of an individual. Women from middle class families who achieve higher professional levels than their parents, perhaps by becoming doctors, can often attract men who are not necessarily from wealthier families but who themselves have the same level of education. For women, the attractiveness of a marriage candidate rises not only if he has the same level of education but also if he has worked abroad in the past or if the possibility of his working abroad in the future exists. Experience abroad is primarily equated with financial success, increased sophistication, and ultimately higher status back in Egypt. These are qualities that can help a man to overcome the stigma of coming from a lower class family than his wife.

In contrast to Western norms, it is not considered advantageous to marry someone above one's rank in family origin. I was told by both men and women that if this occurred, there would be too many expectations on the "better" party's side in terms of both material goods and social obligations and expectations. The intensity of these feelings may be best represented in the case of a young man completing his graduate studies at the American University. Samir was 34 years old at the time of our meeting, and his fiancée, Zeinab, had just turned 28. She was a biology teacher at a local Egyptian school, and he was hoping to gain employment at a foreign language school on graduation. He recounted that his engagement was arranged through Zeinab's sister and that the couple had been engaged for 1 year. They were planning to be married the following month. Samir pointed out that he could easily have met a girl from the American University but that he wanted "someone from the same type of family." Otherwise, his future wife would become dissatisfied with him, he believed, as indicated in his comments:

> If I marry one of these girls that I am studying with, I will have many problems. They have friends who go abroad and wear beautiful clothes. They are used to lifestyles that I do not know much about. The problems would come if we should marry. A wife like this may want a bigger car, more clothes, a nicer apartment. I fear that I may never be able to provide such things. Then she will make my life hell. Why should I subject myself to this? Why not marry a girl who will be a good wife to me?

Samir emphasized that he and Zeinab both are from rather humble families; his father has a sporting goods store, and her father is a low-ranking civil servant. Throughout our conversations, Samir repeatedly pointed out that the young woman he was marrying was a very "normal" girl, "not very beautiful but with good morals like her mother."

I heard the expression of similar beliefs repeatedly from both men and women. One recently married young woman, Aida, pointed out that the disadvantage of marrying someone "above" oneself is that this "could always be used against you." She recounted this situation in her own family:

> My sister married someone from a slightly better off family. They are not so different from us, but they have a German car. My sister is always upset because her husband and his family always sneer at our family for not being wealthy enough. You know, they are not good people. Our family is more religious, and we have a good name. I feel so sorry for my sister.

With ever-increasing economic pressures infringing on many people's lives, cars, clothes, and foreign travel are important status markers. The young people with whom I spoke worried that they were not in a position to compete with others with respect to material possessions. Instead, they emphasized their family names and reputations to make themselves more desirable as potential spouses.

Good Morals (*Akhlaq*)

In contrast to many Western men, many upper middle class Egyptian men do not necessarily cite attractiveness as an important marriage criterion. Many of these men tend to fear "beautiful women" because, as they may put it, "they go out and spend all the money on themselves and attract attention from other men." These are not the qualities men seek in a wife. "One does not want to marry what one admires" was a common response to my questions about attractiveness. Beauty is seen as a necessary criterion in film and television stars, belly dancers, and even women with whom men may have affairs. For brides, however, men tend to seek women who "will make good mothers." As we saw in the case of Samir's recent engagement, he had chosen his bride, Zeinab, because "her mother was a moral woman who kept an orderly house," and he was convinced that his bride would have learned to do the same. Samir, like many men in his generation, viewed marriage choice primarily in terms of setting up a household and starting a family. These men's views are reinforced by both familial and, more recently, fundamentalist discourses that place women in the home— at the center of the family.

It is common for young middle class men and women to take great pains to present themselves in a modest and moral manner so as to make themselves appealing on the marriage market. Unmarried women try to limit their public interactions with men, whereas men are careful to guard their reputations with respect to womanizing and drinking in particular. Validation that these values are really a component of a certain individual's makeup is, according to many Egyptians, found in family background combined with presentations of self. Nevertheless, as the boundaries between classes become increasingly negotiable through the acquisition of wealth and education, it is difficult for young people to apply the traditional criteria that their parents advise them to use when considering marriage choices.

Age at First Marriage

Although marriage choice entails many criteria that have traditionally been considered essential, age at first marriage is becoming a widely disputed aspect of the modern "marriage dilemma" for women and men as well as for their parents. Young women who attend universities generally postpone marriage until after graduation or even until after they become settled in new jobs. Parents and relatives become increasingly nervous as young women reach their mid-20s and continue to find reasons not to get married. Young men, on the other hand, often want desperately to get married at a young age but must wait until they have the means to support families. Among educated young women, it is becoming increasingly common to get married between 22 and 25 years of age. This is in great contrast to their mothers' generation, when many women married between 16 and 19 years of age. Today, these mothers do not understand why their daughters wish to delay this crucial step in life. Women of older generations tend to worry that, by delaying marriage, their daughters will lose their reputations through informal contact with men. These mothers attempt, to the extent possible, to limit the movements of their grown daughters.

Many educated young men face other issues. They must wait until their late 20s to early 30s to marry, depending on their families' financial situations. Although there is also an upward trend in age at first marriage among these men when compared with that among their fathers, it is not as radical a shift. One reason may be that traditionally in Egypt among this class, men have always completed their professional educations and commenced working before starting families. Most of the young women I spoke with stressed that they wanted assurance before marriage that their husbands would have steady jobs to guarantee their welfare and their standing in society. As Aida described,

> The fact that my husband has a good job tells the world that he is a hard worker. A man should always work hard. This is a good sign of his character. A man is not just your husband, he is also the father of your children. They need to look up to him. In today's world, it is important to have stability in your life.

The Formal Aspects of Marriage

Every Muslim Egyptian marriage is characterized by a formalized set of negotiations that begin once the suitability of the marriage partners has been determined. The prelude to the marriage contract is the betrothal (*khutba*), which is the request by the man for the hand of a certain woman in marriage (Nasir, 1990). It is at this point that the man will approach the woman's family with the view of describing his status and negotiating with her family members the contract and their respective demands. For the betrothal to be valid, each party should be aware of the circumstances of the other and should know the potential spouse's character and behavior. As mentioned earlier, this information is obtained through inquiries, investigations, and the direct contact of the couple in the presence of a chaperone. Once the man's offer is accepted by the woman or by those who are legally entitled to act on her behalf, the betrothal will have taken place.

It is usually at the point of the khutba that the man offers his future bride a gift, which in Egypt is referred to as the *shabka*. In some instances, particularly if the man does not know the bride's family through previous contacts or if he wants to make an extremely favorable impression on the young woman, the man will offer her the shabka before the khutba, thereby showing his goodwill, good intentions, and perhaps good financial standing. The shabka is, by middle class American standards, a very expensive gift of jewelry. Most of the young women I met took great delight and pride in showing me their shabkas, which often consisted of a diamond bracelet with a matching ring or pendant or both. A man will put great care into the choice of this gift and usually will enlist the help of his mother and sisters, first in inquiring about the young woman's taste and then in helping to choose a fitting set of jewelry. At times, the shabka is presented after the khutba, but this generally is not looked on favorably by young women, who like to impress their relatives and friends with the fact that men are showering them with this kind of attention.

Betrothal does not constitute a marriage contract; it is merely a mutual promise of marriage between the two parties and is not legally binding for either party. In practice, the khutba is easily dissolved. A general feeling among both women and men is that it is "better to find out before it's too late." Nevertheless, it seemed that the older both parties were, the more reluctant they were to break off the khutba. I met several couples who did not seem very excited about their impending lives together due to economic considerations, yet they continued to reiterate that "God and their families" would make the marriages work.

During the course of this research in Egypt, I witnessed several occasions where betrothals were dissolved due to young women's dissatisfaction with their potential spouses. One case involved a young man who, by Egyptian standards, should have been considered an ideal partner given his education, job (engineer), brand-new luxury car (BMW), and apartment. His potential bride, Olla, was a college-educated young woman who worked at a prestigious new luxury hotel in Cairo. Within a period of 3 months after their betrothal, she informed her family that she refused to marry this man:

> Why should I saddle myself with an indecisive man who is so weak? He will always listen to his mother after our marriage, and I will never have a role in any decisions. Better to find someone who is strong in his family; I will be better off also. Anyway, there are many men to marry, but only one can be my husband.

The betrothal was dissolved, and there was a great deal of pity extended to the young man given that this was the third time a young woman had broken a betrothal with him. At the same time, all of the young woman's relatives commended her for not being taken in by his charming manner. This young woman was not the least bit perturbed by all of these events. She informed me very straightforwardly that several men had already inquired of her family for her hand in marriage and that she had not been thrilled with any of the offers. In this particular case, the young woman's eligibility actually increased through her various refusals. I later learned that this is a tactic employed by particularly "desirable" young women so as to find "better" (usually defined as "richer") husbands.

Among upper middle class Egyptians, the betrothal becomes a public acknowledgment of the young people's right to spend chaperoned time together. It is a general rule now that the prospective groom will join the woman's family for dinner on a regular basis, giving the young man and woman an opportunity to get to know each other in the presence of others. In addition, other members of the two families will start visiting one another. In particular, the man's mother and sisters or female cousins will begin spending long periods of time with the prospective bride, and at family gatherings where they might not be present, someone will inevitably pick up the telephone and call them so as to include them among the group. At all times, the emphasis of each courting family is on the group aspect of marriage: There is a conscious realization that marriage intertwines two families and that it is of utmost importance that they will get along.

Marriage also takes on a unique role in Egyptian society because, for both women and men, it is the only alternative to living at home with their families and so represents independence. Unlike most Western societies, it is socially unacceptable for young people, and especially for women, to live either with friends or by themselves. Young women, as we have seen, are heavily protected by their families, who monitor their movements carefully, whereas older women almost always have to account to their husbands for their actions. Even today, in the contemporary urban context of Cairo, marriage and the associated virtues of respectability, accountability, and morality are seen as crucial to women's identity and status in the society.

Because of the separation of the sexes, women play a vital role in organizing marriages. Women provide their husbands, sons, and brothers with information about marriageable girls and their families. Men are dependent on women to acquire the information they need to form those alliances in which they are interested. By being selective about the information they share, women are able to sway men to courses of action in accordance with their own interests. Therefore, women amass power through the acquisition and dispensation of information.

The Marital Celebration

Once the marriage negotiations have been completed, the formal and public recognition of the marriage takes place at the signing of the contract, or *kabt al-kitab*. Although Westerners tend to assume that the kabt al-kitab is equivalent to an engagement, it is actually a true legal marriage (Nasir, 1990). Nevertheless, the actual consummation of the marriage, *al-dukhla,* often might not take place for months or even years. With the signing of the contract, the legal obligations, privileges, and responsibilities begin for the husband and wife. Any child born to the mother after the signing is legally the husband's, and if the husband dies before cohabitation, then the wife is entitled to maintenance. Mutual rights of inheritance are established 6 months after the date of the kabt al-kitab.

The kabt al-kitab is usually held at the house of the bride, but in Egypt today, it is sometimes performed at the groom's house. If a *mahr* has been agreed on, it will be given to the bride at this time. The mahr is a sum of money that the groom presents to the bride at the signing of the kabt al-kitab. Historically, in the upper middle class, the groom presented a symbolic penny to the bride. Today, women, advised by their extended families, ask for money at the time of the marriage as well as in the case of divorce. The groom will wrap the money, even if it is just one piaster (the equivalent of a U.S. penny), in a white cloth and hand it to the young woman

Traditional Bride and Groom Seated on "Throne"

before the signing of the contract as a symbolic gesture of his gift to her. After this presentation, the bride will be taken into another room by her mother or sister to await the completion of the ceremony. Present at the signing will be her father or guardian, the groom, two witnesses (usually other male relatives), and the official presider the (*maa'zun*). The actual contract consists of a simple form that states the facts of the marriage: who is marrying whom, the families they come from, and the names of the two witnesses. If a mahr is involved, the sums are noted, as are any other specific conditions that were agreed on before the ceremony. The father or guardian of the bride will then place his hand on the hand of the groom, and the maa'zun will declare the marriage to have been completed. On occasion the maa'zun may say some words about the meaning of marriage in Islam, but this is not a necessary part of the ceremony. The maa'zun will then file the contract in his judicial district.

Although at this point the couple is legally married, it is increasingly common for the newlyweds not to celebrate the traditional wedding ceremony, *al-farah,* on the same day or to live together as husband and wife, *al-dukhla.* Even though it was common practice among the older generation to celebrate the kabt al-kitab and the farah on the same day, it has become increasingly fashionable to separate the two ceremonies. Various reasons account for this delay, with the primary ones being either economics or the traditional nature of the families involved; parents do not want their daughters to be seen with men to whom they are not married.

A generational change that has also influenced the lengthy period of time between the kabt al-kitab and the farah is the fact that it is now rare for young brides to agree to live in the same house as (or, often, even in near proximity of) their mothers-in-law. Up until some 30 years ago, it was common for the young couple to move into the groom's natal home. Today, with living quarters being much more cramped due to the overcrowding of the city, young women are quite willing to wait to marry until they can guarantee an independent living space for themselves. Because Egyptian society accords the mother of the groom a great deal of power over her new daughter-in-law, young educated women often try to maintain a physical distance, at least in terms of their living arrangements.

In Egypt, the customary wedding celebration, al-farah, is a major ceremony among all classes in the society. Among many upper middle class Egyptians, the formal marriage ceremony takes on a special meaning because it restates the importance of the family and its standing in society. The status of the family can be seen in every aspect of the rituals that comprise the wedding ceremony. It is customary for the ceremony to be held at a large Western hotel, and the wealth of the families involved is displayed in all aspects of the celebration, including the number of guests, the quality of the food, the fame of the belly dancer, and the choice of the music. The formal celebration is preceded by a procession throughout the hotel, led by the newlyweds and followed by a tambourine-playing all-male band and trilling ululating women who are also wedding guests. At the close of this procession, which lasts for about a half hour, all guests enter a large banquet room where the bride and groom are seated on throne-like chairs, from which they observe the activities and accept everyone's congratulations. Understandably, these wedding celebrations are a significant focus of attention that are much planned for and long remembered. They carry with them the crucial cultural symbols that bind families and social groups more tightly than potentially any other rituals in Egyptian life.

As can be seen from the discussion in this chapter, courtship and marriage in contemporary Egypt represent a complex intermingling of traditional practices and modern circumstances. Concepts such as social equality and good morals still underlie what appear on the surface to be new ways of

Wedding Party Serenaded by Dancers

meeting and arranging marriages. Nonetheless, marriage still remains a central building block from both religious and social points of view. Families undertake great pains to make sure that eligible young people come together under appropriate circumstances and marry as quickly as possible. Western concepts such as dating and premarital sex do not even enter into the discussion. Marriage remains the merging of families as well as the only legitimate channel for sexuality and the bearing of children.

References

al-Misri, A. (1994). *Umdat al-salik wa: Uddat al-nasik* (Reliance of the traveler: The classic manual of Islamic sacred law). Evanston, IL: Sunna Books.

Altorki, S. (1986). *Women in Saudi Arabia.* New York: Columbia University Press.

Ammar, H. (1954). *Growing up in an Egyptian village.* London: Routledge & Kegan Paul.

Aswad, B., & Bilge, B. (1996). *Family and gender among American Muslims.* Philadelphia: Temple University Press.

Baron, B. (1991). The making and breaking of marital bonds in modern Egypt. In N. Keddie & B. Baron (Eds.), *Women in Middle Eastern history* (pp. 275–291). New Haven, CT: Yale University Press.

Fluehr-Lobban, C. (1987). *Islamic law and society in the Sudan.* London: Frank Cass.

Heaton, T. (1996). Socioeconomic and familial status of women associated with age at first marriage in three Islamic societies. *Journal of Comparative Family Studies, 27,* 41–58.

Mir-Hosseini, Z. (1993). *Marriage on trial: A study of Islamic family law—Iran and Morocco compared.* London: I. B. Tauris.

Nasir, J. (1990). *The Islamic law of personal status.* London: Graham & Trotman.

Rugh, A. (1984). *Family in contemporary Egypt.* Syracuse, NY: Syracuse University Press.

Shatzmiller, M. (1996). Marriage, family, and the faith: Women's conversion to Islam. *Journal of Family History, 21,* 235–266.

Tucker, J. (1988). Marriage and family in Nablus, 1720–1856: Toward a history of Arab marriage. *Journal of Family History, 13,* 165–179.

Tucker, J. (1991). Ties that bound: Women and family in eighteenth- and nineteenth-century Nablus. In N. Keddie & B. Baron (Eds.), *Women in Middle Eastern history* (pp. 233–253). New Haven, CT: Yale University Press.

8

Couple Formation in Israeli Jewish Society

Shulamit N. Ritblatt

Rina Ochaion is a 19-year-old girl who lives with her family in the northern part of Israel. She is the youngest child in a family of eight children. Her parents' families came to Israel from Morocco in 1953 and since then have struggled economically. Their families, who knew each other's lineage from Morocco, arranged the marriage of Rina's parents. Rina's mother, Margalit, was 16 years old when she got engaged to 17-year-old Moshe in a special ceremony called Chennee. They got married 6 months later, and the celebrations lasted all week long. At the beginning, the new couple lived with the groom's parents, but after 2 years they moved in with Margalit's parents. Three years after the marriage, they celebrated the arrival of their firstborn boy, Yiftach. As a young couple with a child, they got subsidized housing and finally had their own two-bedroom apartment. In this house, their family grew to include eight children. After the arrival of their first child, Margalit stayed at home and took care of the children. Moshe worked very hard to provide for his large family, and as the kids grew up, they too worked and helped to provide the family's economic needs.

AUTHOR'S NOTE: The author gives special thanks to Eti Rosental, who assisted in finding articles in Israel. Thanks also go to Carolyn Balkwell and Amy Obegi for their helpful comments and feedback on this chapter.

137

Rina, the youngest child, was the only one in her family to graduate from high school and the first girl to go to the army, as is required of every 18-year-old in Israel. Her three older sisters were exempted from the service on the grounds of being religiously observant. In the army, Rina has been stationed in an air force unit as a control room technician. There, she met Yoni Resznik, who is 21 years old and in rigorous training to become a pilot. Yoni is the only child to parents who were born in Israel. His great-grandparents came from Russia to Israel in 1898 and were among the pioneers who helped to establish the state of Israel. His paternal and maternal grandparents met and lived together in kibbutz Nahalal. They got married after they realized that they liked each other's company. Yoni's mother, Masha, and his father, Sasha, were born in the kibbutz and spent their childhoods there. Growing up together, it seemed only natural for the two of them to marry and move to Tel Aviv to go to medical school. They both see Yoni as the culmination of their hopes and dreams. Yoni is very much in love with Rina. They both plan, after Yoni is done with flight training, to take time off and visit their respective parents to introduce them to each partner.

I srael is a country in the Middle East bordering the Mediterranean Sea in the west, Jordan in the east, Syria and Lebanon in the north and Egypt in the south. Although the majority of its inhabitants (80.1%) are Jews, Muslims, Christians, and Druze dwell there as well (*The World Factbook*, 1996). The state of Israel was established in 1948, and in its declaration and the "Law of Return" passed in 1950, it guaranteed to all Jews the right to come and live in Israel and become immediate citizens. This has shaped the demographics and cultural characteristics of its people because many Jews came from all over the world, representing various countries of origin, cultures, and languages as well as various levels of religiosity.

Hence, the two main issues that have ongoing influence on couple formation in Israel are group-of-origin cleavage and the Orthodox-secular division cleavage. Israeli society is characterized by a multifractured social structure that is in opposition to the notion of unity, "melting pot," and Jewish solidarity.

This chapter focuses on the Jewish population in Israel and the couple formation processes that are common among the nearly 5 million Jews living there today. Ethnic and religious makeup, cultural context of the Jewish family, mate selection processes, patterns, ages, and intermarriages in the Israeli Jewish society are discussed.

Ethnic Makeup

There are two main groups in Israel divided according to ethnic lines: the Ashkenazi Jews (of European and/or American [Euro-American] descent) and the Sephardi Jews (of African and/or Asian [Afro-Asian] descent). According to current statistics, 32.1% of Israeli Jews were born in America or Europe, 20.8% were born in Israel, 14.6% were born in Africa, and 12.6% were born in Asia (*The World Factbook*, 1996). The Sepharadim, known also as the *Mizrachim* (Orientals) or *Edot Mizrach* (communities of the East), are euphemized for the poor, underprivileged, or educationally disadvantaged.

Afro-Asian Jews in Israel were unable to compete successfully for economic and political resources with the already established Euro-American Jews (Goldscheider, 1986). The Ashkenazim regarded the Jews from Asia and Africa as primitive and less civilized than themselves (Library of Congress, 1988).

Two current trends play a major role in shaping the ethnic makeup of contemporary Israel: (a) socioeconomic mobility of Sephardi Jews from lower class to middle class and (b) intermarriages. Those Orientals who move upward emulate the Ashkenazi lifestyle (e.g., small family size, type of leisure activities) and loosen their ties with their own ethnic group. This trend has been reinforced by the increased rate of intermarriages.

Religious Makeup

To understand Judaism in Israel, one must understand the trichotomy among *dati* (religiously observant Jews [25%]), *lo-dati* (nonobservant Jews [20%]), and traditionalists who are committed to Judaism in principle only (55%) (Guttman Institute of Applied Social Research, 1993, cited in Elazar, n.d.). The conservative-traditional group is characterized by social control with limitation in the individual freedom to choose. On the contrary, the modern group focuses on individual needs and self-fulfillment, freedom of choice, and low levels of family supervision. These differences are reflected in the way in which mates are selected—either by arranged or free-choice marriages (Shachar, 1988).

Since the birth of the state of Israel, religion and its law (*Halakah*) have dominated in adjudicating matters of personal status. In light of the agreement worked out between Labor Zionists (with Ben-Gurion as the leader) and Orthodox Jews in June 1947, the place of the core traditional Jewish practices had been guaranteed in the new society. Since then, the Rabbinate, a Jewish religious organization, has regulated all matrimonial issues of the Jewish population in Israel (Library of Congress, 1988; Solomon, 1986).

According to the Jewish law (the Halakah), a Jew is one who is born of a Jewish mother or is one who converts to Judaism according to the Halakah and is not a member of another religion. This issue becomes crucial when dealing with marriage. Interfaith couples seeking to marry, but where one partner is non-Jewish, have to do so in a civil marriage outside of Israel. The conflict between the religious Jews and secular Jews continues to take place in contemporary Israel and is reflected in the process of mate selection.

Among the ultra-Orthodox and religious Jews, marriage arrangements are done by matchmakers or relatives (Goshen-Gottstein, 1966). Love and intimacy have no role in these relationships. The religious purpose of marriage is twofold: (a) procreation and (b) maintenance of the family sanctuary. The more contemporary Jews select their mates by individual choice. To understand the Jewish family and the process of mate selection, it is important to go back in history and look at the roots and origin of the patterns and notions regarding couple formation.

The Jewish Family: Cultural Context

During the biblical period (3000 BCE to 70 CE), the Jewish family was a patriarchal family type with inferior status for women. The wife was purchased and taken to the husband's family group, although she was asked for her consent prior to marriage. The bride's father provided the dowry, he and the brothers continued to keep vigilance over the bride's welfare, and the groom's family provided a *mohar* (a marriage price). There was no special ceremony or rite to celebrate this event (Schlesinger, 1971, 1987).

During the later Talmudic period (70 CE to 600 CE), arranged marriages by the parents of the parties still prevailed. The arrangement of a marriage was often made while either the bride or the groom was still a minor—or while both were still minors. A period of at least 12 months was required between the agreement to the marriage and its consummation (in the case of a maiden). During this period of time, a special ceremony for the betrothal, the *kiddushin* (sanctification), finalizes the marital agreement. In addition, the *ketubah,* which is a legal marriage contract, is handed to the bride at the marriage ceremony. The ketubah is in fact a replacement for the prepaid mohar and is like a debt, the ketubah obligation, which is collected by the wife to guarantee her protection in the event of the husband's death or of her being divorced (Friedman, 1986).

The roles in the traditional Jewish family were such that the wife's duties were in the home, whereas the husband was bound to support her and provide for her food, clothing, and other needs (Schlesinger, 1971). These roles are supported by four basic Jewish family values that have endured from the Talmudic period of time to the current time. First, *taharath mishpacha* (purity of the family) relates to chastity prior to marriage and absolute fidelity within the marriage bond. Also, the sexual relationship is seen as a force for good in life to procreate, to enhance the companionship of husband and wife, and to promote their physical and psychological well-being. Second, *gidul uboneth* is the obligation of the couple to take care of and educate all offspring. Third, *kibud horim* (filial responsibility) means that a child has the obligation to honor and respect his or her parents. Fourth, *shalom byyith* (family compatibility) means that the unity of the couple is important. Divorce is the final resort (Schlesinger, 1971).

During the Middle Ages, monogamy became a legal mandate in the Western world around 1000 CE. Jews had been practicing monogamy even before. Jews were in exile and were spread all around the world. Hence, the surrounding community of which Jews are part has influenced each Jewish community. Arranged marriages still were the only acceptable process, but sometimes a *shadchan* (professional matchmaker) was hired to seek out a match. In 1564, *Shulachan Aruch,* which is the standard Jewish law code, was first printed. It was the first time that age of marriage was stated. According to this book, it is the duty of every 18-year-old to marry (although one can be married as early as 13 years of age).

During this period of time, several Jewish marriage customs emerged and have become part of the ceremony. These customs still remain today and reflect the adaptation of Christian and Muslim traditions. The *chuppah* (portable canopy), the wedding ring, the shattering of the glass cup, and the decorated ketubah have appeared in the Jewish wedding. The chuppah was likely adapted from Catholicism, which had used the portable canopy for church rituals since the Middle Ages (Gutmann, 1986). This tradition appeared in Ashkenazi Judaism during the 16th century. In the beginning, the chuppah was simply a cloth or tallit spread over the bridal couple. This custom was given religious endorsement and explained by reference to biblical statements such as "Spread your robe over your handmaiden" (Ruth, 3:9) and "I spread My robe over you" (Ezek, 16:8).

The custom of breaking a glass apparently started in medieval Germany, where Christian Germans smashed a glass before or at the wedding ceremony. It reflected the hope that the shattered glass would hurt or frighten the demons that were believed to reside in the area. During the 15th century, it became customary to shout "Mazel Tov" when the glass was shattered. It was usually shattered against the interior northern synagogue wall. By the 18th century, a stone with the verse from Jeremiah—"the sound of mirth and gladness, the voice of the bridegroom and bride"—was attached to the outside northern wall of the synagogue building. By the 18th century, Sephardi Jews in Holland and other communities adapted this custom, with the glass being placed underneath the chuppah at the groom's feet. Around the 14th century, the Ashkenazi tradition was justified by interpreting the shattered glass as a symbolic remembrance of the destruction of the Temple in Jerusalem. A 17th-century Italian rabbi, Leone da Modena, related to this custom as symbolizing the fragility of life in his book, *Historia dei riti Hebracici* (Gutmann, 1986).

Another custom adapted by Jews in Italy from Christianity was the wedding ring, which came to symbolize unification of the couple. Jews who lived under Islam learned the custom of decorating the ketubah as well as reading the ketubah aloud in the wedding ceremony. What is amazing is that all of these customs, although started in different locations, have spread to include all Jewish communities and became the customs that are adhered to by Jews at the current time (Gutmann, 1986).

As the notions of progress and individualism were spread in the world during the Enlightenment era and emancipation (1650 and onward), Jews began to incorporate these notions into the mate selection process. Although arranged marriage practices continue, the trend is toward individual choice and an emphasis on companionship (Biale, 1986).

Mate Selection Process

Solomon (1986) examined Murstein's Stimulus-Value-Response (SRV) model using 48 Israeli couples entering marriage. In congruence with Murstein's assertion, individuals possessing a high level of self-acceptance tended to choose partners whom they perceived as being similar to themselves, whereas individuals possessing a low level of self-acceptance tended to choose partners whom they perceived as being different from themselves (Solomon, 1986).

Shenhav-Shefer (2000) studied structural difficulties in mate selection decision making in Israel in comparison with the career decision-making process. A total of 210 participants volunteered to take part in this study: 49 men and 161 women ages 19 to 43 years ($M = 23.13$). Results supported that the two decision-making processes, career selection and mate selection, have similar structural difficulties such as unwillingness, lack of motivation, indecisiveness, and myths. Later hindrances to mate selection and career decision making are lack of information, inconsistent information, and inner conflicts. Individuals who reported using more rational thinking processes had fewer difficulties in reaching decisions, whereas those who were high on intuitive thinking rated themselves as having more inner conflicts (Shenhav-Shefer, 2000).

Mate Attributes

The most valued individual characteristics in potential mates were the focus of an international study done by a network of 49 researchers from 33 countries located on six continents and five islands (Buss & Safir, 1990). When comparing the Israeli Jew subsample (n = 473) to the international data (N = 9,474), results indicated no significant differences:

> It differs from the international complement in that it is one of the only three countries (the others being Italy and Venezuela) where both sexes rank intelligence as one of the most valued characteristics in potential mates. Congruent with this finding is the greater than average value given to similar education. Also above average are good-housekeeping skills, heredity, and religious similarity. Health, good looks, and kindness are the main characteristics that Jewish Israelis in this sample consistently placed below the international means. (p. 26)

Peres and Meivar (1986) studied self-presentation during courtship in classified ads (personals) over a period of three decades. A total of 60 advertisements were randomly selected for each year, providing a total sample of 1,800 advertisements. The changes in attributes during these 30 years seem to reflect the changing meaning of marriage. Whereas in the past, marriage was viewed as a partnership, it has gradually shifted toward an emphasis on companionship. The importance of personality traits and appearance has increased for both genders. Data indicate that women spend more money describing their demands for a potential mate and less money advertising their own qualities than do men (Peres & Meivar, 1986).

Core Patterns of Mate Selection

Patterns of mate selection were studied among 206 Israeli youth, ages 18 to 30 years, who had been married for up to 4 years (Shachar, 1988). Level of religiosity was found to be significant in determining behavioral patterns prior to marriage. Ethnic background was not found to be significant in affecting mate selection patterns and premarital behaviors. Factors that play a role in the mate selection process include social characteristics (e.g., family status, socioeconomic status), education and intelligence, emotional expressiveness, dependability, sincerity, vitality, humor, and physical appearance. The social characteristics of family lineage and socioeconomic status account for 41% of the variability of the model, followed by emotional expressiveness (34%) and physical appearance (24%). The score for vitality was low (16%), as was the score for education and intelligence (9%) (Shachar, 1988).

Dor's (1995) study of 182 central Israel teens indicated that couple formation during adolescence is essential to the socialization process of this age group. Having a partner in this age group provided these adolescents with social acceptance and served as an entry ticket to special social events. Results supported the stereotypical patterns in courting in which boys tend to initiate dating and couple formation more often than do girls. Boys also pay more attention to their partners and are more promiscuous in their attitudes toward sexual relations than are girls. The "double standard" regarding sexual relationships was supported. It was viewed as acceptable for boys, but not for girls, to have sex. The adolescents expressed egalitarian notions regarding dating and courting in theoretical terms. Both genders agreed that boys and girls have the same responsibility in deciding on the type of outing and in sharing its cost. The author suggested that no significant changes took place during the 1990s regarding courting practices and couple formation processes compared with those during the 1970s and 1980s in Israel or Western countries (Dor, 1995).

The results of Dor's (1995) study showed that girls are more concerned with the approval of their parents and peers regarding mate selection. Girls tend to link love to sex. Both boys and girls see sexual relations as an outcome of emotional relationships, both tend to think that sex is part of adolescents' relationships, and both tend to share their experiences with friends, although girls do so more often than boys (Dor, 1995).

The contradicting egalitarian notions expressed by both genders reflect the time period in which youngsters are exposed to media influences incorporating feminism and equality between the genders into broadcast messages. Also, in Israel there is a very strong message of equality in sexual relations sent via the images of the pioneers (immigrants who came to settle in Israel before its statehood), Golda Meir as prime minister, and mandatory army service for females. Ironically, the media also convey stereotypical messages of gender relations via movies and programs depicting women in traditional roles (Dor, 1995).

The changes in Israeli society regarding marriage and family life were the focus of Shachar's (1997) study. The purpose was to compare

12th graders' expectations about getting married, attitudes toward role division, and ideas about courtship and sexual promiscuity in 1975 ($N =$ 495) and 1990 ($N = 299$).

Marriage is an acceptable norm, according to most of the 1975 sample (77.1%) and most of the 1990 sample (74.5%) (Shachar, 1997). When examining reasons to get married, as proposed by the respondents, the top two reasons (to love and be loved and to start a family) were shared by the two samples, although in reverse order. The explanation might be related to the new social norms that accept open and free love relations prior to marriage. In 1990, respondents put more emphasis on not being alone as a reason for marriage than did the respondents in 1975, and the 1990 sample put less importance on satisfying sexual needs and the need to love and be loved than did the 1975 sample. When looking at gender differences, boys in both 1975 and 1990 saw the reasons of "satisfying sexual needs" and "to conform to the social norms" as more important than did girls. In 1975, girls saw the reason "to give legal status to children" as more important than did boys. In 1990, however, this result reversed to show boys as being more concerned about this than girls, coinciding with the spread of the norm to raise children in single-woman-headed families (Shachar, 1997).

Another issue of importance is division of roles in the family. In 1975, 61.1% of the respondents believed that both partners are responsible for providing for the family, whereas 85.5% saw it as their mutual responsibility in 1990. Girls demonstrated more egalitarian views than did boys in 1975 and 1990 alike. In 1975, 75.3% of the girls versus 46% of the boys thought that both partners are equally responsible. In 1990, the rate of boys who held egalitarian views increased to 76.8%, whereas the rate for the girls increased to 95.0% (Shachar, 1997).

When asked whether a wife should have a career when there is no economic need for it, no significant differences between the 1975 and 1990 samples were found. However, in 1975, 94% of the girls versus 81% of the boys believed that the woman should have a career. In 1990, 92% of the girls versus 84% of the boys held this opinion. As for preferring the husband's career over the wife's career, results indicated significant differences between the genders and between samples. More than half of the boys in 1975 and 1990 believed that the man's career does not precede the woman's career, whereas the rate of girls who held this position increased from 49.8% in 1975 to 81.6% in 1990 (Shachar, 1997).

Boys and girls were more similar in their attitudes about equality in the courtship process in 1990 than in 1975. In 1990, girls believed that they have the same role in courtship as do boys. The patterns of courtship in 1990 were found to be different from those in 1975. In 1975, there was a division between masculine patterns of courtship (e.g., invites to outings, gives compliments) and feminine patterns of courtship (e.g., remembers important dates, indulges). In 1990, both genders were expected to engage in these behaviors equally. More androgynous courtship behaviors are now expected (Shachar, 1997).

The respondents were asked to answer two questions: "Do you see positively having sexual relations with a partner whom you intend to marry?" and "Do you see positively having sexual relations with a partner who you do not intend to marry?" In 1975, only 54.9% of the respondents answered yes to the second question, whereas 75.7% answered positively to this question in 1990. Although girls increased their sexual activity, boys were still found to be more promiscuous than girls. Both samples approved of sexual relationships when there is a commitment to future marital relationships (Shachar, 1997).

Residential Propinquity and Mate Selection

Tabory and Weller (1986) maintained that residential propinquity plays less of a role in couple formation in Israel than in other places in the world. This hypothesis is based on the fact that all individuals of marriageable age in Israel are called to serve in the army and so are removed from their home localities and reside elsewhere for an extended period of time. A total of 280 couples married during the 1974–1975 period participated in the study. Results confirmed that in Israel a smaller percentage of Israeli marriage applicants lived within a half mile of one another. Findings indicated that persons of Afro-Asian background are viewed as more "local" oriented than are Israelis of Western background. Persons of Afro-Asian background are more traditional and religious and tend to cluster around local synagogues and extended families more than do individuals of Western origin. Therefore, it might be expected that Israelis of Afro-Asian descent are more likely to find spouses within their immediate neighborhoods than are Israelis of Western origin who are relatively less isolated and more open to meeting others (Tabory & Weller, 1986).

Age of Marriage

Historically, Ashkenazi Jews tended to marry later than did Sephardi Jews. However, for those marrying in Israel, the age has increased for Afro-Asian brides and grooms, has decreased for Euro-American grooms, and has remained relatively stable for Euro-American brides. It seems that over time, a process of convergence in the timing of marriage has occurred for the two major Jewish ethnic groups in Israel (Goldscheider, 1986).

Shachar (1997) also found a tendency for both genders to delay the marriage age to 25 or 26 years. In 1990, age 24 or 25 years was more desirable among girls (42.1%), whereas boys' preferred age was 24 or 25 (35.7%) or 26 or above (43.9%). In 1990, fewer people (54.6% vs. 79.8%) believed that it is preferable for the man to be older than the woman. Also in 1990, 45.5% indicated that age differences between husbands and wives is a non-issue, whereas only 17.0% thought this way in 1975. In addition, more girls (84.6%) believed that they should marry older men in 1975 than was the case in 1990 (53.6%) (Shachar, 1997).

Intermarriage

Ethnic intermarriage has been viewed in Israel in the context of exogamy, meaning marrying out of the individual's own ethnic group. According to Goldscheider (1986), the rate of ethnic exogamy increases with time, reflecting the loosening of ethnic constraints and the weakening of ethnic boundaries. Goldscheider maintained that the increase in ethnic intermarriages is not only an indicator of assimilation but also an outcome of ethnic changes.

Stier and Shavit (1994) assumed that older women suffer greater "squeezes" (more pressure due to fewer mate alternatives) that force them to cross ethnic and educational lines and compromise in the pursuit of mates. Results from 147,969 respondents indicated that Afro-Asian women have suffered a more consistently harsh marriage squeeze than have Euro-American women. However, age at marriage does not enhance ethnic heterogamy. Regardless of ethnic origin, women who marry later are more likely to marry men of Euro-American origin than are those who marry early. When education of the mate is controlled for, no significant difference in ethnic heterogamy is found regarding early and late marriage.

The younger generation and its attitudes toward exogamy and endogamy were the subject of a study done by Shachar (1982). Shachar found that second-generation youth in Israel (persons who were born in Israel) did not differ from Israel-residing youth from diverse ethnic groups in their exogamy/endogamy preferences. Youth born in Israel were found to be the most desired partners for marriage. Over the years, the rate of interethnic marriages has increased.

Shavit and Stier (1997) used data that were collected in 1972 (14,545 people) and 1983 (15,488) to study the relationship between exogamy and educational level. Results suggested that ethnicity is a more relevant consideration than education in mate selection in Israel. Members of the Ashkenazi groups, except those who came from Russia, were open to intermarriages. However, members of the Oriental (Sephardi) groups tended to marry within their own group in 1972, whereas in 1983 they tended to cross the ethnic lines more often to marry members from other Oriental groups and fewer partners from Ashkenazi descent. During the early period, the Oriental groups differed significantly from each other in their educational and socioeconomic levels. During the later period in Israel, the Orientals were establishing a global identity that was being strengthened across time, whereas the ethnic distinction in the Ashkenazi groups was losing its importance (Shavit & Stier, 1997).

Engagement and Wedding Ceremonies

The Resniks were very upset with their son's mate selection. Yoni was surprised to realize how strongly his parents felt about his mate choice and her ethnic origin. He told his parents that he is in love with Rina and that he is seriously considering marrying her as soon as possible. The Resniks threatened Yoni that they would not attend the wedding and that they would cut off his financial support. They promised him a great trip to Europe and the Far East on completion of his pilot training and cessation of the relationship with Rina. At the same time, the Ochaions were pleased with their daughter's relationship with Yoni. Although they wished for Rina to find a man within their cultural group, they agreed that Yoni is a great guy.

The families met for the first time at Yoni's graduation ceremony. During dinner, Yoni and Rina announced their engagement. Yoni's parents were speechless and embarrassed to raise any vocal objections in public, and Rina's parents insisted that the engagement be celebrated according to their cultural custom in a Chennee ceremony. Rina explained that in this ceremony, the bride usually wears a traditional ethnic garment and jewelry and that in some cultural groups the groom has a special garb as well. She also mentioned that music, dances, and a special ceremony, the Chennee, take place in this event. In the Chennee ceremony, Yoni gave an engagement ring to Rina and received a beautiful watch from her.

Despite their initial objection, Yoni's parents decided to cooperate given that Yoni is their only son. Yoni and Rina went to the Rabbinate to register, bringing documents and two witnesses each to support their claim of Jewish descent, and got the approval to get married. They met with the rabbi they had selected to perform the marriage ceremony. A special event hall was rented, guest lists were generated, and invitations were sent. Rina rented a beautiful white dress and picked the wedding rings with Yoni.

The evening prior to the wedding day, Rina went with her mother, her sisters, Yoni's mother, her aunts, and her girlfriends to the Mikavh (a religious bathhouse). According to the custom, the bride takes a ritual bath and cleanses herself in a special ceremony conducted by a religious woman. At the end of this ceremony, the bride receives a certificate confirming the performance of this ritual. This certificate is given to the rabbi at the wedding.

The day of the wedding arrived, and the couple's best friend, Shalom, picked Yoni and Rina up in his specially decorated car. All of the guests were waiting for their arrival at the event hall. The band was playing while guests with gifts or envelopes with money/checks shook hands with the parents of the bride and groom. The couple arrived, and Yoni, accompanied by his father and Rina's father, was taken to another room to meet with the rabbi and sign the ketubah. When the signal was given, four relatives picked up the chuppah, and the groom and bride stood under the chuppah with their parents standing next to them. Rina's mother put the veil over her daughter's face, and the mothers of both the groom and the bride held Rina, assisting her in circling Yoni seven times. Special blessings, called the Seven Blessings, were chanted. The rabbi blessed the wine and gave Yoni and Rina a drink. Rings were exchanged, and the ketubah was read and presented. Yoni broke the glass, adhering to the Jewish ritual to commemorate Jerusalem. Yoni and Rina were pronounced husband and wife, and music, food, and dancing filled the rest of the evening. At the end of the evening, Yoni and Rina left for their honeymoon in Eilat, a resort area in the southern part of Israel. Their parents helped pay the wedding expenses, and the money that was given to Yoni and Rina will be used as a downpayment toward their first house.

Although all weddings in Israel are done under the religious guidance and supervision of the Rabbinate, ceremonies share the same core customs but vary by culture and religious observance level. Among all groups, the groom is called *chatan* and the bride is called *kallah*.

Among the religious groups in Israel, arranged agreements between families done by matchmakers, parents, and/or relatives initiate the mate selection process. Families set meetings after the initial agreement to allow the young prospective bride and groom to determine their compatibility. During these encounters, no physical contact is allowed between the two until they are married. The meetings take place in an open public area with other people present (Becher, 1996). As the prospective bride and groom agree to marry, the families negotiate the "conditions." They delineate the

Bride (Afghan origin) Dressed in Special Garment for Chennee Ceremony

specific dates, obligations of each side, and division of responsibilities for the wedding's preparations. An engagement ceremony finalizes the agreement. Some families sign a contract, whereas others shake hands. A week before the wedding ceremony, the bride-to-be and groom-to-be stop seeing each other. On the wedding day, both fast until after the wedding ceremony (Becher, 1996).

Among the more liberal Jews, mate selection is an individual free choice. As a man and woman decide to marry, their families are introduced and the planning stage of the wedding takes place. Oriental families tend to celebrate the engagement in a special ceremony, the Chennee. A special mud-like mixture is prepared and put on the hands of the bride and groom to symbolize their unity. The bride and groom, dressed in special garments, exchange gifts and dance to the special music. Among the Ashkenazi Jews, the engagement ceremony is not as elaborate. An engagement ring is given to the bride, and the arrangements for the wedding are made.

The religiously observant groom is dressed in a *kittle* (white robe), whereas the nonreligious groom is dressed in a suit. The bride is dressed in a white dress. At the wedding, the groom first signs the ketubah, in which his obligations to his future wife are presented. The groom announces to the rabbi and the two witnesses, usually his and the bride's fathers, what sum of money the wife will receive in case of divorce. As the groom and two witnesses sign the ketubah, the veiling of the bride takes place. The two enter the chuppah, and the bride circles the groom seven times with her mother and mother-in-law. This symbolizes the 7 days of creation, and the act of circling represents the bride bringing light and protection into the household. The wedding ceremony takes place with the *kiddushin,* where the ketubah is read aloud, rings are placed on the bride's finger, and the Seven Blessings are recited over a full cup of wine. The blessings praise God, man, and woman. They express hope for the success of the new couple and a prayer for Jerusalem. At the end of the blessings, the bride and groom share in drinking the wine. The ceremony ends with the groom breaking a glass by stomping on it.

At this point, the guests cry out "Mazel Tov!" and the dancing and music start. As the ceremony ends, the couple is sent to a room called the *Cheder yichud* (the room of privacy). This act represents the legitimacy of the marriage by the fact that now the bride and groom can be alone (Becher, 1996). A feast, music, and dance are part of every wedding. At a religious wedding, men and women will dance separately. At a wedding for secular or traditional Jews, the genders will mix and mingle.

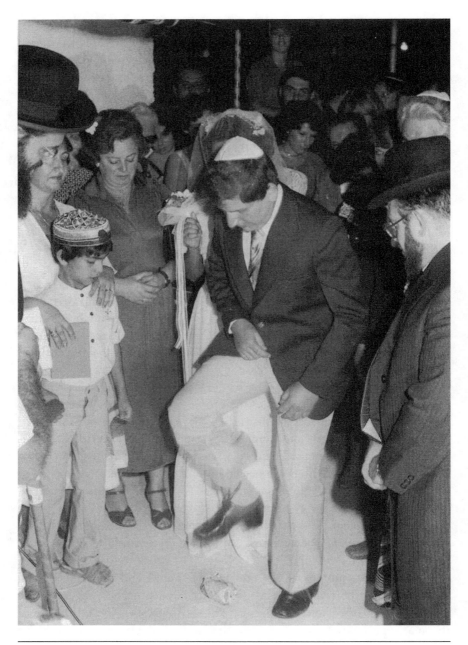

Groom Breaking Glass at Jewish Wedding Ceremony

References

Becher, M (1996). *The Jewish wedding ceremony.* [Online]. Retrieved April 3, 2003, from www.ohr.org.il/judaism/articles/wedding.pdf

Biale, D. (1986). Childhood, marriage, and the family in the Eastern European Jewish Enlightenment. In M. S. Cohen & P. E. Hyman (Eds.), *Jewish family myths and reality* (pp. 45–61). New York: Holms & Meier.

Buss, D., & Safir, M. (1990). International preference in selected mates: A study of 34 cultures. *Journal of Cross-Cultural Psychology, 21,* 5–47.

Dor, O. (1995). *Couple formation and sexuality in adolescence: Attitudes and behaviors.* Unpublished master's thesis, Tel Aviv University.

Elazar, D. (n.d.). *How religious are Israeli Jews?* [Online]. Retrieved April 14, 2003, from www.jcpa.org/dje/articles2/howrelisr.htm

Friedman, A. M. (1986). Marriage as an institution: Jewry under Islam. In D. Kraemer (Ed.), *The Jewish family metaphor and memory* (pp. 31–45). New York: Oxford University Press.

Goldscheider, C. (1986). Family change and variation among Israeli ethnic groups. In M. S. Cohen & P. E. Hyman (Eds.), *Jewish family myths and reality* (pp. 131–147). New York: Holms & Meier.

Goshen-Gottstein, E. (1966). Courtship, marriage, and pregnancy in Geula. *Israeli Annals of Psychiatry and Related Disciplines, 4*(1), 43–66.

Gutmann, J. (1986). Jewish medieval marriage customs in art: Creativity and adaptation. In D. Kraemer (Ed.), *The Jewish family metaphor and memory* (pp. 47–62). New York: Oxford University Press.

Library of Congress. (1988). *Ethnicity and social class.* [Online]. Retrieved on April 3, 2003, from www.1upinfo.com/country-guide-study/israel/israel56.html

Peres, Y., & Meivar, H. (1986). Self-presentation during courtship: A content analysis of classified advertisements in Israel. *Journal of Comparative Family Studies, 17,* 19–32.

Schlesinger, B. (Ed.). (1971). *The Jewish family: A survey and annotated bibliography.* Toronto: University of Toronto Press.

Schlesinger, B. (Ed.). (1987). *Jewish family issues: A resource guide.* New York: Garland.

Shachar, R. (1982). *Attitudes towards ethnic endogamy and exogamy among Israeli youth.* Paper presented at the meeting of the Israeli Sociological Society, Haifa University, Israel.

Shachar, R. (1988). *Mate selection among Israeli youth.* Unpublished dissertation, Bar-Ilan University, Israel.

Shachar, R. (1997). *Attitudes of 18-year-olds toward marriage and family life: Is there any change? Comparing 1975 to 1990.* Paper presented at seminar, "Ahinuch and Svivo" (Education and Related Issues), Michlallet Seminar Hakibbutzim (Kibbutzim Seminary), Israel.

Shavit, Y., & Stier, H. (1997). Ethnicity and educational attainment in the marital patterns in Israel: Changes across time. *Magamot, 38*(2), 207–225.

Shenhav-Shefer, M. (2000). *The structural difficulties in mate selection decision making and how they are related to thinking style: Rational versus intuitive.* Master's thesis, Tel Aviv University. (in Hebrew)

Solomon, Z. (1986). Self-acceptance and the selection of a marital partner: An assessment of the SVR model of Murstein. *Social Behavior and Personality, 14,* 1–6.

Stier, H., & Shavit, Y. (1994). Age at marriage, sex ratios, and ethnic heterogamy. *European Sociological Review, 10*(1), 79–87.

Tabory, E., & Weller, L. (1986). Residential propinquity and mate selection in an Israel town. *International Journal of Sociology of the Family, 16,* 217–224.

The World Factbook. (1996). Retrieved on April 3, 2003, from www.odci.gov/cia/publications/factbook/index.html

9

Marriage in Turkey

Nuran Hortaçsu

Two couples are getting married in different districts of Istanbul, the Turkish city situated on two sides of the Bosphorous separating Asia from Europe. Just like Istanbul, the two marriages represent the East and the West—the traditional and the modern. They reveal signs of both Westernization and perseverance of tradition during an epoch of globalization. As they are about to sign the marriage register, each couple reminisces about the stages leading up to the marriage ceremony. There are similarities as well as differences between the experiences of the two couples.

The families initiated the traditional marriage, and tradition and families guided the marriage arrangements. However, the couple's wishes were usually taken into consideration. The couple had the initiative in the "modern" marriage. The man and woman met and decided to make the decision to marry fairly independently from their families. However, once the decision was made, the families played important roles in wedding and marriage arrangements.

Some information about Turkey and about some facts, practices, and values related to marriage in this culture need to be considered before going into the specifics of each type of marriage.

Turkey: A Modernizing Collectivistic Culture

The Turkish Republic was constituted in 1923 on the relics of the Ottoman Empire following the war of independence against Western occupation. Efforts at Westernization had started during the previous era. Republican governments advocated families based on spousal equality and conjugal affection as part of the campaign toward Westernization and secularization. Thus, it may be argued that Turkey is a traditional and patriarchal culture in the process of modernization. In traditional cultures, marriage is a union of families as well as of individuals. In such cultures, marriage is not based on romantic love or individual choice. The conjugal pair is economically dependent on the extended family and contributes to the extended family by providing children to continue the family name and by participating in the family workforce (Goode, 1971). Work in modernizing non-Western cultures indicates that customs and practices related to marriage and family show variations consistent with the dominant values of the particular culture (Hortaçsu, Baştuğ, & Muhammetberdiev, 2001). Turkey is a modernizing but collectivistic culture. Collectivism is characterized by definition of self in terms of relationships, emphasis on social cohesion and harmony, and value of family integrity. In collectivistic cultures, the line between the individual and the family is thin, similarity rather than distinctiveness from group members is desirable, and interdependence between individual and family is the norm. Thus, collectivism is different from individualism, which focuses on the individual, personal rights, contracts, and independent rather than interdependent self (Kağıtçıbaşı, 1996; Triandis, 1995).

Marriage based on love and spousal equality was introduced to the Turkish scene during the latter part of the 19th century as part of the modernization movement. However, the concept of romantic love led to ambivalent reactions. Love outside of marriage was seen as a threat to the stability of existing marriages and to the norm of female chastity. On the other hand, marriage based on love freed women from the experience of unwanted marriages and offered relative gender equality in marriage (Duben & Behar, 1991).

Currently, it is estimated that half of marriages in Turkey are arranged marriages. The percentages of arranged marriages are lower for the urban, young, and educated sectors of the country (Atalay, Kontaş, Beyazýt, & Madenoğlu, 1992). Currently, about one fourth of marriages in the capital of Turkey are arranged marriages (Hortaçsu, 1999a; Hortaçsu & Oral, 1994). Today, a milder version of arranged marriage has replaced the traditional one in which the bride and groom had no premarital interaction.

In the newer version, the prospective spouses are introduced by their families and are relatively free to make their own decisions after a few dates. On the other hand, Western-style "love" marriages are on the rise, especially among the young, urban, and educated sectors (Atalay et al., 1992). However, these love marriages also involve a high degree of family interference and contribution to marriage arrangements (Hortaçsu, 1995).

Stages of Marriage

A "script" for marriage exists in Turkey. As is true of most scripts, there are essential and nonessential events and roles in this script (Abelson, 1981). The traditional and modern types of marriage vary with respect to the nonessentials. In most cases, modern marriages omit some of the elements of the traditional script. Therefore, stages of the traditional marriage script are described in what follows, and modern variations are noted.

Contemplation

As would be expected from the prevalence of collectivistic values, family is an important value in Turkish culture, and marriage is seen as serving the ends of continuation of the family name, an orderly life, and fulfilling religious obligations (Atalay et al., 1992). Chronological age, which is seen as an indicator of capacity for undertaking the financial and moral responsibilities of marriage, is one of the most important factors leading to contemplation of marriage in the traditional sector. Average age at first marriage in Turkey is 24 years for men and 20 for women. However, it is higher for those with higher levels of educational attainment and for those living in urban regions (Atalay et al., 1992).

According to the traditional script, the prospective groom and/or his parents decide that the time is ripe for marriage. If the young man wishes to get married but sees no signs of marriage plans by his parents, he may deliberately act in a moody fashion—a sign of wanting to get married. This is a good example of indirect communication of desires and is a manner of communication typical of collectivistic cultures (Triandis, 1995). The young man may also convey his desire for marriage to his mother or a relative but not to his father. Open communication between fathers and children is discouraged in the Turkish culture so as to maintain paternal authority. Mothers serve as intermediaries between fathers and children in this situation, as in many other matters (Kiray, 1979). If parents decide that the time for their son's marriage has come, the mother may talk to her son and learn his preferences. Parents may decide that the time for their son's marriage has come without any signs from their son. In this case, the mother talks with her son.

There are a number of disappearing customs that focus on the economic interests of families and treat individuals as goods in exchanges. One such custom is the "cradle match," an arrangement made between families when children are very young (sometimes at birth). This practice serves the function of increasing solidarity between families. Other practices are related to preferred or compulsory spouses. In very traditional sectors, a girl's paternal uncle's son is the preferred spouse for a girl. Her marriage to anyone else depends on whether the cousin states that he does not wish to marry her. This practice is a measure against division of property. Another practice in traditional sectors is the exchange of a daughter for a bride, that is, where two brother-sister pairs from two families get married. This practice is employed among families that adhere to the disappearing custom of "bride wealth."

Bride wealth may consist of money or goods presented to the bride's family. The bride's family may or may not use these resources for marriage expenses. Traditionally, bride wealth is presented to the bride's family as compensation for the loss of the daughter's household labor and the loss of investment incurred in her upbringing. This practice is being abandoned in modern Turkey (Atalay et al., 1992; Hortaçsu et al., 2001). Another disappearing custom associated with bride wealth is the requirement that a woman marry her dead husband's brother provided that he is not already married. This practice is a measure preventing loss of investment (bride wealth) in case of early death of the groom. A third disappearing custom is the substitution of another bride from the same family in the case of the early death of the original bride for whom the family has received bride wealth.

In the case of a "normal" traditional marriage, where none of these disappearing customs are in effect, the groom's parents mobilize their social network in search of a suitable bride. Consistent with the dominant value system, "good family" (e.g., no scandals, respected in community) and similarity with respect to education, monetary means, religion, values, and social status are desired qualities of prospective spouses. Consistent with patriarchal values, male rather than female superiority is preferred with respect to indicators of social status. Spousal harmony (e.g., love, respect, support), good character (e.g., reliability, respectability, absence of deviant habits), indicators of economic security (e.g., education, job, career, ability, skills), and ability to adapt to the family are also desired characteristics in prospective spouses (Atalay et al., 1992; Hortaçsu & Baştuǧ, 2000). Thus, consistent with collectivistic values, harmony both within the conjugal pair and between the conjugal pair and the extended family is stressed.

Once the search for a bride begins, the groom's mother visits the homes of prospective brides with women who act as intermediaries. The prospective bride's family is often informed of the purpose of the visit. The young woman usually opens the door, sits with the guests during some small talk, asks for the guests' preferences for Turkish coffee, and disappears. She comes back with the coffee, waits until the guests finish drinking their coffee, collects the empty cups, and leaves the room. During the greeting and/or coffee offering, the prospective groom's mother may touch the prospective bride (to make sure that her flesh is firm) and try to smell her breath (to make sure that she does not have bad breath). The visitors may also inspect the cleanliness of the room as unobtrusively as possible. There might be oblique inquiries about the young woman's accomplishments.

After some "shopping," the groom's mother chooses a prospective bride and discusses her choice with her husband. If the husband agrees, she informs her son about the young woman, possibly showing him a picture of her. Depending on the degree of traditionalism of the families, the couple may or may not be introduced and may or may not have a few "dates" alone or in the presence of family and/or friends. Such a date might range from an "accidental" meeting at a friend's house to a Western-style dinner date. Parents and the prospective groom usually make a joint decision about the prospective bride. In rare cases, the groom's opinion is not considered.

In the case of modern marriages, courtships are similar to those in the West. A woman meets a man. In most cases, they are friends at school, work in the same organization, or meet through friends. They start going out together and meet each other's friends. They may go on school trips or summer vacations, usually with a group of friends. Depending on the level of conservatism of their families, the relationship may or may not be revealed to the families (this is especially true in the case of the young woman's family). Sexual intimacy may or may not occur. A small minority cohabit (live together), often without the knowledge of their parents (especially the woman's parents). When talk of marriage begins and/or the relationship gets serious, the young people reveal the relationship to their mothers. Each mother (but usually not the father) meets the respective partner. If families are conservative, young people do not meet each other's parents unless they make the decision to marry. Sometimes, a young woman's parents may put pressure on her for getting married because they fear that her dating may compromise her marriage prospects or family honor. When the young man and woman decide to get married, their parents are informed about the decision. If they have not met before, each person meets the other's parents.

Studies conducted with couples on the verge of marriage show that reasons originating from the relationship (e.g., love, spousal compatibility, spouse's personality, desire for a joint future) were rated as more important than normative reasons (e.g., family/friend encouragement, appropriate age, social status, convenience) and reasons related to spouse's market value (e.g., looks, profession, financial condition) (Hortaçsu, 1995; Hortaçsu & Oral, 1994). Although all couples rated relationship reasons as most important, couples involved in modern marriages ascribed greater importance to relationship reasons and lower importance to normative reasons than did couples involved in arranged marriages. In addition, the percentages of respondents classifying their marriages as ones of love or love and logic were higher, and the percentages classifying their marriages as ones of logic or convention were lower, among couples involved in modern marriages relative to those involved in arranged marriages (Hortaçsu, 1997).

Commitment

In the case of traditional marriages, once the groom's family decides on the bride, the groom's mother visits the bride's mother once more and the two women talk about the possibility of a marriage. During this visit, the groom's mother tries to assess the attitude of the bride's family toward the marriage. She may talk about the possible nature of the marriage (e.g., whether or not the young couple will be expected to live with groom's family, financial conditions) and may give a picture of the groom to the bride's mother if the bride and groom have not met each other. Unless something goes wrong, it is fairly certain that an offer will be made at this point. The bride's mother talks with her husband and possibly with the bride. She may show a picture of the groom to the young woman. If the response is positive, word is sent to the groom's family.

Members of the groom's family tell the bride's family that they would like to visit "for a good/benevolent matter" at the convenience of the bride's family. The bride's family sets the time. The visit is usually after dinner but may also take place during tea time. The groom's parents arrive at the bride's home bearing candy and flowers. Aunts, uncles, older siblings, and/or in-laws from both families may be present at this visit. Extended family involvement in the ceremony of asking for the bride's hand and/or the decision to accept the request was reported for 44% of marriages occurring during the 1990s (Hortaçsu et al., 2001). After some small talk, the bride serves coffee and disappears. Sometimes, the bride puts salt in the groom's coffee. If the groom does not make any comments or complaints, that is taken as an indication of his good nature.

After coffee, the groom's father, or a respected relative, asks for the young woman's hand, saying, "With God's permission and the Prophet's approval, we would like your daughter for our son." Traditionally, the bride's family is expected not to show eagerness for the marriage. In accordance with the saying "The girl's house is the place for coyness," the bride's father is likely to say that he and his wife have to consult with their relatives before they give their final answer but that the marriage may take place if God wills. A traditional family does consult with relatives and may ask a trusted relative or friend to pray and sleep, hoping that he or she will have a dream that, when interpreted, will foretell the fate of the marriage.

In the case of traditional marriages, a day is arranged for the groom's parents to visit and ask for the young woman's hand again if the answer is going to be affirmative. If the answer is going to be negative, word is sent and the embarrassment of refusal is usually avoided. The procedure is repeated. The offer is made and accepted. Refreshments are served. Something sweet is served so that the couple may eat sweets and talk sweetly in the future. The bride may be presented with a "commitment ring," that is, a ring with or without a stone depending on the financial conditions of the family. Among couples involved in modern marriages, this ring is often a very thin gold wedding band worn before the involvement of the families in the relationship. Its symbolic meaning is very similar to that of "being pinned" in the 1970s U.S. culture. Negotiations about jewelry to be given to the bride (bride wealth in rare cases), and about each family's contribution to house furnishings and marriage expenses, may or may not be made at this point.

In the case of a modern marriage, the families may meet before the ceremony of asking for the young woman's hand. As a rule, parents' approval of marriage is obtained even if the marriage is a modern one. Parents, rather than the groom, ask for the young woman's hand even in modern marriages. Her father usually accepts the offer, saying that the young man and woman have already decided and that the families should approve. Consultation with relatives and the second visit is skipped. Thus, it may be seen that even in the case of modern marriages, on the surface, parents appear to have the final say.

After Commitment

After the commitment ceremony, the families are likely to exchange dinner invitations in both traditional and modern marriages. These invitations provide opportunities for families to get to know each other and talk about the details of the engagement ceremonies and sharing of expenses. Negotiations about expenses may be direct or indirect. Mothers-in-law do most of the negotiating with help from female relatives, but fathers may have the last word on how much they can (or are willing to) spend.

The average time between meeting the prospective spouse and marriage is more than 3 years for Turkish urban marriages. This period is shorter for arranged marriages than for modern ones. During this time, individuals generally interact with their prospective spouses alone or in the presence of their families about once a week. They also interact with their partners in the presence of friends and relatives. Couples involved in arranged marriages interact more frequently with relatives, and interact less frequently with friends and with their spouses alone, than do those involved in modern marriages. Couples involved in arranged marriages also report lower levels of reciprocal self-revelation, lower emotional involvement with their spouses, and being closer to their families of origin (Hortaçsu, 1997; Hortaçsu & Oral, 1994). Thus, even couples involved in modern marriages interact fairly frequently with their families of origin and with their extended families before marriage. These practices are consistent with the importance ascribed to family harmony and similarity of background—desirable qualities in prospective spouses.

Engagement

The families and the couple agree on the nature and the date of the engagement ceremony. They also agree on the number of guests. In most cases, the two families either invite the same number of guests or limit the guests to similar sectors (e.g., only immediate family, only relatives) of their networks. The engagement ceremony may be skipped for financial reasons or if the wedding is to take place shortly.

In general, engagement is a relatively small celebration. It could be in the form of a small tea or dinner party at the young woman's home or at a restaurant with close relatives. The ceremony may also be a large one in a hotel or banquet hall. Expenses may or may not be paid for by the bride's family. The less traditional the families, the more likely the bride's family will pay for the expenses.

The groom's family arrives with a box or silver tray of candy or chocolate decorated with ribbons on the day of the engagement ceremony. The engagement ceremony takes place after the guests are gathered but before the main refreshments are served. Everyone gathers at a central location. The wedding bands are tied with a red ribbon and placed on a silver tray. A respected family member or friend of the family (usually a male) says a few

Engagement Ceremony in a Modern Marriage

words while putting the rings on the right-hand fingers of the prospective bride and groom. The engagement ring is a simple gold wedding band worn on the right-hand finger and transferred to the left hand at the wedding ceremony. In religious circles, men do not wear gold. They may wear a silver or platinum ring.

After the rings are worn, the young man and woman are kissed and congratulated by their parents and relatives. They, in turn, kiss the hands of relatives from the older generation as a gesture of respect. At this point, the groom and his family may give the bride jewelry or gold coins. Some families give presents to the bride at the engagement, others at the wedding, and some at both ceremonies. The bride's family may also give presents to the young woman at this point. In general, the more traditional the families, the more they give to the new daughter-in-law (as opposed to the daughter) and the more they give at the engagement (as opposed to the wedding). The more the groom's family gives to the new daughter-in-law, the more "honor" this act is supposed to demonstrate. In other words, the more the groom's family gives to the bride, the more honor it bestows on her, and this, in a roundabout way, is a reflection of the family's honor. The daughter belongs to the bride's family anyway, so giving to the daughter does not reflect on her family's honor. This argument is also behind the groom's

Bride Receiving Gift at Wedding

family giving more to the daughter-in-law at the engagement, when she is not part of the family, than at the wedding, when she is part of the family. In very traditional circles, someone announces who gave what to the assembly (e.g., "The groom's uncle gave two gold bracelets"). In modern circles, gifts may be presented privately. After the giving of gifts, the couple may start the dancing and refreshments will be served. Engagement candy brought by the groom is distributed to guests. The bride keeps the tray as a cherished memoir of her engagement. The bride and groom spend a few minutes with all of the guests and thank them for coming.

Between the Engagement and the Wedding

After the young man and woman are officially engaged, they visit relatives and introduce their fiancés to their social networks. They may also spend some time alone and discuss their marriage. They may shop together or with their families for necessities of their future home. Negotiations and conflict may occur between families during this stage concerning choice and price of furniture and place of residence. Because most of the marriage expenses are undertaken by the families, these conflicts may be about who gives how much, excessive demands by one family, place of residence (e.g., with groom's family or not, district of residence), and quality of furniture. They may also be in the form of power conflicts, that is, who will have the last say. Conflict between preferences of the couple and preferences of the families may also take place due to generational differences.

Presents may be given to the bride on the occasion of religious holidays. If the "feast of sacrifice" (a religious holiday involving the sacrifice of a ram or some other animal) occurs between the engagement and the wedding, the groom's family sends a ram to the bride's home. The ram is decorated with gold coins. The bride's family cooks a stew from the ram's meat and sends it to the groom's family. Modern couples often skip this custom.

Families and the couple decide on the day and the nature of the wedding ceremony. Whether or not a wedding reception will be given and/or the number of guests often depend on the financial resources of the groom's family and preferences of the couple. Some modern couples prefer to omit the reception and ask for money instead. Parents, especially traditional ones, usually want to have a feast to enjoy the happiness of their children with their social network.

The young man and woman complete the necessary forms at the main municipality building, present proof that they are single, and get a date for the legal ceremony at one of the marriage offices of the municipality. If they wish, they may have the official ceremony performed at the location of the wedding reception or at one of their homes after office hours. The marriage is announced for 3 weeks prior to the wedding to make sure that there are no legal objections to the marriage (e.g., due to bigamy).

The mothers of the bride and groom go with the bride to the dress-maker for a decision about the wedding dress. Close female relatives may accompany them. The groom's family pays for the wedding dress. In modern marriages, the bride may choose the wedding dress herself. The couple and their mothers may also shop for furniture. Families contribute to the marriage expenses to a large extent, with the groom's family providing most of the necessities. The contribution of the young couple and that of the bride's family to wedding expenses increase with increasing educational level of the families. However, even among those with high levels of education, the couple's contribution to expenses is minimal relative to that of the families. Thus, dependence on families for marriage expenses is generally quite high. Families with higher education are likely to provide the bed-room furniture, the kitchen utensils, and the groom's attire (a Western-style suit or tuxedo) for the wedding ceremony and to undertake the expenses for the engagement ceremony of the bride. Those with less education (and possibly less money) do not spend much toward the young woman's marriage (Hortaçsu, 1995). In all sectors, the bride brings all bedding, pots and pans, tablecloths, plates, and silverware. The bedding and tablecloths constitute the trousseau. In traditional circles, these should be embroidered by the bride and are an indication of her skill. In traditional circles, the contents of the trousseau are displayed for examination by female relatives.

The bride and groom usually deliver the wedding invitations themselves. Before the wedding, the groom's family sends a package traditionally wrapped in an embroidered cloth. This package includes underwear, a nightgown, slippers, clothes, shoes, handbag, perfume, and the like. The bride's family may or may not send packages (usually including clothing) to the groom and his family members (usually the parents).

If the family is very religious, a simple religious wedding ceremony, consisting of prayers and acceptance of marriage in the presence of two witnesses, is performed before the couple may go out together. Many modern couples also have this ceremony shortly before the civil ceremony. Traditionally, the bride should not be present at this ceremony and should give her assent through closed doors. According to Islamic tradition, an (often symbolic) amount of money to be given to the bride is agreed on. This money consists of two parts: a smaller amount to be given to the bride (not to the father) for her own spending and a larger amount to be given in case of divorce. This part of the ceremony is often skipped. A religious ceremony alone is not sufficient for a marriage to be considered legal in Turkey. Thus, a civil ceremony is necessary. However, about 5% of marriages in Turkey involve religious ceremony only, 10% involve only a civil ceremony, and 85% involve both types of ceremonies (Atalay et al., 1992). Thus, the religious ceremony, representing tradition, may be seen as coexisting with the modern civil ceremony.

Henna Night

The "henna" ceremony is the female counterpart of the Western "bachelor's party" and may be viewed as an initiation ceremony for the upcoming marriage. It is also a "good-bye" ceremony. The young woman says good-bye to the happy and protected life at her family home and gets prepared for the hardships of marriage (traditionally) at the home of her in-laws, where she will be the lowest ranking member of the family—being young, female, and inexperienced. Sometimes, men may also get together among themselves.

Women from both families get together. The groom sends the henna (paste made from the root of a henna plant that becomes a reddish brown color when dry), which is placed on the bride's palms and on the palms of those who are present. Food is served. Those who are present sing songs about the bride leaving the parental home and facing hardships with the intention of making the bride cry. (A modest bride should not appear to be happy about getting married and leaving her parental home.) Candy is thrown over the bride's head (for sweet talk in her marriage). The bride may look into a mirror to see her future while candy is thrown over her head. Women dance traditional dances. After the bride has done her crying, she is asked to join the dance. Sometimes, the groom comes and has henna put on his palms, or henna may be sent to the groom. Observance of the henna ceremony is on the decline.

Wedding

The father of the bride or a male relative (usually a brother) puts a red belt around the bride's waist before she leaves for the wedding. This is called a "striving belt" and is a symbol of the bride's virginity. The name of the belt, consistent with the crying at the henna ceremony, also implies that marriage will not be easy for the bride. A married female relative, the *yenge* (wife of a brother or an uncle), talks to the bride about marriage and the wedding night. The groom arrives in a car decorated with flowers to fetch the bride. Relatives may also be present in the car. The bride and groom go to the municipality's wedding hall for the civil marriage. Children or people who see the wedding car may stop the car and ask for money. Sometimes, the driver may honk the car's horn to attract attention.

The civil ceremony is usually a 15-minute affair. Ceremonies of various couples are scheduled in close succession. Guests enter the wedding hall and sit as soon as the previous ceremony is over. The bride and groom, their two witnesses, and the official sit at a table on the stage. The official confirms the identity of the witnesses and may make a short speech about marriage. The official asks the bride and groom whether they want to get married. Each says yes and signs the book. The witnesses also sign. While signing, the bride and groom may try to step on each other's foot under the table. It is believed that whoever steps on the other's foot will get the upper hand in marriage.

After the ceremony, the couple and parents go outside into the entrance of the wedding hall. The guests line up and present their congratulations and presents. Presents may be jewelry or money that is pinned or put on the bride's dress and the groom's suit or tuxedo. If no space is left to place presents, the earlier ones are removed and put into nylon bags held by relatives standing by to make space for new presents. The bags are usually given to the mothers-in-law afterward so that it may be determined who gave the presents.

Traditional Turkish Bride With Striving Belt

A wedding reception that includes refreshments may or may not take place on the evening of the marriage ceremony. The reception may be a small dinner party at the home of the groom's parents or at a restaurant, or it may be a cocktail party or big affair involving a couple hundred guests at a fashionable hotel. If the families are very conservative, male and female guests may be entertained in different parts of the same hall. Otherwise, men and women sit together and liquor is served.

The couple's parents line up at the door and welcome guests. If the civil ceremony is taking place during the wedding reception, it takes place at the beginning of the reception. The bride and groom usually enter with the wedding march. If there is no civil ceremony, they start dancing to "their song" or the classic Italian tango *La Comparcita*. They spend some time at each table and thank the guests for coming to their wedding during the reception. If there is a reception, presents (e.g., gold, jewelry, money) are given at the reception and not at the civil ceremony. Modern couples typically request that money be deposited into their bank accounts rather than being given presents. A less direct way of expressing this wish is to write "Please do not send flowers" on the wedding invitations, meaning "Please give us money." The wedding usually starts with Western-style dancing and ends with folk and/or belly dancing.

Newlywed Stage

The bride and groom retire to their room either at home or at a hotel. The bride has her face covered. The groom presents her with some jewelry and then opens the veil. This jewelry is called "face-seeing jewel." The groom prays before the newlyweds have intercourse. If the family is very traditional, the blood-stained bedsheet is given to the yenge as proof of the bride's virginity. The yenge presents this to the groom's mother and gets a present. The newlyweds may or may not go on a honeymoon, depending on their financial circumstances, work schedules, and preferences. They may or may not live with the groom's family. The covering of the face and praying also may be skipped in modern marriages.

After the newlyweds settle down, friends and relatives visit and view the bride's trousseau. They bring gifts if they have not already done so. Gifts may be brought either to the couple's home or to their parents' homes. Dinner invitations are exchanged between the couple and relatives. Research shows that newlyweds continue to interact rather frequently (about once a week) with their families of origin. Couples involved in arranged marriages interact less frequently with the wife's family than do couples involved in modern marriages. Conflicts with and feelings for families of origin, as well as frequency of interactions with families of origin, are important predictors of feelings for one's spouse (Hortaçsu, 1995, 1997). This is consistent with the argument that a thin line exists between the individual and the family in collectivistic cultures.

A baby is expected from newlywed couples within the first couple of years (Hortaçsu, 1999b; Hortaçsu et al., 2001). Couples involved in arranged marriages are less likely to practice birth control and more likely to have babies within the first year. Most couples want babies because they love them and believe that they will add to the couples' happiness. Parenthood leads to closer relations with families of origin and more gender stereotypical family functioning. Unlike Western marriages, parenthood in Turkey is not associated with a decrease in emotional involvement with one's spouse (Hortaçsu, 1999b).

Conclusion

The preceding description of events and practices that take place before marriage in Turkey demonstrates that the two types of marriage—traditional and modern—have many common aspects, with the underlying theme being interdependence between extended families and the conjugal pair. More autonomy is granted to couples involved in modern marriages than in arranged ones. However, the financial burdens on the families of origin may be very similar. Thus, parents of modern couples seem to have less direct control over the conjugal pair than do those of traditional couples. However, they may be burdened with equal responsibilities. This is consistent with the changing definition of parenthood during modern times, as discussed by Ambert (1994).

The description of modern marriage in Turkey is quite different from that of marriage in the West. Thus, it is consistent with the argument that "modernization" (and/or industrialization) transpires in rapport with the dominant values of each culture (Hortaçsu et al., 2001; Kağtçıbaşı, 1990). It is possible that the coexistence of modern norms of consumerism and limited job and monetary conditions necessitates parental contributions to marriage expenses in Turkey. It is also possible that social status of the young couple reflects on that of their parents, making it necessary for parents to support the young couple for the sake of family integrity.

A few cautionary notes are necessary. First, although there are prototypical modern and traditional marriages, there are variations within each. For example, a marriage may be initiated by parents but may proceed like a modern marriage in that the young man and woman may fall in love and exercise control over most decisions. The reverse may also occur in that families may assume control after the young man and woman announce their decision in a love marriage. Second, although modern marriages are more likely to occur among the more educated and urban sectors and among those with more modern values, this is not always the case. Elopement may occur in rural areas when the young man and woman are in love and their families object to the union, and arrangements may be made when an educated person cannot (or does not wish to) find his or her own spouse.

References

Abelson, R. P. (1981). Psychological status of the script concept. *American Psychologist, 36*, 715–729.

Ambert, A. (1994). An international perspective on parenting: Social change and social constructs. *Journal of Marriage and the Family, 56*, 529–543.

Atalay, B., Kontaş, M., Beyazıt, S., & Madenoğlu, K. (1992). *Türk aile yapısı araştırması* (Investigation of Turkish family structure). Ankara, Turkey: DPT Matbaası (State Planning Organization).

Duben, A., & Behar, C. (1991). *Istanbul households: Marriage, family, and fertility: 1880–1940*. Cambridge, UK: Cambridge University Press.

Goode, W. J. (1971). World revolution and family patterns. *Journal of Marriage and the Family, 33,* 624–635.

Hortaçsu, N. (1995). Prelude to marriage in Ankara: Educational level, reasons for marriage, feelings for spouse and families. *Boğaziçi Journal, 9,* 185–205.

Hortaçsu, N. (1997). Family-initiated and couple-initiated marriages in Turkey. *Genetic, Social, and General Psychology Monographs, 158,* 325–342.

Hortaçsu, N. (1999a). The first year of family- and couple-initiated marriages of a Turkish sample: A longitudinal investigation. *International Journal of Psychology, 34,* 29–41.

Hortaçsu, N. (1999b). Transition to parenthood: The Turkish case. *Journal of Social Behavior and Personality, 14,* 325–343.

Hortaçsu, N., & Baştuğ, Ş. (2000). Women in marriage in Ashkabat, Baku, and Ankara. In F. Acar & A. Güneş-Ayata (Eds.), *Gender and identity construction: Women in central Asia, the Caucasus, and Turkey* (pp. 77–100). Leiden, Netherlands: Brill.

Hortaçsu, N., Baştuğ, Ş., & Muhammetberdiev, O. B. (2001). Change and stability with respect to attitudes and practices related to marriage. *International Journal of Psychology, 36,* 108–120.

Hortaçsu, N., & Oral, A. (1994). Comparison of couple- and family-initiated marriages in Turkey. *Journal of Social Psychology, 134,* 229–239.

Kağıtçıbaşı, Ç. (1990). Family and socialization in cross-cultural perspective. In *Nebraska Symposium on Motivation* (Vol. 37, pp. 135–200). Lincoln: University of Nebraska Press.

Kağıtçıbaşı, Ç. (1996). *Family and human development across cultures: A view from the other side.* Mahwah, NJ. Lawrence Erlbaum.

Kıray, M. (1979). Küçük kasaba kadınları (Little town women). In N. Abadan-Unat (Ed.), *Türk Toplumunda Kadın* (Women in Turkish society) (pp. 349–375). Ankara, Turkey: Çağ Matbaası.

Triandis, H. C. (1995). *Individualism and collectivism.* Boulder, CO: Westview.

Part V

Europe

Part 7

Europe

10

Couple Formation Practices in Spain

J. Roberto Reyes

Two friends in their late 20s met at a café in downtown Madrid one morning. One of them asked the other whether he was happy with his current living arrangement or whether he desired to live by himself, independent from his parents. To this, the young man replied, "Why should I leave my parents? I have it all where I am. My mother washes and irons my clothes, she cooks for me, and I don't have to pay rent. Plus, I don't believe that I earn enough to make it on my own. I have been trying to find a job in my field of study, and I haven't been able to find anything. Things are really hard at the moment." To this, the other man responded, "But what about your girlfriend? What does she think about all this?" "She agrees with me," the young man replied. "I know that she would like to get married soon, but we recognize that we need to be more financially established before we can get married. For instance, we both believe that we should wait until we have enough money to buy and furnish our own apartment. And as it is, we are still able to get away and spend time together as a couple. As a matter of fact, next weekend we will be spending the weekend in Seville. So, I am content with the way things are."

AUTHOR'S NOTE: I thank Carlos Veiga and Monica Miguelez-Pan for their insights on the subject of marriage and wedding customs during my field research work in Spain.

T he above story illustrates some of the many issues affecting couples in Spain today. In examining current demographic data, researchers have found that, over the years, Spaniards have been delaying the age at which they get married. In 1975, for instance, the average age at first marriage was 26.5 years for men and 23.9 for women. By 1995, the average age at first marriage had increased to 28.9 years for men and 26.8 for women (Pérez-Diaz, Chuliá, & Valiente, 2000, p. 46). And by 1998, the average age at first marriage had increased to 30.6 years for men and 28.3 years for women ("Matrimonios," 2001). Meanwhile, the average number of marriages per 1,000 individuals has also decreased. According to the data, the average rate was 7.6 per 1,000 population in 1975, had decreased to 5.9 per 1,000 population by 1980, and had decreased even further to 5.2 per 1,000 population by 1999 (EuroStat, 2000; Pérez-Diaz et al., 2000). However, in comparison with other European countries, the number of couples cohabiting in Spain has not increased even given these changes in the marriage rates. Instead, 75% of single adults report still living with their parents through even their late 20s (Alberdi, Flaquer & Iglesias de Ussel, 1994; Centro de Investigaciones Sociológicas, 1999a).

In trying to understand these and other demographic trends, this chapter examines the unique historical, economic, and cultural factors that have affected, and continue to affect, the process of couple formation and marriage in Spain. The goal of this project is not only to describe current patterns of behavior but also to attempt to understand some of the reasons why these changes may be taking place. To do so, the project examines the position of leading Spanish sociologists and economists regarding this matter and also considers the personal stories and viewpoints of individuals who were interviewed as part of my field research in Spain.

The chapter begins by considering the historical factors that have shaped the current social experience. At the center of the debate between traditional and alternative forms of family life are the political and legal aspects that have provided, or in many cases limited, opportunities for personal liberties. One period that introduced a significant desire for change was the period of the second republic (1931–1936). Chief among the changes brought about during this period was the incorporation of different notions of family life into law. The proposed separation of church and state provided an opportunity for individuals, particularly women, to acquire new liberties (Iglesias de Ussel, 1998).

> Some of the most significant legal changes introduced during this period included: the right to vote; the right to divorce, including by mutual consent; equal rights between the sexes; and equality between spouses. . . . Discrimination

of any kind between legitimate and illegitimate children was abolished, as were the crimes of adultery and cohabitation. Paternity investigation was admitted, obligatory civil marriage was implanted, prostitution was prohibited, the right to abortion was regulated, and family planning centers were set up. (Flaquer & Iglesias de Ussel, 1996, p. 579)

However, regardless of the advances in reforming the legal code during this period, few individuals took advantage of these new measures, for example, in the case of divorce. Some scholars believe that the lack of pursuit by individuals of these new legal freedoms was due, in part, to the short duration of the second republic as well as to the strong opposition to these measures brought about by the Catholic Church (Iglesias de Ussel, 1998).

Eventually, with the onset of the civil war in 1936 and the establishment of Francisco Franco's government in 1939, many of these laws were rescinded as a strong authoritarian form of family policy emerged. As a strong defender and advocate of the Catholic faith, Franco proceeded to conform legal measures to Catholic dogma. For instance, in 1947, the Law of Succession proclaimed Spain to be a "Catholic, social, and representative monarchy," with Franco serving as regent for life (Rinehart & Browning Seeley, 1990, p. 43). The implications of this policy resulted in an authoritarian form of government where stringent standards restricted opportunities for women to pursue professional careers while celebrating their roles as mothers and wives. For example, during this period, Spanish law prohibited wives from nearly all forms of economic opportunities, including employment, ownership of property, and even travel, unless they had the consent of their husbands. These laws were known as *permiso marital* (marital permission) (Clark, 1990). The government advocated a policy of *perfecta casada* (the perfect housewife) and *angel del hogar* (angel of the home), reaffirming women's subordinate roles within the family and in society-at-large. Women were required to enroll in a 6-month training program in preparation for becoming mothers (Sanchez & Hall, 1999). Adultery during this time was considered a crime, as was abortion. Marriages also had to be canonical in nature. This meant that basically all marriages in Spain had to be sanctioned by the Catholic Church. Because the Church did not allow divorce, marriages could be dissolved only through the difficult process of annulment (Clark, 1990).

By the 1960s, social values were changing faster than the existing legal statutes allowed, creating tension between the legal codes and the growing social experience. Many scholars believe that these changes developed as a result of the "rural exodus" that uprooted hundreds of thousands of people, out of economic necessity, from rural settings to new urban centers during that time. In addition, the increasing flow of European tourists to Spain, as well as the migration of Spanish workers to other countries such as France, Switzerland, and West Germany, had a dramatic effect in changing Spain's isolation from the rest of the world (Clark, 1990).

The period that followed was characterized by significant legal and social change, particularly after the death of Franco in 1975. Many of the earlier measures, such as el permiso marital, were abolished in 1978 with the adoption of the new constitution. Divorce was also legalized in 1981. However, it was the increase of women's participation in the labor force (Moral, 2001), as well as the prolongation of the educational preparation of students during the years that followed, that brought about significant changes in the family. These historical and economic factors provide us with a context from which we can understand current trends in couple formation practices.

Attitudes and Practices Regarding Couple Formation in Spain

A central element in understanding the process of couple formation in Spain is language. As in many Latin American countries, the term *noviazgo* refers to a formal and committed relationship where exclusivity and monogamy are understood as central to the definition of the relationship but where there might not be a forgone conclusion that the couple will eventually marry. In English, there is not an equivalent term. In some dictionaries, the term used for noviazgo is *engagement* (*Voz Compact Spanish & English Dictionary,* 1994). Unfortunately, this translation may be misleading because it implies that the partners have made a conscious decision to marry, and this may or may not be true in the case of noviazgo. In Spanish, the term *prometido* or *prometida* is often used instead to refer to someone who is engaged to be married. On the other hand, the term *dating* is a relatively new concept in many Latin American countries. The closest equivalent in Spanish would be *to go out* or *going out* with someone. But this translation does not necessarily denote the basic attraction or romantic underpinnings that may be present when dating someone over a period of time. Therefore, in considering the variations in language and culture for the purpose of this study, the term *noviazgo* is used to denote a committed love relationship where exclusivity and fidelity are expected of each partner but where there has not been a conscious decision to marry.

In Spain, couples usually begin dating during their mid-adolescent years (ages 14 to 15). During this period, friends play an important role in the process. In an effort to be accepted by their peer group and as a sign of transition into adulthood, young men often are encouraged by their peers to ask girls out on dates. If a boy and girl who are dating share similar friends during this period of adolescence, they may go on dates as a group, for example, going to the movies or to a park or discotheque, depending on their financial conditions. This trend was also evident in a recent study that examined the types of activities in which adolescents and young adults (ages 15 to 29 years) participate the most during their leisure time. The study listed playing a sport (20.5%), going out for drinks (17.7%), going out to the movies (17.2%), and dancing (13.9%) as the top four activities in which young people in Spain participate (Centro de Investigaciones Sociológicas, 1999a).

In addition to exerting some peer pressure to initiate contact, friends often serve as messengers (*mensajeros*), making sure that the targeted young man or woman is interested in their friend. Then they relay the information back to the friend. This type of relationship usually does not last very long. Instead, it serves as a way for young people to learn about themselves and about members of the opposite sex. Among older couples (age 23 years or over), personal friends play less of a central role in the development of their relationships. There is also less of an expectation that men are primarily responsible for initiating dates.

The average length of a noviazgo is approximately 43 months. According to a survey conducted by Alberdi and colleagues (1994), among couples that were or had been in noviazgos, 67.6% reported being in committed relationships for at least 3 years, 51.0% indicated being in relationships for an average of 2 years 8 months, and only 29.4% reported being in relationships for less than 1 year. It is important to mention, however, that these couples were in committed relationships without living together. In Spain, as opposed to other European countries, the rate of cohabitation has not increased proportionally to the decrease in the rate of marriage. As a matter of fact, the percentage of individuals cohabiting is very small (approximately 11.1%) in comparison with the percentage of young people ages 15 to 29 years who reside with their parents (75.0%) (Centro de Investigaciones Sociológicas, 1999a). Some scholars believe that this is due in large measure to the economic challenges facing young people in being able to find affordable housing and establish themselves as financially independent in Spain (Alberdi et al., 1994; Marí-Klose & Colom, 1999; Martín, 1999).

The high cost of housing, combined with the limited job opportunities in the 22- to 27-year age group, has encouraged many (particularly women) to extend their educational preparation. Also, the culture in Spain actively encourages home ownership instead of renting as a way of financing personal housing. In light of this, it is not uncommon for couples to delay marriage until they are able not only to buy their apartments but also to have them furnished (Delgado & Martín, 1998). Therefore, these economic and cultural-social factors have not only delayed the age at which individuals marry but also limited the pursuit of cohabitation as a viable alternative to marriage (Delgado & Martín, 1998; Eastaway & San Martín, 1999).

Finally, some scholars have also argued that the notion of cohabitation is less popular in Spain because it is often less associated with the process of reproduction than it is in other Northern European countries. Spaniards, for the most part, often decide to marry when they are seriously considering having children (Cantero, 1994; Delgado, 1993; Iglesias de Ussel, 1998).

Another important aspect in the study of couple formation is the understanding of the types of attributes that an individual may consider attractive or important in developing a love relationship. In a study conducted in 1995 ($N = 1,949$), individuals were asked what kind of attributes or characteristics they considered to be important in developing a short-term love relationship versus a serious/stable long-term relationship (Centro de Investigaciones Sociológicas, 1995). Among the qualities considered important for a short-term relationship were physical attractiveness, a pleasant character, being romantic, sexual accessibility, and sexual ability or dexterity. Among the qualities considered important for a stable long-term relationship were a pleasant character, intelligence, sincerity, sexual fidelity, and similar values or interests (Centro de Investigaciones Sociológicas, 1995).

In comparing the responses of men with those of women regarding the qualities that each gender considered important in developing a serious and stable long-term relationship, the results indicated the following. Among men, physical attractiveness was most important, followed by a pleasant character, sexual accessibility, and sexual ability or dexterity. Among women, physical attractiveness was most important, followed by a pleasant character, being romantic, and being sensitive (Centro de Investigaciones Sociológicas, 1995).

Similar responses were also obtained in another study conducted in Spain where individuals were asked what types of qualities they considered to be important *to achieve happiness* in a relationship. Among the attitudes or situations that were reported, fidelity was most important (98%), followed by tolerance and understanding (97%) and a satisfying sexual relationship (93%) (Centro de Investigaciones Sociológicas, 1999b). These qualities indicate that for many Spaniards, issues of trust and sexual intimacy are very important in developing meaningful and stable love relationships. This is understandable given that, because of the presence of "machismo" in Spanish

CONSEJO N° 5 DE GENTE SIN COMPLEJOS

¿Tu novia es demasiado alta?

Probad en horizontal

www.dyc.es

Billboard in Spain Reflecting Concerns About Sexual Performance

society, a double standard exists between men and women regarding the issue of sexual promiscuity. Because of this cultural practice, men's promiscuity has often been accepted and even understood as being part of their basic gender identity, whereas women's values of personal restraint, modesty, and chastity have been valued. These concerns over trust and infidelity are evident in Spanish society on local billboards and in magazine advertisements. In one, we see a young man smiling while standing in front of a set of bull's horns, which traditionally has been a symbol of male virility and sexual prowess. The slogan of the announcement says, "If your girlfriend cheats on you, do the same." The slogan clearly illustrates the presence of these concerns over trust in interpersonal relationships as well as the inherent expectation that this is what men would do anyway. What is interesting, however, is the way in which women are portrayed in this ad. Here, women are portrayed not in a passive subservient role but rather in an active role in pursuit of their own personal happiness. Concerns over sexual performance or dexterity are also present in the culture, as illustrated in another billboard where a short man who is dating a tall, beautiful young woman is encouraged not to develop an inferiority complex because of his height. The ad suggests that at the moment of making love, the height difference does not matter because they both will be in a horizontal position.

The next section considers the following questions. What happens when couples decide to formalize their unions? What concerns do couples have to overcome in entering marriage? What are the unique characteristics or traditions associated with the wedding ceremony in Spain?

Formalization of the Union: Attitudes and Practices Regarding Marriage in Spain

To this point, we have observed how economic factors play a critical role in delaying the formalization of the union between a young man and woman in Spain. But beyond the economic challenges that individuals or couples may experience, there are other interpersonal factors that influence this process. Chief among them is the change in personal values and the increasing tensions between pursuing individual liberties and conforming to traditional role expectations. The shift has been more pronounced among working/professional women. With the increase in education for women and their greater participation in the labor market, more and more women want to establish themselves professionally before getting married or before having children (Martín, 1999). This trend has raised a number of questions regarding the nature of personal liberties, particularly for women within the marital relationship.

This trend toward the pursuit of individual liberties is also evident even when considering the individual's religious commitment. According to Marí-Klose and Colom (1999), there seems to be a generational split when considering the relationship between commitment to religious beliefs and the individual's view on the importance of marriage. In their study, only 45% of 16- to 32-year-old practicing Catholic women reported being married, and only 50% indicated that they considered marriage very important during this stage of development. On the other hand, among women ages 33 to 49 years, 90% reported being married and 55% considered marriage to be important. The latter percentage increased from 55% to 69% when examining the responses of practicing Catholic women age 50 years or over (Marí-Klose & Colom, 1999). Scholars believe that the reason for this disparity, even among practicing Catholic women, may be due to how women historically were socialized during the Franco regime to see themselves first and foremost as mothers and caretakers in the home. During the period when women from the older generation married, the policy of national Catholicism (*el nacional catolismo*) was at the center of Spanish society (Marí-Klose & Colom, 1999). The younger generation, meanwhile, benefited from a shift in mind-set in and outside of the Catholic Church. The end of the Franco regime, as well as the changes instituted in the Church as a result of the second Vatican Council, encouraged church officials to distance themselves from promoting civil law as a way of maintaining a desired moral/social order (Iglesias de Ussel, 1998).

In addition, there has been a growing change in mind-set among men and women regarding the importance for women to get an education and work outside the home. For instance, in a study conducted in 1997 by the Centro de Investigaciones Sociológicas (1999b) ($N = 2,462$), men and women ages 15 to 29 years were asked which model they would consider to be the ideal among the existing family models. Fully 75% indicated that they preferred the type of family arrangement where both the husband and the wife could work outside the home and where they could share domestic/child care responsibilities as well. Only 16% indicated that they preferred a model where the wife would work fewer hours outside the home so that she could attend to the domestic/child care responsibilities. This contrasts with an opinion poll conducted in 1975 where 81% of men and 83% of women agreed with the statement, "Household chores are a woman's job, and only when the wife is sick should they be performed by the husband" (cited in Valiente, 1998, p. 144).

This change in perspective has also been evident demographically in the number of women who identified themselves as being full-time housewives during the past 20 years or so. Between 1978 and 1998, the number of women who identified themselves as housewives dropped from 54.1% to 32.1% (Carrasco & Rodriguez, 2000). However, when examining the relationship between expressed egalitarian beliefs and actual participation in domestic and child care activities, the results indicate a different experience. In a survey conducted in 1993 and 1996, Spanish women reported spending 22 fewer minutes per day in household activities over that time period. The average time spent in domestic activities each day had decreased from 7 hours 50 minutes in 1993 to 7 hours 28 minutes in 1996. Among men during the same time period, they reported that their involvement in household activities increased by only 35 minutes per day, from 2 hours 30 minutes to 3 hours 5 minutes (Marí-Klose & Colom, 1999). And although men's involvement in household responsibilities has increased, particularly among middle class, college-educated individuals (Landwerlin, 1998), the fact remains that the amount of men's participation in these activities is significantly less than that of women.

This lack of support of men to participate in domestic responsibilities can be seen in the following story. José is in his late 30s or early 40s, is from Seville, and currently lives in Córdoba. He has been married for 6 or 7 years, and he and his wife have a 4-year-old girl. José currently stays at home and cares for their daughter while his wife works full-time as an administrative assistant. Since making the decision to stay home, José has endured a lot of criticism and ridicule from his male friends when he goes to the nearby bar. For example, they ask him "*Qué vas a hacer de comer hoy en tu casa?*" (What are you planning to make today for dinner?), "*Qué, estás hoy de amo de casa?*" (Are you now a househusband?), or "*Qué, tu mujer es la que trabaja? No hombre*" (So is your wife the one who works? No way). Through these questions, the friends affirm that José should be the one working and that his wife should be the one staying at home taking care of the couple's daughter. This interaction also illustrates, in an explicit manner, how machismo still operates in the culture and how it may still be an important factor to consider in studying the quality of interpersonal/love relationships.

All of these factors, combined with an increasing desire to devote more time to the pursuit of personal happiness, have led many to question the validity of marriage. The result, however, has not been to abandon the idea of marriage but rather to delay it and, in so doing, to decrease the number of children that a couple may have. As a matter of fact, research shows that as individuals grow older, they become more supportive of the institution of marriage (Centro de Investigaciones Sociológicas, 1998). The issue for couples is whether to have children and, if so, how many and when.

It almost seems that couples, in attempting to cope with the competing demands of work and family, are opting to have fewer children as a way of managing their hectic lives. This is understandable given that women are not receiving the type of assistance from their husbands that they need. This mind-set has resulted in a significant decrease in the fertility rate in Spain. For instance, in 1980, the average number of children born to a woman during her lifetime was 2.20, whereas by 1998 and 1999, the average numbers had decreased to 1.15 and 1.18, respectively (EuroStat, 2000), representing one of the lowest fertility rates in Western Europe.

Before we minimize this process to a simple correlation between the decrease in fertility rates and a practical approach to managing familial resources, however, consider that Alberdi (1999) called our attention to an underlying shift in the way in which young couples are thinking about the future. As opposed to the previous generation, whose members were willing to sacrifice immediate personal happiness for the rewards of a better tomorrow, today's generation refuses to do so. According to Roussel and colleagues (cited in Alberdi, 1999), what is taking place in these kinds of situations is not the result of changes in cultural characteristics but rather is the result of a shift in personal priorities. What is important to couples forming new relationships is the pursuit of personal happiness now instead of waiting for an uncertain future that may never materialize. At a time when Spain has experienced so many social changes, and where the economy continues to represent a significant challenge for young professionals, the focus has become the pursuit of happiness in the here and now. In so doing, love and the expression of romantic ideals become central to the formation and maintenance of many relationships.

It is common, for instance, to see adolescents and individuals in their early 20s, in parks or on public transportation vehicles, being very physical and public in their expression of love for one another, almost as if to declare to anyone who sees them that their love is the most important thing in the world to them. This example illustrates two other important values that have contributed to the shift in mind-set. One is the increase in tolerance in the society-at-large regarding personal lifestyle choices, and the other is an increasing sense of individualism that permeates every aspect of society today (Alberdi, 1999). These changes have produced a society that appears to be in conflict with itself, that is, a society that is divided between the pursuit of individual or personal liberties and the maintenance of cultural traditions that have centered on family obligations and conservative religious values for many centuries. At the same time, it is important to consider how quickly and dramatically these social changes have occurred given that it has been only 24 years since the inception of many of these new legal freedoms. And it may be that this dramatic shift in personal priorities has come as a reaction to decades of authoritarian governmental control of personal choices and/or is the result of experiencing the benefits of living and growing up in a more open, technologically advanced, and more "consumerist" society (Moral, 2001, p. 40).

Finally, this chapter concludes by exploring the unique cultural traditions and customs associated with a very significant symbol of the formalization process: the wedding ceremony.

Formalization of the Union: The Wedding Ceremony

As in many countries, in Spain the wedding ceremony represents one of the most important symbols of the formalization of a couple's relationship. Various wedding traditions or customs are associated with particular regions of the country. What follows is a general description of some of the more common traditions associated with this experience.

Prior to a couple's engagement, it was customary for the man to meet with the father of the woman he hoped to marry to ask for the father's permission and/or blessing to marry his daughter. Today, this tradition is less common. Instead, the man will ask the woman he loves to marry him, and on her acceptance, they announce their decision to their respective families.

As in other countries, couples can choose to marry either by civilian-government authorities or by their religious institutions. Historically, as mentioned earlier, individuals in Spain could marry only through the Catholic Church. Today, the Spanish government recognizes the legality of ceremonies officiated by other religious groups such as Muslims, Protestants, and Jews as well as by civilian government authorities (*por lo civil*).

On the day of the wedding, it is customary (primarily in the province of Cataluña) for the brother of the bride to read to his sister a poem, which he either selected or wrote, just before departing for the church. The bride is usually dressed in white or wears a new dress, and it is customary for her to have four articles of clothing or jewelry for good luck (a new one, an old one, a blue one, and a borrowed one). It is also acceptable for the bride to be 5 to 10 minutes late. Therefore, it is not until the bride arrives, accompanied by her father, that the ceremony begins. During the ceremony, the groom gives the bride 13 coins (*las arras*) that symbolize his promise to provide for her financially. Las arras also represents the groom's good economic standing and his intent to care for his bride as well as any children that may come in the future. This tradition is believed to be an old one, rooted within a traditional delineation of family roles.

If the wedding is officiated by a judge at city hall, the number of invited guests is usually small and the ceremony consists primarily of the exchange of wedding vows. When the ceremony takes place in a church (i.e., the Catholic Church), it is more elaborate, consisting of the wedding liturgy along with some readings and prayers. It is also a larger affair; anybody who knows the bride and/or the groom is welcome to attend. Invitations are sent, but only for the reception. After the ceremony is over, the bride and groom go to the vestry or sacristy of the church, followed by the priest or minister, the best man, the bridesmaid, and some witnesses, to sign *las actas matrimoniales* (the wedding record or certificate). After that takes place, the bride and groom are legally married and then go to the reception.

The *convite* (reception) is an important part of the wedding celebration because it is through this activity that the newlyweds are able to receive from friends and loved ones an initial financial start in their life as a married couple. Guests typically do not bring wedding gifts. Instead, they are encouraged to bring money for the couple. The minimum amount per guest is usually $30 (or $60 per couple). The parents of the couple generally pay the cost of the reception (approximately $3,000 to $3,575

Friends and Family Celebrating With the Newly Married Couple After the Wedding Ceremony

depending on the number of guests), and the newlyweds keep the money that was given to them as gifts. Often, the amount given can vary between $3,000 and $6,000.

Bride and Groom at the Wedding Reception

The reception typically consists of a banquet dinner followed by a dance. The dinner lasts approximately 3 hours and consists of an appetizer, two principal dishes, a dessert, and wedding cake. In Cataluña, it is customary to have prawn or crayfish as an appetizer. This custom is so prevalent in this region of the country that it is often understood that *sin langostinos no hay boda* (without prawns or crayfish, there is no wedding). After the dinner, the bride and groom go table to table, greeting all of their guests and giving them a small keepsake that commemorates the occasion. For instance, it is common for men to receive a cigar with the names of the couple attached to it. In some regions of Spain, it is also customary for the friends of the couple to take the tie from the groom and the garter from the bride, cut them into little pieces, and distribute them among the guests. As the guests take a piece of either the tie or the garter, they give money in return as a contribution to help offset the cost of the wedding. After this, the dancing begins with a dance by the newly married couple, followed by the rest of the guests. After the dance, it is popular among youth to prolong the celebration by going with the bride and groom to a nearby discotheque to continue dancing until sunrise.

Finally, regarding the honeymoon, although taking a honeymoon is practiced in Spain, it does not occupy the position of importance that it does in the United States. Couples usually do not travel that much. Instead, they may take a week off in an area of Spain that they enjoy, or they may wait until they are able to take their summer vacation to have their honeymoon. These and many other traditions, practices, and values represent an important array of factors that help to explain the experience of couple formation and marriage in Spain.

References

Alberdi, I. (1999). *La nueva familia Española* (The new Spanish family). Madrid, Spain: Tauros.

Alberdi, I., Flaquer, L., & Iglesias de Ussel, J. (1994). *Parejas y matrimonios: Actitudes comportamientos y experiencias* (Couples and marriages: Contemporary attitudes and experiences). Madrid, Spain: Centro de Asuntos Sociales, Centro de Publicaciones.

Cantero, P. C. (1994). *Percepción social de la familia en España* (Social perceptions of the family in Spain) (Opiniones y Actitudes, No. 9). Madrid, Spain: Centro de Investigaciones Sociológicas.

Carrasco, C., & Rodriguez, A. (2000). Women, families, and work in Spain: Structural changes and new demands. *Feminist Economics, 6*(1), 45–57.

Centro de Investigaciones Sociológicas. (1995, July). *Actitudes y conductas afectivas de los Españoles* (Attitudes and affective behaviors among Spaniards) (Datos de Opinión, Boletín 7, Study No. 2157). [Online]. Retrieved January 9, 2002, from www.cis.es/boletin/7/est2.html

Centro de Investigaciones Sociológicas. (1998, March). *Hijos y parejas* (Children and couples) (Datos de Opinión, Boletín 17, Study No. 2283). [Online]. Retrieved July 3, 2002, from www.cis.es/boletin/17/hijos.html

Centro de Investigaciones Sociológicas. (1999a, October–November). *Informe sobre la juventud Española, 2000* (Report on the Spanish youth, 2000) (Study No. 2370). Madrid, Spain: Author.

Centro de Investigaciones Sociológicas. (1999b, January–March). *Los jóvenes de hoy* (Today's youth) (Datos de Opinión, Boletín 19, Study Nos. 2257, 2262, and 2265). [Online]. Retrieved January 9, 2002, from www.cis.es/boletin/19/familia.html

Clark, R. P. (1990). The society and its environment. In E. Solsten & S. W. Meditz (Eds.), *Spain: A country study* (pp. 69–129). Washington, DC: Library of Congress, Federal Research Division.

Delgado, M. (1993). Cambios recientes en el proceso de formación de la familia (Recent changes in the process of family formation). *Revista de Investigaciones Sociológicas, 64,*123–153.

Delgado, M., & Martín, T. C. (1998). *Encuesta de fecundidad y familia 1995 (FFS)* (Survey of fertility rates and the family 1995) (Opiniones y Actitudes, No. 20). Madrid, Spain: Centro de Investigaciones Sociológicas.

Eastaway, M. P., & San Martín, I. (1999). General trends in financing social housing in Spain. *Urban Studies, 36,* 699–714.

EuroStat. (2000, March 7). *First results of the demographic data collection for 1999 in Europe.* [Online]. Retrieved September 28, 2001, from http://europa.eu.int/comm/eurostat

Flaquer, L., & Iglesias de Ussel, J. (1996). The sociology of the family in Spain: An attempt at interpretation. *Marriage and Family Review, 23*(1–2), 575–598.

Iglesias de Ussel, J. (1998). *La familia y el cambio político en España* (The family and the political changes in Spain). Madrid, Spain: Tecnos.

Landwerlin, G. M. (1998). Changing domestic roles in the new urban family in Spain. *South European Society & Politics, 3*(2), 75–97.

Marí-Klose, M., & Colom, A. N. (1999). *Itinerarios vitales: Educación, trabajo, y fecundidad de las mujeres* (Vital statistics: Education, work, and fertility rates among women) (Opiniones y Actitudes, No. 27). Madrid, Spain: Centro de Investigaciones Sociológicas.

Martín, T. C. (1999). Pautas recientes en la formación de pareja (Recent norms in couple formation). *Revista Internacional de Sociología, 23,* 61–94.

Matrimonios según estado civil y edad de los contrayentes (Marriages according to civil state and age of participants). (2001). In *Anuario Estadístico de España 2000* (Statistical yearbook of Spain 2000). Madrid, Spain: Instituto Nacional de Estadística.

Moral, F. (2001). *Veinticinco años después: La memoria del franquismo y de la transición a la democracia en los Españoles del año 2000* (Twenty-five years later: The memory of the Francoist regime and the transition to democracy among Spaniards in the year 2000) (Opiniones y Actitudes, No. 36). Madrid, Spain: Centro de Investigaciones Sociológicas.

Pérez-Díaz, V., Chuliá, E., & Valiente, C. (2000). *La familia Española en el año 2000* (The Spanish family in the year 2000). Madrid, Spain: Fundación Argentaria, Visor Dis.

Rinehart, R., & Browning Seeley, J. (1990). Historical setting. In E. Solsten & S. W. Meditz (Eds.), *Spain: A country study* (pp. 4–62). Washington, DC: Library of Congress, Federal Research Division.

Sanchez, L., & Hall, C. S. (1999). Traditional values and democratic impulses: The gender division of labour in contemporary Spain. *Journal of Comparative Family Studies, 30,* 659–685.

Valiente, C. (1998). More than just breadwinners? The role of men in Spanish family relations (1975–1996). *Revista Española de Investigaciones Sociológicas, 79,* 221–243. (English ed.)

Voz compact Spanish & English dictionary (2nd ed.). (1994). Chicago: National Textbook.

11

The Development of Intimate Relationships in the Netherlands

Manfred H. M. van Dulmen

Jan and Ria meet each other at a village feast during their late teens. They both are single and have had romantic relationships with others in the past. They still live with their respective parents and work full-time. Over the next couple of years, they see each other regularly and develop a close relationship. After several years, Jan and Ria decide that they are ready for the next step: marriage. They officially announce their verloving (engagement) to family and friends. They develop wedding plans and, at the same time, look for a home. Following the wedding, they move out of their parental homes and into the new home they bought. The year is 1960.

Karel and Muriel meet each other at a party when they both are in their early 20s. They have seen each other at times in college classrooms but do not know each other well. A few days after the party, Karel invites Muriel for dinner at his apartment. Over the course of a year, their relationship becomes

AUTHOR'S NOTE: I thank Joseph and Riet van Dulmen for the availability of family pictures and helpful discussions regarding recent changes on rituals surrounding couple formation. I also thank Frans Vrolijks for his perspective regarding couple formation policies and the process of couple formation during the earlier parts of the 20th century.

closer and they decide to move in together. Their friends approve and congratulate them on the next step in their lives. They hold a housewarming party to celebrate. After living together for several years, Karel and Muriel decide that they are ready for the next step: a home. They have their attorney draft a cohabitation contract so that they can legally organize their living arrangement. Within a few weeks, they move out of their apartment into their newly purchased home. The year is 2000.

As the above examples illustrate, mate selection in the Netherlands has changed significantly during the past 40 years. The process of couple formation has become more diverse, not only due to changes in individual values and legal arrangements but also due to an increasingly diverse Dutch society. In 1999, 17% of the Dutch population was foreign born (Sociaal en Cultureel Planbureau, 2000).

Not only has the process of couple formation changed, but the outcome of couple formation has changed as well. There has been increasing individualization in Dutch society. This has led to multiple lifestyle options from which people may choose, including cohabitation, marriage with children, marriage without children, single parenting, and living alone (Wilterdink & van Heerikhuizen, 1989). Whereas the beginning of the 20th century showed a trend toward standardization (one model fits all) of living arrangements, with marriage being the predominant living situation, the latter part of the 20th century showed a trend toward diversification of living arrangements (Garssen, de Beer, Cuyvers, & de Jong, 2001). This trend toward diversification of living arrangements has resulted in more people opting for either staying single or choosing a non-marital relationship arrangement. As alternative living arrangements are actually becoming more the norm than an alternative, it is important to understand the underlying motivations of individuals and couples to choose these living arrangements.

Why Do People (not) Marry?

The reasons why people in the Netherlands have gotten married, and increasingly have decided not to marry, can be explained through the interplay among familial, social, political, historical, legal, and religious factors. This section specifically discusses the role of social, political, historical, legal, and religious factors as they relate to the development of intimate relationships in the Netherlands.

Social Norms

Social norms affect whether individuals choose marriage or a different living arrangement by providing rules and regulations as to what is considered *normative* in a particular society regarding the ways in which people live together in that society at a particular time point. Changes in social norms in the Netherlands regarding relationship arrangements are specifically reflected in the definitions that the Dutch society has used to define a household. In 1947, the Dutch government defined a household as requiring individuals to have a relationship through blood, marriage, or adoption; in 1996, a family was defined as a household in which one or more people have responsibility for one or more children (van Praag & Niphuis-Nell, 1997). Thus, the marriage requirement is not part of this definition anymore.

Changes in social norms regarding relationship arrangements are reflected not only in definitions of households provided by the Dutch government but also in attitude surveys among people residing in the Netherlands. In 1996, 96% of the population considered a cohabiting couple with children to be a family, 56% considered a married couple without children to be a family, and 43% considered a cohabiting couple without children to be a family (van Praag & Niphuis-Nell, 1997). Thus, the definition of family is viewed by Dutch residents as more dependent on whether a man and woman have children than on whether the partners are engaged in a marital or nonmarital relationship.

Changes in social norms in the Netherlands are reflected not only in attitudes toward what comprises a family. Attitudes toward sexual permissiveness have also changed in the Netherlands during the past 50 years. Kraaykamp (2002), in a cohort study from 1965 to 1995, showed that Dutch society has become more accepting of premarital sex. From 1965 to 1975, there was a trend toward increasing acceptance of extramarital sex, but since then there has been a countertrend due to the negative effects of extramarital sex, especially among respondents who were in marital relationships at the time when they participated in the study (Kraaykamp, 2002). Thus, these results suggest that sexuality in Dutch society is not as strongly linked to the marital relationship as it was 40 years ago and that sexuality in nonmarital committed relationships is becoming more acceptable. However, once individuals are in a committed relationship, they see sexuality as being limited to that particular relationship.

Political Changes

Political changes in the Netherlands are a reflection of changes in values while at the same time directly affecting the coming of age of legal changes. From 1945 to the late 1980s, the Christian Democratic Party was the majority party in the Dutch government. It was not until 1994 that a government was in place that did not include the Christian Democratic Party. During this time period (1994 to 2000), many legal changes took place, enabling individuals to formalize relationships in a variety of ways. Thus, the previously described diversification of living arrangements was formalized by law. Although political changes did not directly affect the mate selection and couple formation process for individuals, they have affected the legal options that a man and woman have once a relationship is formed.

History

The period from 1986 to 1990 was the first time in modern Dutch history when the number of single people exceeded the number of married or cohabiting people for first-time home leavers. First-time home leaving is defined as the *first* point at which a son or daughter leaves his or her parental home to reside in a different home. Thus, first-time home leaving also refers to, for example, the situation where someone leaves his or her parental home to go to college.

Of all first-time home leavers during the period from 1986 to 1990, 36% lived alone, 30% cohabited, and 27% were married. In comparison, from 1961 to 1965, 15% lived alone, 78% were married, and 2% cohabited (van Praag & Niphuis-Nell, 1997). These percentages vary greatly, however, among the various minority groups in the Netherlands. The majority of young adults from Turkey, Morocco, Suriname, and the Netherlands Antilles are married when they first leave home, although the latter two groups are somewhat more likely to cohabit than are young adults in the former two groups (Garssen et al., 2001). Thus, couple formation and first-time home leaving are directly affected by the cultural and ethnic backgrounds of various individuals and couples.

A second macro-level change in Dutch society that affects couple formation is the *ontzuiling* (undoing of the pillars). Until the 1960s, Dutch society was structured by different *zuilen* (pillars), each representing a major group of people within Dutch society. Four main pillars grouped individuals in Dutch society: the Catholic pillar, the Protestant pillar, the Liberal pillar, and the Socialist pillar (Wilterdink & Heerikhuizen, 1989). Each pillar had its own political party, newspaper, television/radio station, youth organizations, and the like. Not surprisingly, many first romantic relationships of young people started in organizations within these pillars, and individual and family life was also structured through the pillars. Individuals often would meet each other at special leisure events organized for youth by organizations within each pillar. These events, such as Friday evening dances and board game nights, were opportunities to meet age mates with the same cultural background.

Since the 1960s, the ontzuiling has taken place (Wilterdink & Heerikhuizen, 1989), leading to weaker connections among organizations *within* each pillar and less clear boundaries *between* pillars. Without doubt, these macro changes affect the individual choices people have regarding whom they select as mates and where they go to meet age mates. Activities organized within a pillar became less popular, and many youth opted to spend their free weekend evenings in discotheques or dance clubs where religious or cultural affiliation was not (in)directly affecting the meeting arena.

Legal Prescriptions

Legal prescriptions have undergone major changes during recent years. Three partnership contracts currently exist in the Netherlands: the registered partnership, cohabitation, and marriage. Since 1997, there has been legal recognition for the status of cohabitees or partners due to the Registered Cohabitees Act (Mills, 2000). This act amended the Dutch Civil Code to provide that all Dutch citizens or persons can register cohabitation. Dissolution of registered cohabitation was to be formalized as a court decision. As of January 1, 1998, relationships could also be legally formalized by a registered partnership or cohabitation contract. These union options make it possible for partners of the same sex to legally formalize a relationship. A *registered partnership* and a *marriage* are considered to be legally equivalent, with virtually identical judicial consequences (Ministry of Justice, 1997). In both relationship types, the legal requirements are the same, for example, those related to taxation, pension, and social security. The main distinction between a registered partnership and a marriage lies in the relationship with the children, with the registered partnership having no consequences for the relationship with children (Ministry of Justice, 1997). The *cohabitation contract* differs from both a marriage and a registered partnership by the essential distinction that it regulates only what the two parties agree between themselves (Mills, 2000).

Essentially, recent changes in Dutch law have provided a variety of options for couples to legalize long-term partner relationships outside of the traditional legal form of marriage, either through registered partnerships or through cohabitation contracts. Marriage is no longer seen as a logical next step in the process of relationship development. Rather, couples have various options as to how to legally bind their relationships.

Religion

The Netherlands is a widely diverse country in terms of religion. Roman Catholicism and Protestantism are the two major religions. During recent years, the number of people who are not affiliated with a church has outgrown the number of church-affiliated people. In 1997, 60% of the people in the country were not affiliated with a church. Among people who do affiliate themselves with a religion, the majority affiliate with the Roman Catholic Church (22% of total population), followed by various Protestant church groups (Sociaal en Cultureel Planbureau, 2000).

Mills (2000) showed that religion is one of the factors associated with whether or not individuals will participate in the mate selection process in the Netherlands. People who affiliated themselves with a religion had a 15% greater chance of getting married or cohabiting than did people who did not affiliate themselves with a religion.

Kraaykamp (2002) showed that there are some differences among religious groups in the Netherlands regarding premarital sex. He showed that Dutch Reformed, Jews, Muslims, and Hindus were somewhat more likely to disapprove of premarital sexuality than were Dutch Protestants and Catholics. Thus, the decisions that one makes regarding *stages* of couple formation may be affected not only by whether one is affiliated with a religion but also by the specific type of religion.

Although religion still plays a role in determining whether or not people participate in the mate selection process in the Netherlands, research on lifestyles has revealed some interesting trends toward the decreasing importance of religion so far as explaining individual differences is concerned. More specifically, recent data showed that the role of women in the household is more a function of women's educational level than of their religious affiliation. Women who assumed a traditional household role, where they were primarily responsible for the household tasks, were more likely to be from a low educational background. Women who assumed a modern household role, where they shared the household tasks with their partners, were more likely to have a higher educational level (Garssen et al., 2001).

What Does It Mean Not to Marry?

It is becoming more common for individuals not to be married in the Netherlands. Recent statistics (1995 data) show that 31% of the Dutch adult population is single, as compared with 12% of the population in 1965 (van Praag & Niphuis-Nell, 1997). Considering this issue from a long-term historical perspective, it should be noted that marriage rates in Western Europe were low until the late 18th century, especially among peasants and the lower class, and increased as a result of modernization in that part of the world (Stearns, 1975). Thus, deciding not to marry/cohabit is not a new phenomenon in Dutch society, although the reasons why people decide not to marry have changed over the years. During the 18th and 19th centuries, economic factors—specifically poverty—prevented people from marrying. During the latter part of the 20th century and the first part of the 21st century, the decision to stay single has been based more on individual choice.

Furthermore, a 1988 survey showed that only 2% of the Dutch population disapproved of staying single (Sociaal en Cultureel Planbureau, 1988), establishing that there is little stigmatization regarding the decision to stay single. More so now than in the recent past, the choice to stay single has become a viable lifestyle option. However, the values and behaviors regarding staying single differ among the various ethnic groups in the Netherlands. There are few women from Turkish or Moroccan descent in the Netherlands who live alone for any period of time. On leaving home, many Turkish and Moroccan youth move in with brothers or sisters or otherwise enter into marital relationships (Garssen et al., 2001). Unfortunately, information on the values regarding staying single, broken down by various ethnic groups, is not available.

It should be clear from the discussion earlier in this chapter that the decision not to marry does not imply that one stays single. Many Dutch couples choose to commit themselves to enduring relationships through cohabitation contracts or registered partnerships. In 1995, 31% of Dutch households consisted of a single person and 10% consisted of nonmarried partners (van Praag & Niphuis-Nell, 1997). These percentages compare with 12% single-person households in 1960 and 5% nonmarried households in 1981, the first year for which data on nonmarried households are available. Only a small percentage (about 10%) choose to be single as a life course option (van Praag & Niphuis-Nell, 1997).

Relationship Dissolution: Are There Differences Between Marital and Nonmarital Relationships?

The chance that a marriage will end in divorce in the Netherlands is currently about 32% (Sociaal en Cultureel Planbureau, 2000) and has been at this level since 1980 (Garssen et al., 2001). This percentage is somewhat lower than divorce rates in other countries in Northwestern Europe, such as Denmark and Sweden, but is higher than divorce rates in Southern European countries, such as Italy and Spain (Sociaal en Cultureel Planbureau, 2000).

The chance that a nonmarital relationship will be dissolved is much higher than the chance that a marital relationship will end in divorce. Based on data from the early 1980s, statistics were obtained showing that 25% of nonmarital relationships ended within 8 years of the start of the relationships. This figure compares with 7% of marital relationships that ended in divorce involving women between 20 and 24 years of age (van Praag & Niphuis-Nell, 1997). Statistics were similar for women between 25 and 29 years of age, where 10% of marital relationships and 24% of nonmarital relationships ended in dissolution within 9 years of the start of the relationships (van Praag & Niphuis-Nell, 1997).

Differences in dissolution rates between marital and nonmarital relationships can be partially explained by the fact that nonmarital relationships, especially cohabiting ones, are often viewed as "trial marriages" (Garssen et al., 2001). Many couples see cohabitation as a stage during which the relationship can be "tested"; cohabitation is seen as trying out the relationship as in a trial, that is, getting all of the facts before making a decision. As such, partners who decide to get married after a period of cohabitation have been in the relationship longer than have partners who decide to get married without cohabitation, and the former may potentially have a more stable relationship because they cohabited first.

However, in actuality, partners who live together before marriage are not less likely to get divorced than are those who do not live together before marriage. On the contrary, partners who live together before marriage are about three times more likely to get divorced within the first 9 years of marriage than are those who do not live together before marriage. One possible explanation for this statistic is that the group of individuals who marry without living together before marriage may have moral beliefs that view both cohabitation and divorce as unacceptable (Garssen et al., 2001). This is a small group given that only 1 in 10 women marries without having cohabited before marriage (Garssen et al., 2001).

What Are the Cultural Values Associated With Couple Formation?

During the 1950s and 1960s, the Netherlands was a couple-oriented society (Weeda, 1981), as it was generally assumed that people would get married. However, the cultural values associated with marriage changed during the latter part of the century. A 1994 survey among eight European countries (Sweden, Ireland, the United Kingdom, Germany, Austria, Italy, Spain, and the Netherlands) showed that participants from the Netherlands were the least likely of these eight countries to ascribe to the statement, "Married people are happier than unmarried people" (Sociaal en Cultureel Planbureau, 2000). One might surmise that the Dutch do not see marriage as an important part of individual happiness. The question remains, however, as to how the Dutch would have responded if the statement were rephrased as follows: "People in committed relationships are happier than people who are single."

The Process of Couple Formation in the Netherlands

During the first part of the 20th century, the process of couple formation was much more formalized than it is today. For example, a man would ask permission from a girl's parents before dating her (Mak, 1999). Today, the first stages of mate selection generally occur informally. The first stage of the dating relationship is generally symbolized by the term *verkering* (organized love relationship) (*Het complete Nederlandse Woordenboek*, 1999). The term reflects the informal nature of the relationship in that it is organized through informal rules such as seeing one another on a regular basis.

The majority of Dutch women cohabit at some point in their lives. Beginning with the cohort of women who were between 20 and 29 years of age during 1985 to 1989, the majority of women who married also cohabited before marriage (Garssen et al., 2001). Although the likelihood of cohabitation increased during the latter part of the 20th century, the same is not true for the likelihood of marriage. The likelihood that someone will marry during the life course in the Netherlands is currently about 67%, down from 90% during the early 1970s (Garssen et al., 2001).

Although there is somewhat of an inverse relationship between cohabitation and marriage trends in the Netherlands, these trends are not reflected in all ethnic groups in Dutch society. There are some important differences regarding cohabitation and marriage trends among the population of non-Dutch descent as well as between the population of Dutch descent and the population of non-Dutch descent. For example, only 10% of Turkish women cohabit before marriage. This percentage is somewhat higher for women of Moroccan descent (Garssen et al., 2001). Percentages of cohabitation among individuals originating in Suriname and the Netherlands Antilles are comparable to rates among individuals from Dutch descent

ONDERTROUWD:

STEPHANUS JANSSEN
EN
ANNA VAN DREUTEN
HUWELIJKSVOLTREKKING OP DONDERDAG 1 JUNI
A.S., 'S MORGENS 9 UUR, IN DE PAROCHIEKERK
VAN DEN H. MARTINUS TE DIDAM

DIDAM, MEI 1939

TOEKOMSTIG ADRES: DIDAM, GREFFELKAMP C 137

Wedding Invitation From 1939

(van Praag & Niphuis-Nell, 1997). It is fair to say, however, that trends in marriage and cohabitation are not reflected within all of the various ethnic groups in the Netherlands. Especially the Turkish and Moroccan populations maintain more traditional patterns of couple formation than do the population of Dutch descent and individuals originating from Suriname and the Netherlands Antilles.

Young men and women who intend to get married generally *verloven* (connect through the promise of marriage sometime before they get married) (*Het complete Nederlandse Woordenboek*, 1999). The function of the *verloving* is to publicly announce the intention of the couple to get married and is symbolized by the exchange of verlovings, that is, rings for both the man and the woman.

In the past, it was also common for individuals to go into *ondertrouw* (under the marriage) just before getting married. Ondertrouw reflects the time period just before marriage and serves both religious and public functions. Ondertrouw was publicly announced for 3 consecutive weeks in the local newspapers of both the bride- and groom-to-be. During this period, it was possible for anyone to object to the marriage for valid reasons, for example, either the young man or young woman still being married to someone else.

Ondertrouw served a similar function in the Church. For example, a priest/father in the Roman Catholic Church would announce for 3 consecutive weeks all of the couples in ondertrouw, thereby providing an opportunity for church members to object to any of these marriages based on committed sins. After the period of ondertrouw, the bride and groom were *ondertrouwd* (undermarried). They were able to send out wedding invitations (such as the one shown in the accompanying photo) that included the information that the bride and groom were ondertrouwd and so fulfilled the public requirements to be married.

Marriage and Weddings

The photo of a decorated home has some important details about marriage rituals. Both the bride and groom are married out of the parental home. The groom would meet the bride at her parental home on the day of the wedding, and the family of the bride would be present. On the wedding day, the door of the home would be decorated with green ivy and white paper roses. The color white symbolizes the bride's virginity. This ritual is still conducted in large parts of the Netherlands, especially in rural areas.

Home Prepared for Wedding Celebration in 2003

The process of decorating the door is referred to as "green making" and is conducted by people in the neighborhood on the evening before the wedding. Because many couples cohabit before they get married, the door of the home of the cohabiting couple is decorated with green.

At wedding anniversaries, with the major ones being 12.5 years and 25 years, green making is also part of the anniversary celebration, although a different color is used for the paper roses. For example, at the 25-year celebration, the color silver is used for the paper roses.

If people decide to get married, they can be married by the city/state, the church, or both. In other words, a wedding ceremony may take place twice during the same day or on different days, with one wedding ceremony in the city hall reflecting the marriage for the city/state and one wedding ceremony in the church reflecting the marriage for the Church. It is important to note that a church marriage is not recognized as a legal marriage under Dutch law. Thus, any couple getting married in a church would also conduct a wedding ceremony in the city hall to legalize the marriage vows. In other words, a public marriage is a necessary and sufficient condition for a marriage to be legal, whereas a religious marriage is neither a necessary nor a sufficient condition for a marriage to be considered legal according to Dutch law.

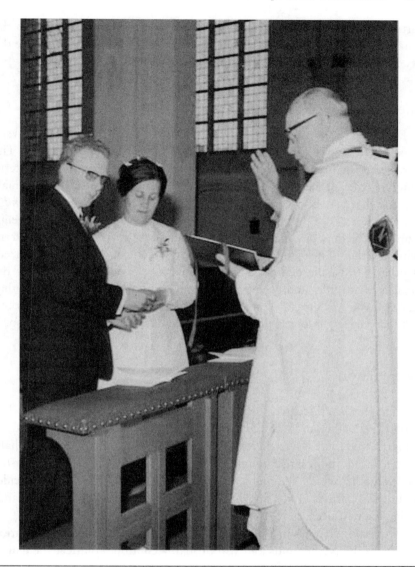

Church Ceremony in 1970

At the wedding ceremony, the bride and groom each bring one person to witness the marriage. These are comparable to the maid of honor and best man in many U.S. weddings. In the Dutch language, they are referred to as *getuigen* (witnesses). They are present not only to support the individuals who are entering the marital relationship but also to act as legal witnesses to the ceremony. In addition to the witnesses, most couples have a wedding party that includes flower girls. The flower girls toss small flowers on the walking path at the city hall or church when the bride and groom leave the city hall or church after the wedding ceremony.

The Language of Marriage

The Dutch language refers to the process of marriage with the verb *trouwen* (to attach) (*Het complete Nederlandse Woordenboek*, 1999). The Dutch language refers to the wedding with the word *huwelijk* (long-term living together of men and women after certain formalities have been finalized and that may be accompanied by festivities) (*Het complete Nederlandse Woordenboek*, 1999). It is interesting to note that the definition for huwelijk is broad. The only binding part of the definition is the mention of long-term living together of men and women after legal documents have been finalized. In other words, the definition of huwelijk, as provided here, reflects the changes in attitudes and behavior of the majority of the Dutch, that is, that they still want to develop long-term committed romantic relationships but that marriage is no longer the only binding contract with which to do so.

Conclusion

This chapter has discussed the process of couple formation and mate selection in the Netherlands. Dutch couples are deciding in decreasing numbers to marry, and there is a trend toward marriage becoming replaced by cohabitation. In addition, larger numbers of Dutch couples are deciding to stay single. In other words, the couple formation process, and whether one decides to choose a partner in life, has undergone major changes in the Netherlands during the past decades.

Two major changes in Dutch society have affected the couple formation process in the Netherlands and will probably continue to affect the course and outcome of the couple formation process: legal changes and increasing ethnic diversification of Dutch society.

Legal Changes

Legal changes have allowed couples to choose a contract that binds two people together. However, the contract is not the equivalent of marriage. The question remains how this will affect the behavior and attitudes of the Dutch. Future research should investigate whether the choices that Dutch couples make are at all affected by these legal changes. For example, are couples less likely to choose marriage now that alternative contracts are available? Likewise, questions should be asked regarding the motivations of couples to choose marriage now that alternative relationship contracts are available. Who are the people who continue to choose marriage as a life choice, and what are their motivations? Is this simply a function of religious affiliation, or do people who are not affiliated with a formal religion continue to choose marriage as well? What might be the motivating factors to choose marriage beyond values based on religion?

Ethnic Diversification

Dutch society is becoming more diverse as a result of an increasing number of immigrants and settlers from former Dutch colonies, such as the Netherlands Antilles and Suriname, as well as from former Eastern European countries, African countries, and Asian countries. There is a clear need for research that investigates the development of intimate relationships among the various cultural groups in Dutch society, especially considering that they emigrate from countries with more traditional values and norms. How do these families view the Dutch laws regarding couple formation? How do these families balance their own values and norms with the Dutch legal options that are available for relationship contracts? What are the couple formation decisions their children make, and what are their motivations?

This chapter has provided an overview of the changes in couple formation and mate selection during the past century in the Netherlands. However, many questions remain to be answered. The legal changes in the Netherlands, combined with increasing ethnic diversity, provide opportunities for cross-cultural research on couple formation and mate selection in an effort to investigate factors that affect the decisions that individuals and couples make across the life course of developing close relationships.

References

Garssen, J., de Beer, J., Cuyvers, P., & de Jong, A. (2001). *Samenleven: Nieuwe feiten over relaties en gezinnen* (Living together: New facts about relationships and families). Voorburg, Netherlands: Sociaal en Cultureel Planbureau.

Het complete Nederlandse woordenboek: Nieuwe officiele spelling (The complete Dutch dictionary: New official spelling). (1999). Amsterdam, Netherlands: Atlas.

Kraaykamp, G. (2002). Trends and countertrends in sexual permissiveness: Three decades of attitude change in the Netherlands 1965–1995. *Journal of Marriage and the Family, 64,* 225–239.

Mak, G. (1999). *De eeuw van mijn vader* (The century of my father). Amsterdam, Netherlands: Atlas.

Mills, M. (2000). *The transformation of partnerships: Canada, the Netherlands, and the Russian federation in the age of modernity.* Amsterdam, Netherlands: Thela Thesis.

Ministry of Justice. (1997). *Geregistreerd Partnership* (Registered partnership). The Hague, Netherlands: Information Department, Internal and External Communication Section.

Sociaal en Cultureel Planbureau. (1988). *Sociaal en cultureel rapport 1988* (Social and cultural report 1988). The Hague, Netherlands: Author.

Sociaal en Cultureel Planbureau. (2000). *Sociaal en cultureel rapport 2000: Nederland in Europa* (Social and cultural report 2000: The Netherlands in Europe). The Hague, Netherlands: Author.

Stearns, P. N. (1975). *European society in upheaval: Social history since 1750* (2nd ed.). New York: Macmillan.

van Praag, C. S., & Niphuis-Nell, M. (1997). *Het gezinsrapport* (The family report). Rijswijk, Netherlands: Sociaal en Cultureel Planbureau.

Weeda, C. J. (1981). *Huwelijk, gezin, en samenleving* (Marriage, family, and society). Assen, Netherlands: Van Gorcum.

Wilterdink, N., & van Heerikhuizen, B. (1989). *Samenlevingen: Een verkenning van het terrein van de sociologie* (Societies: An exploration of the field of sociology). Groningen, Netherlands: Wolters-Noordhoff.

Part VI

Asia

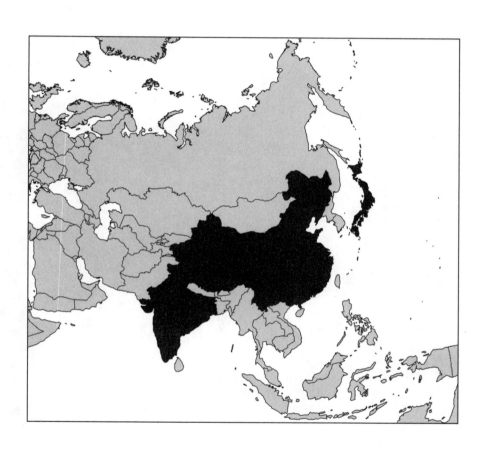

12

Mate Selection in Contemporary India

Love Marriages Versus Arranged Marriages

Nilufer P. Medora

Sita, one of my young respondents, was a college graduate with a degree in political science. She had been waiting [more than] a year while her parents were arranging a match for her. I found it difficult to accept the docile manner in which this well-educated young woman awaited the outcome of a process that would result in her spending the rest of her life with a man she hardly knew—a virtual stranger picked out by her parents. "How can you go along with this?" I asked her in frustration and distress. "Don't you care who you marry?" "Of course I care," she answered. "This is why I must let my parents choose a boy for me. My marriage is too important to be arranged by such an inexperienced person as myself. In such matters, it is better to have my parents' guidance." (Nanda, 1995, p. 113)

Stutely (2001) wondered how an executive in a Bombay-based, European-owned company could submit to an ancient tradition that denied free choice. He was told by the groom's great-uncle, "But it is his choice. Family tradition and commitment have bound young Indian couples together for centuries, and today's generation is no different. Your Western ideas of individualism have proved to be a fragile notion as far as modern marriage is concerned" (p. 12).

I ndia is one of the world's oldest civilizations and has a rich cultural, social, historical, and religious heritage. Historically, India was part of the British Empire for nearly 300 years. India attained independence in 1947, and since then it has achieved multifaceted socioeconomic progress. India is the seventh largest country in the world and has a population that recently went over the 1 billion mark, making it the second most populated country in the world after China. It is bound by the great Himalayan Mountains in the north, and the Indian peninsula stretches southward to the Tropic of Cancer, and tapers off into the Indian Ocean between the Bay of Bengal on the east and the Arabian Sea on the west (Consulate General of India, n.d.).

India is a secular and pluralistic society made up of 29 states and 6 union territories. There are 18 different languages and more than 300 different dialects spoken by the inhabitants of India. Indian people belong to varied ethnic groups, share a multicultural heritage, and practice various religions. The religious distribution is as follows: Hindus (82.41%), Muslims (11.67%), Christians (2.32%), Sikhs (1.99%), Buddhists (0.77%), Jains (0.41%), and others—Bahai, Zoroastrians, Jews, and other tribal religions (0.43%) (Consulate General of India, n.d.). Most Indians tend to view religion as a way of life rather than as a set of strict dogmas and perceptions.

Transmission of culture and values is intricately interwoven with religious affiliation. Indians define themselves simultaneously as individuals who are affiliated with a particular religion and as belonging to a specific geographical region/state in India. Religion prescribes the form of worship and guides daily behavior, whereas the geographic region usually identifies the language one speaks; the literature, art, and music one enjoys; the food one eats; and the clothing one wears (Segal, 1998).

It is imperative to understand that, based on regional and cultural differences, there is quite a bit of variation that makes it difficult to generalize the mate selection practices and marriage customs to all Indian families. It should be noted that even though a large majority of Indians are Hindus, people belonging to other religious faiths (e.g., Muslims, Christians, Buddhists, Zoroastrians) have some practices that are similar to those of Hindus and others that are quite different. Non-Hindus have adopted some of the beliefs, rituals, and marriage and family practices from Hindus as part of the assimilation process because people of many faiths have resided and coexisted in India for centuries. They are governed by different precepts and laws dictated by their religion, making many of the beliefs and ceremonies different. Given space limitations, and given that the large majority of Indians are Hindu, this chapter focuses attention on mate selection practices among the Hindu community. Before discussing the process of mate selection, it is of paramount importance to get an insight and understanding about individualistic and collectivistic models, and about the structure and function of the Indian family, that seem to significantly guide and influence the process of mate selection and marriage practices.

Individualism Versus Collectivism

Some cultures in the world are individualistic, whereas others tend to be collectivistic. Triandis and his colleagues (Triandis, 1990; Triandis, Bontempo, Villareal, Asai, & Lucca, 1988) have examined the concepts of individualism and collectivism across various cultures and concluded that individualism is correlated with personal initiative, personal autonomy, self-reliance, and personal freedom. In less industrialized, Eastern, and more traditional societies, collectivism is related to family integrity, family unity, and family loyalty. Hui and Triandis (1986) defined individualism as "the subordination of the goals of the collectivities to individual goals and a sense of independence and lack of concern for others" (p. 245). Collectivism, on the other hand, was defined as "a sense of harmony, interdependence, and concern for others" (p. 244). India, along with most Eastern cultures, has been placed on the higher end of the collectivism continuum. Collectivistic cultures assume that any person through birth belongs to either a family, an extended family, or a clan that takes interest in the individual's well-being and safeguards his or her interest but in turn expects that person's permanent loyalty. Collectivism manifests itself in the beliefs and practices that reflect the individual's embeddedness in his or her family and the influence of the family and extended family on the individual in all important aspects of life, including mate selection and subsequent marriage (Verma, 1989). More specifically, in collectivistic societies, there is a greater emphasis on the views, needs, and goals of the family than on the individual. Social norms and duty are defined and prescribed by family and kin. The beliefs a person has are those that are similar to and shared by family rather than those that distinguish the person from his or her family, and there is a greater readiness to cooperate with and among family members (Triandis, 1983; Verma, 1989).

Although India is a multicultural society, there seem to be certain basic patterns and practices that are followed and that underlie family life in the various Indian communities. The Indian family, like most families in Oriental cultures, is considered to be strong, well knit, resilient, and enduring (Sriram & Verma, 1992).

The Indian Family

Srivastava (1995) defined the Indian family as a transmission belt for the diffusion of cultural standards to the next generation, a psychological agent of society, a shock absorber, and an institution of many enhancing and valuable qualities. The joint or extended family system has always been the most important institution and one that has been integral to the Indian culture. Despite the many social, cultural, and technological changes and adaptations to a pseudo-Western culture and a move toward the nuclear family form among the middle class and upper class Indians in the urban areas, the extended family system still continues to prevail in modern India (Medora, Larson, & Dave, 2000; Segal, 1991). Even in the most modern and nuclear families in contemporary India, the deep-rooted jointness in various structural and functional aspects still exists (Bhatnagar & Rastogi, 1989).

Traditionally, Indians lived in an extended family where the family was hierarchical (Segal, 1991). In general, three or more generations may have lived together, with age, gender, and generational status of individuals serving as the primary determinants of power, behavior, and role relationships (Sue, 1981). During contemporary times, it is common to find two generations in the extended family, as sons bring their wives to their parents' home. Even though there are regional and religious differences, most Indians follow the same basic kinship patterns. Their residential patterns are guided by the principles and practices of patrilineal descent. In the Indian family, the father or grandfather is typically the head of the household and females assume subordinate roles. Females usually perform most of the household chores, take care of the children and elderly, and are responsible for socializing, communicating, and instilling cultural values in children.

Today, in most urban areas throughout India, both men and women work outside the home so as to maintain a decent standard of living. Despite the fact that women are employed full-time, most of the cooking, cleaning, child rearing, and other household responsibilities are still performed by women with occasional help from men. Male children are greatly desired and preferred over female children. Patrilineal inheritance, patrilocal residence, and ancestor worship are practiced and endorsed. As such, the status of men is generally higher than that of women (Kakar, 1998; Mullatti, 1995).

As in most Asian families, cooperation and conformity are also stressed in the Indian family. Interdependence among family members is promoted, and self-identity is inhibited. The belief in the integrity of the group provides the family with a group identity and strengthens family stability, albeit at the cost of individual autonomy (Triandis et al., 1988). Family life is characterized by closeness, mutuality of interests, strong group controls, and mutual assistance during times of need (Khatri, 1988). Moreover, it is considered a person's duty to maintain the noble "name and fame" of the family and its tradition in all aspects of one's life (Mullatti, 1995).

Significance of Love and Marriage in India

In some countries, including India, love and romance are not considered to be prerequisites to getting married, nor is courtship a necessary prelude for testing the relationship. Levine, Sato, Hashimoto, and Verma (1995) examined college students' perceptions about the importance of love for both the establishment and the maintenance of a marriage in India, Pakistan, Thailand, Mexico, Brazil, Japan, Hong Kong, the Philippines, Australia, England, and the United States. Love was given more importance in Westernized nations and less importance in the underdeveloped Eastern nations. The differences were stronger and more significant for dimensions regarding the establishment of a marriage than for dimensions regarding the maintenance and dissolution of a marriage. Individualistic cultures assigned greater importance to feelings of love in marriage decisions than did collectivistic cultures. Also, respondents who assigned greater importance to love tended to come from countries with higher economic standards of living, higher divorce rates, and lower fertility rates. Gupta (1976) reported that love generally is considered a weak basis for marriage because it often overshadows suitable qualities in a spouse.

Medora, Larson, Hortaçsu, and Dave (2002) distributed Knox and Sporakowski's (1968) Attitudes Toward Love scale to 641 young adults in the United States, Turkey, and India to investigate their perceived attitudes toward romanticism. They found that American young adults were most romantic, followed by the Turkish students and then Indians. Once again, it appears that in Westernized countries such as the United States, romance is given a lot more importance than it is in India.

In the traditional Hindu society, marriage was considered a sacrament and not a contract; as such, marriage was for life. It is also important to point out that *vivaha* (wedding) is generally obligatory for every person. One of the primary motives in a traditional Hindu marriage is progeny, particularly sons. According to Kapadia (1966), the primary aim of a Hindu marriage is *dharma praja* (progeny) and *rati* (pleasure). Furthermore, marriage is regarded not only as a union between two individuals but also as the establishment of an enduring bond between two extended families (Chekki, 1996; Sureender, Prabakaran, & Khan, 1998). Marital unions are religiously, economically, politically, and socially oriented, and marriages are arranged by the elders and extended family members (Chekki, 1996; Lessinger, 2002; Mullatti, 1995).

Even today, many traditional Hindus regard marriage as a social and cultural duty and as a lifelong commitment (Lessinger, 2002). It is not viewed as a means of attaining personal happiness nor as a means of sharing one's life with a person one loves. Instead, family unity, family togetherness, and sharing common family goals are of primary importance, and personal considerations are only secondary. It is not really important whether the young man and woman feel that they are in love with each other because love is expected to come after marriage. It is not considered important whether the man and woman share common goals and interests, or even whether they know each other in advance, so long as the family line and family traditions can be maintained.

During the past few decades, several social, cultural, and economic changes have occurred with regard to selecting prospective partners and marriage practices, but marrying within the religion and caste still continues to be an important determinant in marriage. In India, it is still customary for individuals to marry within their religion, caste, and subcaste. Although the caste system that divides Hindus into four main castes— Brahmins, Ksatriyas, Vaishnavs, and Shudras—and subcastes has been officially abolished, it still plays a crucial role and is unchanged in most of its essential features (Katti & Saroja, 1989; Mullatti, 1995). Caste is an exclusive phenomenon highly characteristic of Indian society (Katti & Saroja, 1989). There are more than 100 subcastes in India (Mahalanobis, 1968). Each caste is generally bound together by a common occupation and common customs, especially regarding mate selection and marriage. The most important consideration in a Hindu marriage is caste endogamy. Endogamy refers to the traditional custom where members belonging to a certain caste marry among themselves and where marriage outside the caste is taboo.

Arranged marriage, the most prevalent form of marriage, works effectively to ensure that the marriage takes place within the caste and thereby prevents romantic attractions from interfering with endogamous principles (Das, 1980; Katti & Saroja, 1989; Uplaonkar, 1995). Marriage is expected to bind the two families belonging to the same caste in a very special form of familial and social relationship. It is customary to ensure that the potential partner's family history and background, as well as his or her social, educational, and economic statuses, are compatible with one's own (Nanda, 1995; Raman, 1983; Sprecher & Chandak, 1992). Most Indian parents are not aware of or attuned to the tensions and problems that their children experience in the social arena. Inadequate and ineffective communication in many Indian households is the cause of severe tensions between parents and children. The following statement of a 23-year-old Gujarati Brahmin girl attending a large Indian university explains her predicament:

"I was living in the dormitory while I was pursuing a graduate degree in child development and family studies. I had been dating and was in love with a 26-year-old young man who was also a Gujarati but belonged to the Patel caste and community. In spite of the fact that my dad was educated in the U.S. and had a terminal degree from there, he was very traditional and conservative in his way of thinking. My parents wanted me to marry a boy of their choice from their Brahmin community. They were waiting for me to complete my graduate education before the so called "search" was initiated. I confided in my older brother and told him about my plans to marry Pravin. My brother betrayed my confidence and went and told my parents about my plans. My parents called me and told me to come home immediately because there was a family emergency.

"I was disturbed to hear about this, but totally unsuspecting, I left with nothing except the clothes on my back. Once I came home, my parents confronted me and asked me if what they heard from my brother was true. I told them it was. They proceeded to tell me that they were very disappointed with me, that I had let them down, and they seriously reprimanded me and forbade me to go back to continue my studies. I begged and begged, but eventually my parents' wishes prevailed. I cannot believe that my parents would ruin my education and my whole life." (J. T. Kumar, personal communication, September 15, 2001)

The Mate Selection Process

Contrary to what most young Americans think, most Indian young adults do not believe that they have the knowledge and wisdom to select their prospective mates. In addition, they do not believe that it is essential to date many partners before picking the right mate. Instead, many of them believe that because their parents raised them, no one knows them as well as their parents do and their parents have their best interests at heart. So, they leave the so-called "search" up to their parents. The type of family that the prospective spouse comes from is given the most important consideration. In addition, occupational and cultural compatibility, class compatibility, and moral history of the family are qualities taken into consideration by the respective parents on both sides (Mullatti, 1995). This implies that the prospective family has to have a good and solid social, political, and economic reputation in its caste and community (Nanda, 1995).

Arranged marriages carefully and thoroughly screen family ideals and values, look for partner compatibility, and assess educational and social homogamy factors. In arranged marriages, love is expected to grow and blossom after marriage. Arranged marriages stem from a cultural concern with family unity and family cooperation (Lessinger, 2002). According to Rao and Rao (1976), the Hindu belief system regarded mate selection by self-choice as undesirable and feared that freedom of choice might upset the process of adjustment of the bride in the new family.

Most marriages are arranged to a greater or lesser extent. Even among the educated and upper class families in modern urban India, marriage is as much a concern of the families as it is of the individuals (Mullatti, 1995; Nanda, 1995), although there now is an increasing trend to consult and get input from the children. Typically, the parents or kin select a pool of potential partners who have been screened by them first to ensure a similar social, cultural, familial, and economic background. One of the most common ways in which the partners are selected is from among the children of friends and extended family members who have a similar sociocultural background.

The use of matrimonial advertisements is increasing and so is becoming an integral part of the mate selection process (Mullatti, 1995). Das (1980) pointed out that in no other country, except maybe Egypt, does one find marriage being advertised through matrimonial advertisements in newspaper columns. These advertisements are becoming so commonplace that the major newspapers, such as *Times of India,* are using a quarter to half of the page in advertising for prospective partner inquiries.

Advertisements like the ones that appear in the extracts that follow are placed in a newspaper that is likely to attract a wide readership. If many persons apply, screening is done on the basis of photographs. During recent times, after the photographs are sent and a specific person seems to fit the specified criteria and appears to be attractive, the young man and woman correspond via the Internet to find out whether they are compatible before they actually meet. It is important to point out, however, that this is a common practice only among the upper class, Westernized, and educated families living in metropolitan areas.

Grooms Wanted

ALLIANCE INVITED from North Indian Hindu gentlemen based in US/Canada for tall, slim, beautiful, 28yr., educated, professionally employed, Girl has East/West values. Respond to matrisearch01@yahoo.com with bio-data/photo.

SEEKING SUITABLE match for fair, charming girls (30) and (27). Interior Designers, hailing from respectable Tamil Roman Catholic Family. Correspond with photos to: Mr. Joseph Thomas, Delhi, India.

Brides Wanted

SEEKING ALL pretty professional with Indian values for very handsome Jat-Sikh boy, 26, 6'4" clean shaven, software engineer, six figures, from very well connected, affluent and high status family. Returnable photograph to PO Box M-9145 c/o India-West or ruby_2000@yahoo.com.

A WELL SETTLED Hindu/Punjabi businessman educated, good natured, smart 35/5'11 is looking for a simple, educated, beautiful and affectionate girl. Please send bio-data with recent photograph to uncle, Mr. Vinod Khanna richman50@hotmail.com.

As the pool is narrowed down to two or three members of the opposite sex, the young adults are allowed to meet, talk over the phone, and occasionally go out on a date accompanied by a chaperone who is usually an adult family member and who accompanies the young man and woman while they try to determine the person with whom they are most compatible. It is important to point out that while this exchange and interaction are occurring, marriage is foremost on the minds of both parties and all forms of premarital sex are discouraged.

After the man and woman go out a few times, the man generally proposes marriage to the woman. If the woman accepts the proposal, the respective parents are informed about their children's decision. If the woman is not interested in accepting the marriage proposal, she will let her intentions be known to her parents, who will politely and gently give some excuse to the man's parents. The man's parents may be disappointed but will not pursue the matter any further. Instead, they will try to pursue another match for their son.

An adaptation of the arranged marriage to modern life is the introduction of a relatively new form of marriage referred to as the "semi-arranged" marriage. This form of marriage is more prevalent among young adults belonging to the urban middle class. According to Lessinger (2002), the semi-arranged marriage "is intended to retain parental control while accommodating the youthful yearning for romantic love which is fed by both Indian and American media" (p. 103). During recent years, many urban, professional Indian families have initiated the process of introducing suitable, prescreened young men and women to each other. The young man and woman are then allowed a brief courtship period, during which they can decide whether they are suited for each other and whether they like each other adequately to get married and spend the rest of their lives together. This is different from American-style dating in that parents and extended family members (e.g., grandparents, uncles, aunts, cousins) are still involved in the initial screening, the courtship is much shorter, little or no premarital sex is involved, and there is a realistic recognition by both parties that the purpose of the meeting is marriage (Lessinger, 2002).

Even today, in rural and urban India, most Hindu families consult an astrologer to ensure that the two prospective partners are well suited for each other based on familial backgrounds as well as on social and economic factors (Sureender et al., 1998). The astrologer matches the partners' horoscopes and predicts whether or not the couple will enjoy marital happiness, find financial success, and be blessed with children. As a rule, Indians are fatalistic and believe that what is predestined to happen will happen. They believe that their lives are predestined, their fate is preordained, and they are helpless so far as choice is concerned—hence, they must succumb to the celestial forces of the universe (Gupta, 1976). In a comparative study on the concept of marriage by professional and nonprofessional degree students, Umadevi, Venkataramaiah, and Srinivasulu (1992) reported that nearly 50% of the participants favored matching of the two horoscopes before the marriage was finalized.

Basically, the couple's compatibility is checked out on the basis of parameters such as mental compatibility, physical compatibility, ability to deal with crises, longevity of attraction between the partners, longevity of life of each partner. All of these factors together are supposed to make up 36 points or *gunas*. If the partners score less than 18 points, the match is rejected. If they score 18 to 24 points, the alliance is expected to be average. If they score 25 to 32 points, the match is supposed to be very good.

If they score more than 32 points, the match is supposed to be excellent (*Love Matters/Marriage/Compatibility,* 2000).

The influence of Western movies, Western television shows, and the Internet has caused many Indian youth to desire and emulate their Western counterparts. A minority of urban youth belonging to the middle and upper social class, who are educated, independent minded, and Westernized, are selecting their own prospective mates and so are involved in "love marriages." Most Indian parents do not approve of their children having love marriages. It is a great source of anxiety and concern to them. During contemporary times, some Westernized Indian men living in the urban areas are meeting young women at universities or at their workplaces. They socialize with them, go out on dates, and eventually plan to marry them. The complex emotions expressed in the following statement summarizes the torment and confusion that some Indian youth experience during young adulthood:

> "In the 21st century, and in this day and age, my parents are very insistent that I follow and adhere to the Hindu tradition of having an arranged marriage. Since the last 2 years, I have been in love with a young man who is attending the same university as I am. We are in a serious committed relationship and someday plan to get married. Obviously, my parents don't know about this relationship. If they found out about it, they would coerce me to break off the relationship and marry someone of their choice." (A. R. Shah, personal communication, June 8, 2001)

Attitudes Regarding Arranged Marriages

Youth in modern India are experiencing significant transformations regarding their values, attitudes, beliefs, and perceptions due to changes occurring as a result of industrialization, urbanization, and technological advancements. Likewise, the influence of widespread education and mass media has caused young people, especially those in urban areas, to marry at a later age, seek greater freedom, assert themselves more, desire greater independence to express themselves, and make their own independent decisions regarding mate selection. The average age at marriage is 19 years for Indian females and 24 years for males (*Chennai, India,* n.d.).

These changes are likely to be reflected in young people's attitudes and beliefs about the acceptance and/or rejection of an arranged marriage. What do contemporary youth in India think regarding arranged marriage? Researchers have concluded that most young adults in India favor the system of an arranged marriage over a love marriage or a free choice marriage (Saroja & Surendra, 1991; Sprecher & Chandak, 1992; Umadevi et al., 1992; Uplaonkar, 1995). Researchers found that although young men and women prefer an arranged marriage, most of them want to be consulted and want a final say in whom they marry. If they happen to fall in love and so select their own prospective mates, approval from parents is deemed of paramount importance for a large majority of Indian youth. A gender difference was found, with more females desiring an arranged marriage and more males opting for a love marriage (Raman, 1983; Sex Education, Counseling Research Training and Therapy, 1993). As indicated earlier in this chapter, some Indian youth experience tremendous turmoil, conflict, and anger toward their parents but do not know how to deal with the situation. A young Indian male summarized his feelings in the following statement:

> "I have been dating a girl for the last 3 years. She is also a Hindu but belongs to another caste and community. We are very much in love and are in a committed relationship. We have been sexually intimate for the last 6 months. My parents don't know about my girlfriend, and I don't want them to know about her. Recently, they started looking for a girl for me to marry. The main thing that they are concerned with is that the girl belong to the same caste and community as themselves and that the family has social prestige and plenty of money. They don't understand my need to get to know the girl, share mutual interests with her, develop a sense of intimacy, and fall in love with her before I marry her. My parents were introduced on a Saturday, and they got married 10 days later. They are hoping the same for me and my siblings. Could I get married to a girl without knowing her and bonding with her? I certainly couldn't." (N. Patel, personal communication, May 22, 2001)

Criteria for Mate Selection

When Indian youth were asked to specify the most important reasons for getting married, a majority of the respondents specified companionship and a means of achieving security and stability (Sex Education, Counseling Research Training and Therapy, 1993), and love was given secondary importance (Verma, 1989). Schwartz and Bilsky (1987) identified three clusters of individualistic values (self-direction, achievement, and individual enjoyment) and three clusters of collectivistic values (prosocial values, conformity, and security) that influence criteria for mate selection.

Suman (1990) reported that male respondents were interested in a girl who was physically attractive and sexually responsive and who had the attributes to make a good housewife. Female respondents, on the other hand, tended to look for economic security, affection, and tenderness in a

Hindu Bride in Traditional Wedding Attire

partner (Sex Education, Counseling Research Training and Therapy, 1993). Some researchers found that Indian youth envisioned a prospective spouse as being kind, having a sense of humor, being expressive and open, having a potential for career success, and being a good conversationalist (Sprecher & Chandak, 1992). Verma (1989) found that both male and female respondents chose friendship as the most important attribute. The male respondents ranked the following other attributes as desirable qualities in a prospective partner: (a) being a good parent, (b) having good looks, and (c) being from a good family. The female respondents also ranked (a) being educated, (b) having someone to share household responsibilities, and (c) having financial security as being other important attributes.

Das (1980) analyzed 1,327 matrimonial advertisements that appeared in newspapers and found that Indian men desired education in a woman and that Indian women preferred to have a mate who did well in his profession. Pal and Mathur (1989), in their study of 221 Indian men and women, reported that members of both genders desired life partners who belonged to the same social class as they did but that a higher percentage of women than men preferred life partners from richer families. In the same study, it was found that serious commitment to one's job was an important attribute for respondents of both genders. However, more women valued and desired this quality than did males.

In an interesting study, Sprecher and Chandak (1992) surveyed Indian youth living in India and Indians living in the midwestern part of the United States and assessed their attitudes about dating and arranged marriages. Participants were asked to identify and rank order the advantages and disadvantages of an arranged marriage and a love marriage.

Participants mentioned that the three most important advantages of an arranged marriage are (a) support from families, (b) quality and stability of an arranged marriage, and (c) compatible or desirable background. The three most important factors identified as disadvantages of arranged marriages are (a) not knowing each other well, (b) dowry, and (c) incompatibility/unhappiness. On the other hand, the three most important factors identified as being major advantages of a love marriage are (a) getting to know the partner, (b) stimulation and fun, and (c) being able to socialize with the opposite sex. The three most important factors identified as disadvantages of a love marriage are (a) sex, pregnancy, and immoral behavior, (b) disapproval by parents, and (c) cause anguish.

Buss (1989) interviewed 247 Indians and found that having good financial prospects, being ambitious, and being industrious were more important qualities in a potential mate for women. Men tended to prefer a younger mate, whereas women preferred an older mate. Good looks and chastity were slightly more important to males than to females.

From the studies just cited, it is obvious that in the Indian culture, being in love, or the feeling of being emotionally or physically close to one's partner, were not considered to be important attributes in the mate selection process by most participants. Instead, being physically attractive, sharing household chores, being a good parent to one's child, and being a good provider were qualities deemed as being important in a potential mate.

Dowry System

A unique feature of the mate selection process is the giving of the dowry by the bride's parents to the groom's family. The amount of the dowry varies and is dependent on the couple's social class. Dowry gifts could be cash, pots and pans, furniture, gold jewelry, land, cars, or apartments. The Indian dowry system traditionally was never a financial burden but rather was voluntary and initiated to provide security for the bride in case of adversity or unexpected circumstances after marriage. Today, the dowry custom is more or less ritualized and widespread (Shangle, 1995). According to Mullatti (1995), "The custom of dowry has taken the form of a market transition in all classes and castes irrespective of the level of education" (p. 99).

During recent years, the custom has deteriorated to the point where the groom and his family sometimes become very greedy. They may make tremendous demands, and if these demands are not met after marriage, the result may be a dowry death, that is, burning a bride alive if the dowry is insufficient so that the groom can remarry another woman for a higher or better dowry (Mullatti, 1995). Educated and urban youth generally tend to have more liberal ideas about marriage and so oppose the dowry system more than do rural youth. The greater focus on dowries may have contributed to a preference for sons and a dislike and poor treatment of daughters among the less educated and in rural parts of India.

The Marriage Ceremony

The wedding season in India is mostly from November to March. Hindu weddings are very festive and elaborate affairs that extend over several days, with religious ceremonies interspersed with parades, fireworks, flowers, music, dancing, rich food and drink, and exchanges of clothing, gifts, and jewelry. A wedding is the celebration of the joining of two individuals and two families. Mullatti (1995) explained that a Hindu marriage is not merely a union of two individuals but rather an extremely elaborate ceremony that unites two families almost like blood relations. Thus, a marriage ceremony is shared by all family relations from the father's and mother's sides, friends, neighbors, and caste members. In rural areas, the entire village is invited to attend the wedding. It is also a prime opportunity to show off one's wealth. An average wedding costs approximately a half-million rupees ($10,000) (Stutely, 2001).

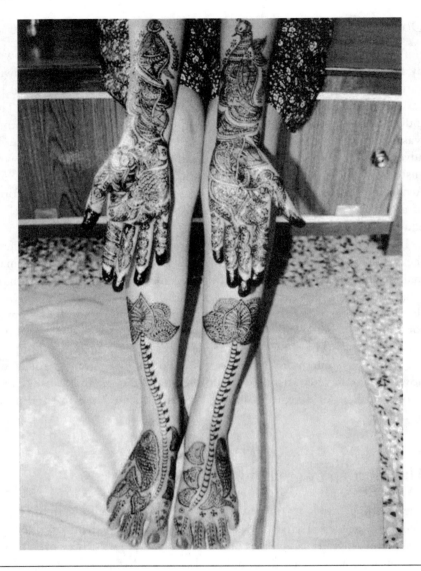

Hindu Bride With Intricate Patterns of Henna on Her Hands and Feet

Prior to the wedding ceremony, there are festive preceremonial activities in which a band plays, trumpets sound, flowers are thrown, fireworks explode, and immediate family members and close friends engage in dancing and singing. In the midst of these festivities, the *varraj* (groom) rides on a white horse, dressed in a colorful turban and brocade jacket and adorned with flowers that cover his head and face. The *bahu* (bride) is dressed by

Hindu Wedding Ceremony With Bride and Groom Seated in Front of Fire and Family Members in the Background

her family and friends in a red, white, and gold inlay work sari, adorned with heavy 22-karat jewelry, and has elaborate makeup on her face, hands, and feet. The use of *mehndi* (henna) is an integral and important aspect of an Indian wedding. Henna is applied to the bride's hands and feet in a pre-marriage ceremony to signify the strength and power of love in marriage. The bride and groom are led to the *mandap,* a colorful and ornately decorated canopy under which the ceremony takes place.

The wedding ceremony lasts for approximately 2 hours, during which the priests invoke Sanskrit chants to the Hindu deities Shiva, Lakshmi, Ram, and Krishna and throw grains of rice on the couple and into a small fire to signify blessings for a long, happy, and contented married life. Immediately after the religious invocations, one end of the bride's sari is tied to the sash from the groom's turban. The bride and groom are made to hold hands and walk hand-in-hand as they take seven steps around the sacred fire pit, accompanied by appropriate Vedic verses chanted by the priests, in the presence of witnesses and invitees. The family, kin, and well-wishers cheer the couple on and offer their blessings. This formalizes the completion of the marriage. The band starts playing again, and the bride and groom and their families make their exit and get ready for the reception that follows.

For the wedding reception, the bride and groom change their clothes. In urban areas, the groom usually wears a Western suit and the bride usually wears an expensive, colorful, silk brocade sari. The bride and groom are made to sit on the stage, where the guests approach them and offer their hearty congratulations and give them wedding gifts. Family and kin generally hand the couple envelopes filled with cash that are discreetly placed in the folds of the bride's sari. After the groom and bride have met their invited guests, a sumptuous dinner consisting of a variety of rich foods and sweets is served to the guests (Stutely, 2001). The ceremonies and celebrations are the same among the poor, but on a smaller scale. Many families borrow money from more affluent relatives and are in debt because Indians believe that a child's wedding, especially a son's wedding, must be celebrated with a lot of pomp and show.

Status of Single People in India

Because the Hindu culture believes that *vivaha* (marriage) is obligatory for every person, an individual who remains single and never marries does feel out of place both socially and culturally. Also, an unmarried girl of marriageable age is considered shameful and a reproach to her family. Traditionally, single persons are supposed to be the responsibility of the extended family. Remaining single is more acceptable for men than it is for women. When a woman is not married, it is assumed that there is something wrong with her, that she may be difficult to get along with, or that she may be uncompromising. Single men and women are not allowed to participate in religious festivities and marriage celebrations because it is considered unlucky, unholy, and inauspicious. Traditionally, parents who could not find a suitable match for their daughters were ostracized and looked down on (Kapadia, 1966). Because there are very few single men and women in India, they receive minimal social support and so many of them experience loneliness and alienation.

Conclusion

It is important to point out that India is a secular and pluralistic society with tremendous diversity in terms of languages, customs, food habits, clothing, beliefs, and values. The joint or extended family is the norm in rural and urban areas and among individuals residing in the lower, middle, and upper socioeconomic classes. In India, a marriage is seen not only as a union of two individuals but also as a merger between two families. Love and romance are not considered to be prerequisites or co-requisites to getting married. The cultural belief is that love blossoms after marriage. Having an arranged marriage is still the norm for most young Hindu adults. The arranged marriage is negotiated and arranged by parents or extended family members of the potential partners. It is customary for the parents to select partners based on caste endogamy as well as social, political, religious, cultural, and social class similarities. In addition, occupational and educational compatibility and moral character of the family are qualities taken into consideration by parents of both partners. The extended family has a built-in support system that assists the newlyweds in the adjustment process and during times of crises later on in their married life.

With the advent of industrialization, urbanization, and technological developments, there is an increasing tendency—especially among educated individuals in urban areas—to have some input into the mate selection process. In other words, if the parents have selected three of four potential partners, a young Indian adult would like to meet them, sometimes go out on dates with them, and have a say in the final decision as to who he or she marries. On the other hand, if the Indian man or woman has fallen in love and selected his or her own partner, parental approval is still of paramount importance to the Indian man or woman.

Among Hindus, marriage is considered to be a sacrament, so singlehood and divorce are socially ostracized. Therefore, their occurrence is relatively uncommon.

India is a collectivistic society in which the family's needs, goals, and interests supersede those of the individual. The family safeguards the individual's well-being for life, and social norms and duties are specified and prescribed by family and kin. Finally, it could be said that the Indian family structure is different from that in the West. Furthermore, India has its own dating and culture-specific marital patterns. Indian families are strong, resilient, and enduring.

References

Bhatnagar, P., & Rastogi, M. R. (1989). Development of a family scale. *Psychological Studies, 34,* 61–63.

Buss, D. M. (1989). Sex differences in human mate preferences: Evolutionary hypotheses tested in 37 cultures. *Behavioral and Brain Sciences, 12,* 1–49.

Chekki, D. A. (1996). Family values and family change. *Journal of Comparative Family Studies, 27,* 409–413.

Chennai, India. (n.d.). Health statistics: Average age at marriage—India. [Online]. Retrieved April 13, 2003, from www.medindia.net/health_statistics/general/marriageage.asp

Consulate General of India. (n.d.). *Indian information: Land and the people.* [Online]. Retrieved April 13, 2003, from www.indianconsulate-sf.org

Das, M. (1980). Matrimonial advertisements: An examination of its social significance in mate selection in modern India. *Man in India, 60,* 187–200.

Gupta, G. (1976). Love, arranged marriage, and the Indian social structure. *Journal of Comparative Family Studies, 7,* 75–85.

Hui, C. H., & Triandis, H. C. (1986). Individualism-Collectivism: A study of cross-cultural researchers. *Journal of Cross-Cultural Psychology, 17,* 222–248.

Kakar, S. (1998). Asian Indian families. In R. L. Taylor (Ed.), *Minority families in the United States: A multicultural perspective* (pp. 208–223). Englewood Cliffs, NJ: Prentice Hall.

Kapadia, K. M. (1966). *Marriage and family in India.* Bombay, India: Oxford University Press.

Katti, M., & Saroja. K. (1989). Parents' opinion towards intercaste marriage and their preference in mate selection for their children. *Indian Journal of Behavior, 13,* 28–34.

Khatri, A. A. (1988). Some dimensions of a state family. *Journal of Comparative Family Studies, 19,* 261–272.

Knox, D. H., Jr., & Sporakowski, M. J. (1968). Attitudes of college students toward love. *Journal of Marriage and the Family, 30,* 638–642.

Lessinger, J. (2002). Asian Indian marriages: Arranged, semi-arranged, or based on love? In N. V. Benokraitis (Ed.), *Contemporary ethnic families in the United States: Characteristics, variations, and dynamics* (pp. 101–104). Upper Saddle River, NJ: Prentice Hall.

Levine, R., Sato, S., Hashimoto, T., & Verma, J. (1995). Love and marriage in eleven cultures. *Journal of Cross-Cultural Psychology, 26,* 554–571.

Love Matters/Marriage/Compatibility. (2000). Love Compatibility Report. [Online]. Retrieved April 13, 2003, from www.indianastrology2000.com/astrology/romance.html

Mahalanobis, P. C. (1968). *The problems in Indian society.* Bombay, India: Popular Prakashan.

Medora, N. P., Larson, J. H., & Dave, P. B. (2000). East-Indian college students' perceptions of family strengths. *Journal of Comparative Family Studies, 31,* 408–424.

Medora, N. P., Larson, J. H., Hortaçsu, N., & Dave, P. B. (2002). Perceived attitudes toward romanticism: A cross-cultural study of American, East-Indian, and Turkish college students. *Journal of Comparative Family Studies, 31,* 155–178.

Mullatti, L. (1995). Families in India: Beliefs and realities. *Journal of Comparative Family Studies, 26,* 11–25.

Nanda, S. (1995). Arranging a marriage in India. In J. K. Norton (Ed.), *India and South Asia* (pp. 113–116). Guilford, CT: Brown & Benchmark.

Pal, M., & Mathur, S. S. (1989). Socioeconomic factors in mate selection. *Indian Journal of Applied Psychology, 26,* 16–21.

Raman, M. V. (1983). Opinion of Calcutta men on arranged marriage. *Indian Journal of Social Research, 24,* 34–37.

Rao, V. V., & Rao, V. N. (1976). Arranged marriages: An assessment of the attitudes of the college students in India. *Journal of Comparative Family Studies, 7,* 433–453.

Saroja, K., & Surendra, H. S. (1991). A study of postgraduate students' endogamous preference in mate selection. *Indian Journal of Behavior, 15,* 1–13.

Schwartz, S. H., & Bilsky, W. (1987). Toward a universal psychological structure of human values. *Journal of Personality and Social Psychology, 53,* 550–562.

Segal, U. A. (1991). Cultural variables in Asian Indian families. *Families in Society, 74,* 233–242.

Segal, U. A. (1998). Career choice correlates: An Indian perspective. *Indian Journal of Social Work, 69,* 338–348.

Sex Education, Counseling Research Training and Therapy. (1993). Attitudes of youth towards marriage, partner selection, and dowry. *Journal of Family Welfare, 39,* 7–18.

Shangle, S. C. (1995). A view into the family and social life of India. *Family Perspective, 29,* 423–446.

Sprecher, S., & Chandak, R. (1992). Attitudes about arranged marriages and dating among men and women from India. *Free Inquiry in Creative Sociology, 20,* 59–69.

Sriram, R., & Verma, A. (1992). *Women and families in transition: The Indian situation.* Alexandria, VA: International Federation of the Home Economics.

Srivastava, S. (1995). Family, deviance, and delinquency. *Trends in Social Science Research, 2,* 95–96.

Stutely, T. (2001, February 24). First marriage, then love in India. *Daily Telegraph.* (London)

Sue, D. W. (1981). *Counseling the culturally different.* New York: John Wiley.

Suman, H. C. (1990). Some antecedents of mate selection: An experimental study on perception of spouse. *International Journal of Psychology in the Orient, 33,* 123–127.

Sureender, S., Prabakaran, B., & Khan, A. G. (1998). Mate selection and its impact on female marriage age, pregnancy wastages, and first child survival in Tamil Nadu, India. *Journal of Social Biology, 45,* 289–302.

Triandis, H. C. (1983). *Collectivism vs. individualism.* Champaign-Urbana: University of Illinois Press.

Triandis, H. C. (1990). Cross-cultural studies of individualism and collectivism. In J. Berman (Ed.), *Nebraska Symposium on Motivation* (pp. 41–133), Lincoln: University of Nebraska Press.

Triandis, H. C., Bontempo, R., Villareal, M. J., Asai, M., & Lucca, N. (1988). Individualism and collectivism: Cross-cultural perspective on self in group relationships. *Journal of Personality and Social Psychology, 19,* 323–338.

Umadevi, L., Venkataramaiah, P., & Srinivasulu, R. (1992). A comparative study on the concept of marriage by professional and non-professional degree students. *Indian Journal of Behavior, 16,* 27–37.

Uplaonkar, A. T. (1995). The emerging rural youth: A study of their changing values towards marriage. *Indian Journal of Social Work, 56,* 415–423.

Verma, J. (1989). Marriage opinion survey and collectivism. *Psychological Studies, 34,* 141–150.

13

The Transition of Courtship, Mate Selection, and Marriage in China

Yan R. Xia

Zhi G. Zhou

Daolin Yang, 77, a grandfather, is retired and lives in Hebei Province, China. In 1940, at 15 years of age, he married his wife, Yufen, then 13, in a village. Yufen's father was a rich farmer and a longtime friend of Daolin's father, who was a Chinese medical doctor, an occupation that provides both money and fame. A matchmaker proposed the marriage on behalf of the Yang family. Yufen's father accepted it. Daolin had not seen his fiancée until the wedding when he lifted up the red veil that covered her head. They have been married for 62 years and reared three children. "Mutual respect and caring" is how Daolin describes their marriage. He says that they married first and dated later. It is "cold at the start but hot in the end." He does not approve of "modern marriage" marked by free choice. "It's just the opposite," he says. "It starts hot but ends cold. That's why there are so many divorces today."

This was one of the stories heard by the authors during their 2002 study examining the perceptions of Chinese mate selection and marital values. The stories of the Yang family's three generations illustrate the dramatic changes in modern Chinese marriage.

231

"Men and women should marry when they come of age." As this old Chinese proverb suggests, courtship, mate selection, and marriage are natural human behaviors fundamentally governed by biological laws. The expectations that one has for a potential spouse and the way in which a marriage partner is chosen, however, are greatly influenced by social norms and conventions. The criteria for an ideal mate may vary not only from culture to culture but also within one culture as time goes by.

Mate Selection Process

China has 1.2 billion people and 267 million families. Each year, approximately 10 million people get married. The legal years of age for marriage are 22 for males and 20 for females. For first marriages, the average age is between 22 and 23 years. The average age is somewhat lower in rural areas and somewhat higher in the cities (Chen, 1997).

History has witnessed tremendous social and economic changes in China during the past 50 years. These changes have had a great impact on the lives of the Chinese people. Traditional beliefs have been challenged, and conventional marriage customs have been questioned or abolished. Marriage has gone through a process of reforms from prearrangement to free choice. Mate selection criteria and the decision-making process have also changed dramatically as a result of social, economic, and political transformations.

The Feudalist Society Before 1949

For thousands of years before the 20th century, marriage had been primarily prearranged in China. Whom to marry was more a parental decision than an individual choice. Typically, the parents chose the potential spouse for their child with the help of a professional matchmaker. The arrangement was generally made before the child entered puberty and sometimes even before the child was born.

> This form of mate choice is more common when extended kin groups are strong and important. Essentially, marriage is seen as of group, rather than individual, importance, and economics is often the driving force rather than love between the principals. (Ingoldsby, 1995, p. 145)

A matchmaker was usually a married elderly woman who knew the birthday, temperament, and appearance of every unmarried man and woman in her community. She would constantly visit families with children ready for marriage and propose potential mates. If a young woman's parents were interested in a man the matchmaker proposed, the matchmaker would meet the man's parents and tell them about the young woman. Like a real estate agent or broker, the matchmaker would be rewarded with hefty gifts or money if parents on both sides were willing to "tie the nuptial knot." A professional matchmaker was noted for her broad network, good relationships with the target households, and strong "people skills."

The basic rule for matchmaking was *men dang hu dui,* that is, to match families of the same social and economic status. The rule was not strictly observed, however, because matchmaking was profit driven and the matchmaker's income was associated with the number of successful marriages promoted. She would not hesitate to exaggerate the facts about a young man or woman in her introduction, telling the respective parents how beautiful and obedient a young woman was and how much wealth and talent a young man had.

The matchmaker would obtain the year, month, date, and time of the young woman's birth from her parents if they approved of the candidate and then would take the information to the parents of the man. The information would be written on a piece of paper and placed on the man's family ancestral altar for 3 days. If no ominous thing happened, such as breaking a bone or catching cold in the family, the parents of the man would proceed to consult a Chinese astrologer to see whether the young man's and woman's signs of the zodiac were a compatible match for each other. If it turned out to be a bad horoscope, there would be no further contact between the two families. If all went well with the young people's fortune, the man's family would give the same information about his birth to the woman's parents, who in turn would repeat the process. The matchmaker could at least save face or avoid embarrassment for the parents in case a rejection had to be made. A matchmaker was often well liked as a person by many for her warmhearted and caring nature. But as an occupation that was full of superstition and manipulation, matchmaking was generally despised and often equalized with professions such as witchcraft.

Love and marriage were not inextricably tied together. Marriage did not mean that two people fell in love and decided to exchange vows to become lifelong partners. Marriage was first utilitarian, that is, valued as an important way in which to extend family ties. China's patrilineal kinship system regarded the husband's foremost role in the family as having male children to carry on the family name and ancestral line. Therefore, a marriage was conducted to continue the family heritage rather than to please the individuals involved (Baker, 1979).

In a self-reliant economy, an extended family often functioned as the basic economic entity as a result of scarce resources. It was a common practice for several generations of the extended family to live and work together in a male-dominated hierarchical system. Therefore, mate selection was viewed as too important a task to be left to the young, especially when they had little contact with the opposite sex in their age group. Parents believed that with their experience, they could help their children find appropriate mates. The young, with little financial independence and decision-making power, could do nothing but follow their parents' decisions.

"A man marries a woman's pretty face, while a woman marries a man's smart head." This old Chinese saying illustrates the longtime criteria by which parents searched for their children's spouses. To carry on the family line, a woman was first valued for her potential ability to produce and care for children expressed in youth and physical attractiveness. Men, on the other hand, needed to show a potential to provide valuable resources for the offspring in a poverty-stricken economy.

Children were taught from an early age that a man and a woman could not enter into an intimate relationship without a formal introduction etiquette procedure performed by a matchmaker. They needed to accept their fates and take whoever their parents chose as their wives or husbands. Once they were married, the marriages would be sealed forever. A virtuous husband could marry more than one wife but should not disgrace his wife and her family by divorcing her. A chaste wife would remain faithful to her husband and would not remarry even after his death.

The Socialist Society After 1949

The custom of arranged marriages was legally abolished by the Marriage Law passed in 1950, a year after the foundation of the People's Republic of China. The element of no-fault divorce was added in 1980 when this marriage law was amended during the third session of the Fifth National People's Congress ("Evolution of the Marriage Law," 2001). The change reflected the emphasis on freedom of choice and the quality of the marital relationship that was brought about by social and economic reforms. In 2001, no substantial revision was made after a heated debate of whether the law should be amended to curb the rapid increase in the Chinese divorce rate.

The government's first marriage law stipulated the following:

The feudal marriage based on arbitrary and compulsory arrangements and the supremacy of man over woman, and in disregard of the interests of the children, is abolished.

The New-Democratic marriage system, which is based on the free choice of partners, on monogamy, on equal rights for both sexes, and on the protection of the lawful interests of women and children, is put into effect. (*Marriage Law*, 1950, General Principle section, para. 1–2)

One goal of the new marriage law was to shift the power over the marital decision making from the extended family to the individual. The government promoted love and mutual companionship as major criteria in mate selection (Pimentel, 2000). Traditions die hard, however, especially in the rural areas. Arranged marriages greatly decreased in number, especially in the urban areas, by the end of the 1950s. However, the practice continued among farmers, who made up more than two thirds of the country's population. A 1996 survey found that 43.1% of the marriages taking place in the rural areas before 1959 were decided by the parents (Shen, Yang, & Li, 1999). Another study reported that the rate of parent-decided marriages was as high as 74.9% in rural areas of Gangsu, a northwest province, from 1967 to 1976 (Xu, 1998).

Apart from the new marriage law and family policies, the government helped to abolish the traditional marriage system by promoting gender equality and encouraging women to join the labor force. From the beginning of the 1950s, the traditional family economic system was replaced by a collective economy in the country. Farmers living in the same area formed communes where they worked together on the commonly owned fields. The harvest was distributed based on the labor provided by each household. Enticed by the government's policy of "equal jobs and equal pay," many women, particularly unmarried women, began to work outside the home to contribute to their families' income. In urban areas, many large state-owned enterprises were established and job opportunities were created. Young people, both rural and urban, began to enjoy not only economic freedom but also a broader social circle in which to meet each other. As a result, dramatic changes took place in the shift from an arranged marriage system to a pattern of greater freedom of choice (Whyte, 1990; Xu & Whyte, 1990).

The courtship-marriage practice from the early 1950s to the late 1970s was marked by two characteristics. First, parents had less control over their children's marriages. Arranged marriage still existed, especially in the remote rural villages, but it became less common and less acceptable. Parents generally still reserved the right to approve or veto their children's marital choices, but they had to take their children's opinions into consideration. A study of who made the final marital decisions showed that before 1959, 6.3% marriages in the city of Shanghai and 31.2% of those in Qingpu (a neighboring rural district) were the joint decisions of parents and children. In 1989, these rates increased to 18.8% and 41.2%, respectively (Shen et. al., 1999).

Second, mate selection was greatly affected by the political and social environment. The political background of an individual and his or her family became a primary concern in courtship, especially in the cities. From 1949 to 1987, China was flooded by a series of nationwide political campaigns. The government initiated these campaigns to strengthen its power and socialist system and to purge potential saboteurs. Each movement, while labeling certain groups as "anti-revolutionaries" (a synonym for political enemies), made other groups favorites. Family background and political identity became crucially important in deciding whether an individual could be admitted to a college, employed, or recruited by the military. People with the government's trust and protection were more likely to have secure and successful careers, thereby ensuring income and privileges.

During the 1950s, cadres of the Chinese Communist Party were on the top of the "most desirable" list of young women. They were preferred for their political standing, good incomes, and upright personalities (Xia, 2000). Technicians and workers, especially those in railway transportation, big state-owned enterprises, and military factories, became women's favorites during the 1960s. Apart from having secure jobs and great fringe benefits, they were regarded as the leading class with superior political and social status. Military officers and soldiers dominated the list during the 1970s. They could help their spouses' families move to urban areas, thereby providing a great improvement in living conditions. With the government's tight residency control policy, such moves were very difficult at that time. The spouses and parents of servicemen also received government-issued certificates that entitled them to many benefits and privileges. Xu (1998) found that between 1967 and 1976, 54.1% of young people married in the cities ranked family political background and personal political status as the third most important criterion for mate selection, after health and reliability.

The marriage of Songlan, Daolin's daughter, is an example of political tragedy. She was a high school Chinese teacher when she met and fell in love with a chemistry teacher working at the same school during the mid-1970s. Songlan told her parents about him and that he proposed to marry her. At that time, China was engaged in the "Great Cultural Revolution" and the educated were perceived as a threat to the Communist regime. Daolin and his wife rejected this young man because his father, a university professor, was being persecuted as an anti-revolutionary. Songlan threatened to kill herself, but she caved in later for fear that the man's political stigma would ruin the life of her children. Instead, she married a worker for whom she did not have affection but who had higher political status. She said that she was not sure whether her husband loved her. The two have been separated for 5 years. "Living with him was like serving a life sentence in prison," said Songlan. She wanted to divorce but was not sure of the consequences.

The Modern Society After 1978

Unprecedented changes have taken place in China since 1978, when the large-scale social and economic reforms began. The state-controlled economic system gave way to a market economy. Being rich was no longer equated with being anti-revolutionary. In fact, the government headed by Deng Xiao-Ping issued a policy encouraging some people living in the coastal areas to get rich first so as to become role models for people in the other areas to follow. Wealth replaced political status as the primary yardstick for success. Privately owned businesses mushroomed in the coastal areas, prompting an exodus of young people looking for job opportunities. The increased mobility enabled the young people to make not only more money but also more friends. People became more respectful of individual choice and more lenient toward diverse behaviors concerning dating and marriage. The values and beliefs of the young were greatly influenced by Western cultures through books, newspapers, radio, television, and other public channels. A demand for the emancipation of humanity emerged in terms of human rights, individualism, and sexual liberation. The central government, although disapproving of some socially deviant attitudes and behaviors, was very tolerant in policymaking and law enforcement.

The revised Marriage Law in 1980 explicitly stated that marriage should be based on mutual affection and that divorce should be granted with complete alienation of mutual affection (*Marriage Law*, 1980, Divorce section, para. 3). This was the first time in Chinese history that a person was allowed no-fault divorce by law. Chen (2002) observed, "The ethical foundation of marriage has shifted from the family's stability to the individual's happiness. Marriage is seen as a purely personal matter" (p. 11). Chinese began to enjoy the unprecedented freedom in choosing who to date and marry. Divorce became more acceptable than it was previously, although it was still a stigma. Sex, premarital cohabitation, and trial marriage became less a taboo. A 1990 national survey involving more than 20,000 respondents in 15 provinces revealed that 30% of the Chinese youth engaged in premarital sex and that 86% approved of premarital sexual behavior (Liu, 1998).

In terms of mate selection criteria, wealth, advanced academic degrees, and body height are most important for Chinese women today (Chen, 2002).

Chinese men are more attracted to women who are beautiful, healthy, gentle, chaste, and youthful (Xu, 1990). Beautiful women and smart men, the traditional criteria of Chinese mate selection, still hold today. However, they are not the only factors that people consider when they choose their mates. Women have higher expectations for men's emotional commitment. They want quality marriages with high emotional compatibility, sexual enjoyment, and freedom to act independently. They want husbands with great self-cultivation, social status, reputation, and wealth, although most women no longer depend on their husbands for material survival (Chen, 2002).

The new concepts of love permeate the story of Xinyi, Daolin's grand-daughter, a 23-year-old college senior majoring in finance. She had her first date when she was 18 years old. She had dated a dozen young men—"good enough to know what I want from a husband." She had dated her current boyfriend for 4 months, and she thought that she would marry him if he proposed to her. He was a marketing graduate who had just been hired by a German food processing company. He was offered a good starting salary of 60,000 YMB (approximately $7,317 U.S.) per year with great benefits, including a bonus, medical and dental insurance, and vacation time. Xinyi said that she did not want to marry him for his money given that he was a poor college student when the two first met. But she agreed with her college roommates that men should be more responsible for family financial security. "Love and money are not enemies," Xinyi said. She appreciated the fact that he earned more than three times her salary (18,000 RMB or approximately $2,195 U.S.), which she considered average. She dreamed of buying her own apartment and a car by the time she married. She believed that she could realize her dream and marry in less than 5 years. "Knowledge is money," she said. She had great confidence in her boyfriend's ability to provide financial security for the family.

According to Xinyi, she was not attracted to her boyfriend because of his income. "Love and mutual affection brought us together," she said. Their romance started at a college dance. He was "charming," and she "had a crush on his smile." She felt that he was the man she had been looking for when he asked her to dance. She expressed, "He made me crazy. I felt so much loved and treasured." They have been together since then. They rented an apartment and lived together. Neither her parents nor her grandparents liked the idea of a trial marriage, but it did not bother Xinyi because "it is about my marriage and my future, not theirs anyway."

Cohabitation is not popular among Chinese of Xinyi's age. However, her emphasis on love and affection within the couple relationship may well reflect the value of her generation.

Courtship and Engagement

Dating used to be a very serious matter in China. Asking someone for a date was perceived as a marriage proposal. Multiple dating was generally disapproved of and was viewed as frivolous and as inappropriate behavior. A study of 586 women who married between 1933 and 1987 showed that more than 90% had never considered marrying any other persons besides their husbands and that more than 70% had not had other boyfriends (Xu & Whyte, 1990).

Nowadays, most young people meet at school, at work, or through a mutual friend (Xu, 1997). During the authors' recent investigation, some urban young people reported that they first met their dates through Internet chat rooms. Jiang was a second-year graduate student of computer science at a university in Beijing. He expressed that he and some young people he knew started dating through the Internet. He said, "You can be honest when you start through the Internet. You don't need to hide anything. If the other person is still interested in you given your weaknesses, you can think of sending a picture and arranging the first meeting in a public place." Dating through the Internet began during the late 1990s when using computers became popular among college students.

Xu An-Qi, a renowned Chinese marriage researcher, surveyed more than 3,200 married couples at four different regions in China (Xu, 1997). She found that 80.4% of the surveyed couples from Shanghai, a developed metropolitan city, met at school, at work, or through mutual friends, whereas only 37.2% of those from Gansu, an underdeveloped rural inland province, met in this way. In contrast, 12.5% of the couples from Shanghai were neighbors or were introduced by relatives when they began dating, whereas this was the case with 45.3% of the couples from Gansu. Overall, dating classmates and colleagues or dating people met through friends increased, whereas dating neighbors or people met through relatives decreased, over the past 30 years. Higher percentages of dating through a person's social network were observed in the more developed economic area, whereas lower percentages were noted in the underdeveloped area. Higher percentages of dating through kinship connections were observed in the underdeveloped area, whereas lower percentages were found in the more developed economic area (Table 13.1).

Although many youth experience their first loves in high school, it is very difficult to develop these first loves into serious relationships. The young people can hardly acknowledge their relationship openly. "Early love" or dating is forbidden by parents and prohibited by school authorities because they believe that it will distract the adolescents from their schoolwork. Young

Table 13.1   Social Networks for Mate Selection During Various Time Periods
(percentages)

Social Network	Time Period of Marriage				
	Until 1966	1967–1976	1977–1986	1987–1996	Total
Kinship	46.1	39.5	31.7	27.2	33.6
Neighbor	26.2	26.7	20.3	15.8	20.9
Friend	27.1	32.8	47.5	56.2	44.4
Other	0.6	0.4	0.3	0.2	0.2
Total	100	100	100	100	100
	(n = 477)	(n = 613)	(n = 1,013)	(n = 2,866)	(N = 6,032)

SOURCE: Adapted from Xu (1997, p. 43).

NOTE: Kinship = family members and relatives. Neighbor = neighbors. Friend = classmates, teachers, coworkers, colleagues, friends, and acquaintances.

people cannot find good jobs without college degrees. The competitiveness of the national college entrance examination leads to a demanding curriculum at the high school level. Love has to wait so as to ensure a successful passage to college.

College, however, is a love haven. For the first time in life, young people are free to pursue love relationships. The education environment provides more opportunities for the young people to meet. Students of the same major are divided into classes varying from a dozen to a hundred in number, depending on the availability of teachers and facilities. People in the same class often hang around together during their college years, taking the same classes and doing lots of extracurricular activities together. Most of them live in the school dormitories and eat in the cafeterias. As a result, they get to know each other fairly well after 1 or 2 years of college. Love relationships often evolve during the senior year of school. In the meantime, many couples break up because either the partners find that they now know each other too well to keep the attraction they had for each other before or they realize that they cannot be together after graduation.

Young people enjoy more freedom to express their affection than did those before the economic and social reforms that started in 1978. They can openly express their love by holding hands and hugging. People are rarely seen kissing in public because it goes against the Chinese behavior code of reservation. Sex and cohabitation are no longer taboos for many young people. They can rent an apartment off campus if they can afford it. Premarital sex is a hot topic of debate on campus. More and more students think that sex is justifiable if it is based on love. Before the mid-1980s, kissing and holding hands on campus were rarely seen and could be prohibited by student codes. Disciplinary actions could be imposed on those who violated the conduct codes. In the case of a pregnancy, both the man and the woman could face expulsion from school. Today, students are seldom disciplined for dating, but school authorities generally discourage it. Many parents approve of college courtship and believe that college is a place where their children may have many excellent mate choices given that fewer than half of high school graduates can pass the national college entrance examinations and go on to college.

If a young man or woman cannot find a mate in college or at work on his or her own, the whole network of parents, relatives, friends, and coworkers will be motivated to help. They will stay busy, like the matchmakers of the past, out of a sense of obligation or concern as relatives or friends of the young people or their parents. They often work in pairs, with one knowing the man and the other knowing the woman. They help to set up the first meeting if the man and woman involved agree to meet after seeing pictures and learning the basic information about each other. The first meeting is often short and is set up at a public area such as a park, a restaurant, or the home of a warmhearted matchmaker. The man and woman are formally introduced and left alone. They have a short talk and then later tell the go-between whether they want to meet again or not. If they feel good about each other and decide to start dating, they can get each other's telephone or cellular phone number through their mutual friends. Another round of searching will kick off if they do not want to continue.

The dating period in China is generally short, from a few months to 1 or 2 years. Most of the young couples the authors interviewed had dated for less than 2 years. One of the main reasons is that the young lovers can rarely live together unless they get married. Premarital cohabitation is a new phenomenon that is not easily accepted by the parents. The majority of the authors' interviewees started cohabitation after engagement. Many state-owned businesses and institutions provide subsidized housing only for the married couples. Some young lovers today want to delay marriage and save more money to help pay for commercial housing and the wedding expenses.

Age, financial resources, education, and trust seem to determine what the young lovers do while dating. In their study, the authors found that adolescents like to go to discotheques and movie theaters. College students, although often thronging the weekend dances on campus, visit these places only occasionally because they generally have tight budgets and do not like the choices of music and movies. Window shopping is popular with new couples. The partners will walk, talk, pick up some knickknacks, and eat at inexpensive restaurants or buy food from street vendors. They are cautious not to invest too much money before they are sure about their relationships. Parks, movie theaters, and restaurants are for those who have gained a level of trust. Serious lovers with financial resources favor traveling. Traveling is easier now, with two major week-long national holidays available.

A young man and woman will formally introduce each other to their respective parents after they get serious about their relationship. This is an important occasion. The parents will invite the young couple to their homes and treat them to grand dinners. The parents may receive some precious gifts in return from their potential son-in-law or daughter-in-law. Although parents' opinions on the prospective marriage do not carry as much weight as they did previously, they are always respected and seriously considered. The parents' disapproval of the marriage, although rare, can complicate the relationship.

Formal proposals rarely happen because they are not a Chinese matrimonial custom. Although a young man and woman are legally married the moment they obtain a marriage certificate from the government office, according to the secular view or custom, they are just engaged when they get the marriage certificate. Engagement celebrations are simple in the cities. The prospective bride and groom will treat their friends to a nice meal at a restaurant and receive congratulatory gifts and money. Engagement is more formally celebrated in the rural areas. In the authors' study, one interviewee who came from a village said that young couples usually express their appreciation to the people who connect them with gifts and money and invite all of the village officials, relatives, friends, and neighbors to a lavish meal. Besides gifts and money from the guests, the future daughter-in-law receives 5,000 RMB (approximately $610 U.S.) from her fiancé's parents. The interviewee said the woman always took the money, whether the fiancé's family needed the money more than hers or not, because she was afraid of being belittled if she did not.

Wedding

To regulate marriage and birth, the central government requires people who plan to marry to officially register with the local government. The government officials check their legal ages and their premarital physical checkup reports before issuing a marriage certificate. The physical examination is intended to check for any unknown or inheritable serious health problems. The man and woman are legally married once they get the certificate.

Groom and Bride in Traditional Costume

The first important thing that a young couple will do is take wedding photos months before the wedding. In these expensive glamour shots, the prospective bride wears a *qipao* (wedding gown), a traditional long dress for women, whereas the groom wears a *magua* (suit), an old-fashioned Manchu jacket for men. Afterward, there is planning for housing and the marriage ceremony as well as shopping for furniture and clothes. Housing may be a problem for young couples living in the urban areas. More commercial housing is available now, but the price is generally beyond their

Car Used to Take Bride to Join Groom's Family

incomes. Many live with their parents until they have their own apartments. Some live in dormitories provided for single employees. One study reported that 65% of couples in Shanghai would have liked to live alone after marriage but that only 33% could do so. The majority (54%) had to live with their parents due to housing problems (Shen et al., 1999).

It is a custom that the groom and his family take care of all the wedding expenses, although the bride's family may help with some furniture and clothes. From 1990 to 1998, the average expenses for a wedding were 31,383 RMB (approximately $3,900 U.S.) in Shanghai and 23,155 RMB (approximately $2,900 U.S.) in Qingpu, a rural area close to Shanghai (Shen et al., 1999). This is a lot of money for families with average incomes. Parents start saving early for their children's weddings.

Modern weddings tend to mix the latest fashion with traditional rituals. In the past, an astrologer would consult the Chinese astrological calendar and pick an auspicious wedding date. Today, many weddings are scheduled on the "lucky days" by the Chinese lunar calendar. For example, August 8, 2000, was considered to be a lucky day not only because all of the numbers are even—symbolizing double happiness—but also because the number *eight* (*ba*) sounds similar to *prosperity* (*fa*) in Chinese. During earlier times, the bride was carried to the groom's home in a decorated sedan chair by four or eight people. Today, the groom picks her up by car. On the wedding day, a fancy motorcade drives to the home of the bride's parents to pick up the bride early in the morning. The cars are decorated with fresh flowers and "double happiness" paper cutouts. At the door, the brides-maids tease the groom by asking him to answer many funny questions and to perform a series of mischievous tests to prove himself worthy of his bride. For example, he may be asked to sing out his love in front of many people and to drink something that tastes horrible. He will be allowed to enter the house and meet the bride only after he has passed the tests and given the mischievous bridesmaids enough *hongbao* (little red paper bags full of cash). The groom may get help or hints from his close friends who go with him if he has trouble passing the tests.

A typical wedding is held at a fancy restaurant. The ceremony starts with the bride and groom marching to the front in a Western wedding gown and suit, respectively. Firecrackers are fired to greet the young couple and "scare off any evil spirits." The wedding is often presided over by a gentle-man who is a close friend of the couple or their families. He also helps to organize all of the preparations and activities. A marriage witness from the family planning department of the local government may be invited to announce the union of the couple. The bride and groom will be led to three bows: one to their parents, one to each other, and one to the guests. Then the bride's father and the groom's father each may make a short speech, thanking the guests and giving their good wishes to their children. The cer-emony often ends with the bride and groom drinking *jiaobeijiu* (marriage wines) with their arms entwined. Each of them may be asked to call the other's parents "mother" and "father" and to get hongbao in return as the parents' wedding gift. A large feast follows, with wines and dozens of courses full of traditional dishes symbolizing happiness and prosperity.

China covers a large territory and has 56 ethnicities. Courtship and mar-riage rituals may vary from ethnicity to ethnicity and from region to region. The majority of the population lives in the rural areas, where traditional values and customs are more maintained. The customs just discussed are more from the urban and northern perspectives. Chinese mate formation and marriage have gone through a process of reforms, from prearrange-ment to free choice, over the past 50 years. Mate selection criteria and the decision-making process have changed dramatically as a result of social, economic, and political transformations. Statistics and stories show the patterns and changes in Chinese mate selection.

References

Baker, H. (1979). *Chinese family and kinship*. London: Macmillan.

Chen, X. (1997). Chinese marriages and families: Social changes are affecting Chinese marriages and households. *China Today, 46*(5), 18–20.

Chen, X. (2002). Women and marriage in China. *China Today, 51*(3), 10–17.

Evolution of the marriage law. (2001, March 15). *Beijing Review*. [Online]. Retrieved April 16, 2003, from www.beijingreview.com.cn/index11.htm

Ingoldsby, B. B. (1995). Mate selection and marriage. In B. Ingoldsby & S. Smith (Eds.), *Families in multicultural perspective* (pp. 143–160). New York: Guilford.

Liu, D. (1998). *Zhongguo dangdai xin wenhua: Zhongguo liangwanli "xingwenhua" diaochabaogao, disanban* (Sexual behavior in modern China: Report of the nationwide "sex civilization" survey in China) (3rd ed.). Shanghai, China: Sanlian Press.

Marriage Law. (1950). The Seventh Session of the Standing Committee of the Central People's Government. Retrieved October 29, 2002, from www. law.duke.edu/curriculum/coursehomepages/spring2001/508_01/marriage_law 5080.pdf

Marriage Law. (1980). The Third Session of the Fifth National People's Congress. Retrieved October 29, 2002, from www.law.duke.edu/curriculum/course-homepages/spring2001/508_01/marriage_law5080.pdf

Pimentel, E. E. (2000). Just how do I love thee? Marital relations in urban China. *Journal of Marriage and Family, 69*, 32–47.

Shen, C., Yang, S., & Li, D. (1999). *Shiji zhijiao de chengxiang jiating* (Urban and rural families at the turn of the century). Beijing, China: Social Science Press.

Whyte, M. K. (1990). Changes in mate selection in Chengdu, China. In D. Davis & E. Vogel (Eds.), *Chinese society on the eve of Tiananmen* (pp. 181–213). Cambridge, MA: Harvard University Press.

Xia, L. (2000). Love and marriage in China. *China Today, 49*(5), 28–35.

Xu, A. (1997). *Sijizhijao zhongguoren de aiqing he hunyin* (The Chinese love and marriage at the turn of the century). Beijing, China: Chinese Social Science Press.

Xu, A. (1998). Zhuanxingqi zhongguoren de aiqing he hunyin (Love and marriage of the Chinese at the time of transition). In A. G. Fan (Ed.), *Zhuanxingqi zhongguoren de aiqing he hunyin* (pp. 46–64). Beijing, China: Chinese Women's Press.

Xu, Z. (1990, Autumn). China's unmarried millions. *Nexus: China in Focus*, pp. 48–51.

Xu, X., & Whyte, M. K. (1990). Love matches and arranged marriages: A Chinese replication. *Journal of Marriage and the Family, 52*, 709–722.

14

Multiplicity of Paths to Couple Formation in Japan

Colleen I. Murray

Naoko Kimura

Ayumi met her husband, Kazuyuki, in college. They have a lot in common; both majored in pre-law, have similar political views, and enjoy traveling overseas. She is 3 years older than Kazuyuki. Ayumi says that they were very much in love when they married. They did not have a wedding ceremony; they just signed the marriage license paper and registered it with the city government.

Ayumi's sister, Minako, moved to Tokyo for employment. There, she dated one man for 7 years, but despite their love for each other, the high demands of their jobs got in the way and the relationship ended. Shortly afterward, she met the man she was to marry, Kouichi, through her friends from work. They all met together at a local restaurant, much like a "blind date." The couple had been dating for 2 months when she found out that she was pregnant. Minako, 29 years of age, viewed her pregnancy as en (a sign of their fate to marry each other). She believed that real love could grow over the years after they got married. Kouichi agonized over what to do because he was recently divorced and not ready to marry. A month later, he decided that he wanted to marry Minako. They had a small wedding in a restaurant in her hometown with just their relatives present.

Hiroyuki, Ayumi and Minako's brother, says that he is ready to marry but cannot take the time to go about finding the right person. He has used

Internet dating services and looked for a partner via e-mail through online discussion groups that share his interest in skiing and "J-pop" (Japanese popular) music. So far, he has not found anyone interested in the kind of dating that could lead to marriage; they are only interested in deto (dating just for fun). When he finally finds a partner, Hiroyuki expects to have a Christian wedding, even though he is not Christian himself. He expects to ask his boss and his wife to fill the role of honored nakodo at the wedding and during the years afterward, when this respected married couple will continue to serve as role models and sources of marital guidance.

Ayumi, Minako, and Hiroyuki's cousin, Sachiko, was introduced to her husband, Takuya, by a relative. Their two families met formally for dinner, during which time either the couple or their families could have rejected the arrangement. This was the sixth man Sachiko was introduced to in this manner; the first five were not acceptable to her. After this meeting, they dated for 2 years before he proposed to her. He gave her a ring and she gave him an ink pen. They had an elaborate engagement party where Takuya's family gave money to Sachiko and her parents to purchase a dresser and large bureau that she would be expected to fill with her things to bring with her after the wedding when she became a part of his family. Their Buddhist-style wedding 6 months later was followed by a traditional, expensive reception party during which Sachiko changed into three different styles of rented wedding costumes (each with an accompanying hairstyle), ending with a Western-style wedding dress.

Grandmother Ina's experiences before World War II had been quite different from those of her grandchildren today. During her young adulthood, transportation was expensive and quite limited, so most people married individuals from nearby. Ina legally married her first cousin. She met her husband once before the wedding day at a formal meeting of their families. Her wedding was at home and was not religious; instead, it could be described as "in front of people" (getting their approval), with all relatives and neighbors attending. On the wedding day, Ina said to her sister, "I am not sure which one I am marrying. I hope my husband is a good-looking one." Ina did not receive a wedding ring. She has been a widow for 10 years, but she has no interest in dating or remarrying. None of her widowed friends has remarried; they prefer each other's company to that of men.

As the above scenarios indicate, the desire for close intimate relationships is evident in Japan. This family demonstrates that although there are many possible paths taken during the couple formation process, the typical end point is marriage. The beliefs and practices related to marriage have undergone many changes during Japan's long recorded history. The concept of couple formation as a private experience involving two individuals has not been a dominant pattern; rather, it was seen as the union of two groups or families. During the period from the Heian era through the Edo era (794 to 1868 CE), marriage was a custom represented in the form of a ceremony (Kaku, 1999). Only since 1868 has marriage been a legal status requiring registration. During the later half of the 20th century, marriage was nearly universal in Japan; it was viewed as an essential stage in the transition to mature responsible adulthood (Goldman, 1993). Today, there is less social stigma attached to people who are not married, particularly in the cities. In Japan, marriage is not primarily for religious purposes; rather, it is to fulfill one's needs (emotional or economic) or the needs of one's family. Other types of dyadic relationships (e.g., same-sex couples, cohabiting couples) are not legally recognized, although there have been calls to acknowledge diversity in coupled relationships (Yoshizumi, 1994).

In the past, people usually married because it was what was expected of nearly everyone. Today, they marry for a variety of reasons, including financial stability, emotional/psychological stability, love, family expectations, becoming part of society, and having a family. The Japanese people recognize both the pros and the cons of marriage, including its ability to provide psychological tranquility, create more responsibility, provide an opportunity for experiencing the joy of raising children, and prevent partners from doing what they enjoy doing individually (Takeishi, 1998).

Several recent trends related to marriage began during the late 1970s. Although most people choose to marry, there has been a steady rise in the proportion of young adults (ages 20 to 34 years) who are remaining single (Yamada, 1999, 2000). These unmarried young adults comprise approximately 10% of the Japanese population. The reason they often give for not being married is that they have not met the person they want to marry yet and do not feel a need to rush into marriage when they are unsure of their choice of partner (Institute of Population Problems, 1994). It is not yet clear whether they will eventually marry or continue to remain single throughout adulthood (Raymo, 1998). However, Japan's Ministry of Health and Welfare has predicted that 14% of women born after 1980 will never marry (Conover & Gaouette, 1997). Among those who do marry, the percentage of same-age couples has increased and the percentage of couples in which the wife is older has doubled during the past decade, accounting for more than 23% of marriages today. The husband is older in less than 60% of new marriages today. The legal age for marriage is 16 years for females and 18 for males. However, the age at which people enter their first marriage in

Japan has increased dramatically. The average age of first marriage in 1950 was 23 years for women and 26 for men; today, it is approximately 27 years for women and 29 for men. These trends may be related to the following factors: recent economic problems and high unemployment (especially among young adults), an increase in women's economic independence and higher expectations for one's partner as more women are employed, the freedom that comes with the single life, the fact that women today view marriage as a less desirable alternative, the lack of pressure to hurry into marriage given the long life span in Japan, the desire to enjoy romance freely, the desire to give more importance to oneself rather than to family, encouragement from family members to continue living with one's parents, and the *kekkon kanbatsu* ("marriage drought" or lack of available acceptable men) (Applbaum, 1995; Hirano, Sodei, & Kin, 2000; Lester, 1996; Sugiyama, 2001).

Cultural Context

Japan has typically been represented as a collectivistic society with a focus on subordinating one's personal goals to the goals of the group or family (Hatfield & Sprecher, 1995), adjusting one's behavior to avoid interpersonal conflicts at all costs so as to maintain harmony (Nakanishi, 1998), responding based on pragmatism rather than on principles (Iwao, 1993), and accommodating to the context of a specific situation and with an aversion to absolutes. In contrast, the United States has been identified as predominantly a society centered on the individual, based on the belief that personal goals take preference over integration of people into stronger cohesive groups and that conflict (which is viewed as potentially healthy) is inevitable. From this perspective, social behaviors of individuals in the United States (including those who are dating or married) would be primarily for the purpose of influencing a situation, whereas the behaviors of individuals in Japan would be primarily for the purpose of adjusting to the current situation (Kitayama, 2000). If these representations are accurate, we would expect to see the couple formation process in Japan emphasizing accommodation to the needs of one's partner, empathy, and compliance while minimizing autonomy, verbal expressiveness, and exploration. Recent research suggests that although there is support for these representations, dichotomizing cultures as either individualistic or collectivistic is insufficient because both sets of characteristics are present in the experiences of the majority of couples in Japan (Takahashi, Ohara, Antonucci, & Akiyama, 2002). Most Japanese adults place a high value on the individual, personal happiness, and personal freedom (Prime Minister's Office, 1999), whereas much of the focus in the United States is on the couple rather than on the individual (Kimura & Murray, 1998). Those in Japan who are married indicate that their primary reasons for marriage were that they wanted to have a life together, they were ready for a family, and they believed they had reached the appropriate age for marriage (Takeishi, 1998). Those who are not married indicate not only that they have not met the person they want to marry but also that they want to engage in hobbies and do what they enjoy, their priority is work or study, and single life is easier.

Visitors to Japan report that individualistic and collectivistic beliefs, attitudes, and customs seem to coexist—a situation that, to outsiders, appears to be full of inconsistencies and contradictions. Writers generally assume that the emphasis on the individual (a) emerged in response to Western influences, initially during the 1800s but primarily after World War II when Allied countries helped to rebuild Japan, and (b) increased in response to exposure to European American culture through the recent global technological climate. Such mistaken beliefs have led Western authors to assume that *omiai* or *miai* (arranged marriage), in which the family makes the choice of marriage partner without input from the bride or groom, has been the norm throughout Japanese history and that *ren'ai kekkon* (romantic love marriage), based on attraction to a freely chosen partner, emerged only as Western influence spread during the past century. Today, approximately 90% of marriages are classified as ren'ai kekkon, and 10% are classified as miai. However, a closer look indicates that the reason for this is not that Western influences are overshadowing Japanese traditions but rather that many of these supposedly emerging beliefs and practices coexisted within Japanese civilization long before the spread of post-World War II Western influences. These individualistic and self-expressive values and behaviors appear to be catching on quickly, in part, because they already existed in the long recorded history of Japanese civilization and are just being reinvigorated (Yamazaki, 1994). Early Japanese history (through 645 CE) contained polygamous families (two or more spouses) in which wives and husbands often lived separately and practiced gender equality (Sougou joseishi kenkyuukai, 1992). Until 1186 CE, polygyny (two or more wives) was practiced, sexual abstinence before marriage was not a concern, and husbands married into their wives' families (*muko-iri*). During the 13th and 14th centuries, monogamy became the dominant custom (at least for wives) and wives began to marry into their husbands' families (*yome-iri*), a system that largely survives today. From the 17th to 19th centuries, marriages among the samurai class were arranged by families (with no input from the bride or groom), but commoners typically chose their own spouses (marrying "for love").

It was not until the latter half of the 19th century that arranged marriages spread through all social classes (Kaku, 1999; Sougoou joseishi kenkyuukai, 1992) and marriage changed from being a ceremony to becoming a legal arrangement with wives and husbands having the same family name. These policies were promoted by the Meiji government and emphasized that Japan was "one big family" with the emperor at its head. Prospective marriage partners were brought together by a *nakodo*, whose role was to help the family identify an acceptable compatible partner, participate in the wedding ceremony, and provide guidance for the new couple even during the years after the wedding. During the period from mid-1800 through 1926 (the Meiji and Taisho eras), the ideal of romantic or courtly love, brought by Western Christians, began to emerge; however, it was seen by many in Japan as dangerous, and the value of *ie* (family) had much greater influence when it came to marriage (Notter, 2000). In response, during the early 1900s, men had to be at least 30 years old and women had to be at least 25 to marry without the permission of their parents.

Until World War II, marriage was typically seen as a link between two families rather than as a joining of two individuals; it preserved family lineage and social standing. The Western Christian influence after the war brought a focus on the ideal of romantic love based on individual attractions and an emphasis on sexual purity before marriage for both men and women (Kaku, 1999). By the mid-1960s, romantic love marriages had replaced arranged marriages as the social norm and dating had become the new fashion. Intimacy and public displays of affection were still considered undesirable, in line with the Confucian philosophical teaching that men and women should not mix after 7 years of age. Today, young adults distinguish dating that is just for fun (*deto*) from dating that is leading toward marriage (*otsukiai*), high school students are beginning to show affection in public, and sexual abstinence before marriage is less of a concern (Institute of Population Problems, 1994). With improved transportation and increased urbanization, there are fewer remaining distinct regional traditions related to couple formation.

General beliefs developed over centuries guide behavior and shape couple formation. There is a belief that words cannot adequately explain many matters (Doi, 1986) and that some things have a shared understanding and do not need to be discussed (Iwao, 1993). For example, romantic love, if experienced, is thought of more as an aspect of the new couple relationship. Once there is a commitment, there is more emphasis on the aspects of the relationship that provide assurance, including loyalty, compassion, mind reading, and the support of the couple's social network, with little discussion of the relationship (Rothbaum, Pott, Azuma, Miyake, & Weisz, 2000). In contrast, in the United States, romantic love is assumed to be an ongoing essential element. There is an emphasis on keeping the relationship new and exciting, maintaining passion and intimacy to sustain attraction, and using high levels of verbal communication (even if it is conflictual). Such Western relationships emphasize trust, including the hope and faith that although one's partner could choose other commitments, he or she will remain in the current relationship. It is ironic that Japanese marriages are more stable, whereas Americans try harder to keep the romance alive (Rothbaum et al., 2000).

Another distinction is in the use of the phrase "romantic love marriage." For ease of classification, the Japanese discuss marriage types today as being either arranged (miai) or romantic love marriages, but they know that these dichotomous terms do not represent the actual experiences leading up to marriage. Today's arranged marriages are not strictly arranged by relatives who allow no input from the couple; their partners' feelings for each other are considered. Relatives or a paid nakodo, who is higher in status or age, may be used to bring the young man and woman together. Or, a nakodo may be largely a formality, offered by a man to his boss and spouse, with only the expectation that the nakodo take a special role in the wedding ceremony and be available during the years afterward as a role model and source of marital advice. The couple in a miai may actually be in love at the time of the wedding. In contrast, today's romantic love marriages (ren'ai kekkon) in Japan might not contain romance, love, or passion at the time of the wedding. The term is used to refer to any marriage that is not arranged. The expectation is that love will be nurtured after the wedding. Rather than marrying for romance, the man and woman marry for practical reasons, generally because they like each other and are compatible. The Japanese know that these terms for marriage do not really reflect the reality of the situation, but they are comfortable with them because they have a shared understanding of the concept and know the context without having to speak about it. In English, where words are expected to adequately represent a concept, a Japanese romantic love marriage might be called a "free choice marriage," emphasizing the element of autonomy of choice rather than the romance or love.

Rather than focusing on these variations as inconsistencies, one can view the Japanese as maintaining a pool of many coexisting beliefs, reflecting the fluid multiplicity of self contained within each individual and the culture (Lebra, 1994). As such, Japan is a multiple religious culture (Kumagai, 1995) in which individuals usually identify themselves as both Shinto and

Buddhist, practice a basic moral code of social interaction derived from Confucian philosophy, and partake in Christian festivals and rituals. Thus, although only 1% of Japanese people are Christians, more than 65% of weddings are Christian ceremonies (Abe, 2001).

This multiplicity of self can also be seen in the gender issues related to the pressure to marry today. The stigmatized image of an unmarried woman past the *tekireiki* (marriageable age), "like a stale Christmas cake after 25," seems to be disappearing, particularly in urban areas (Applbaum, 1995; Prime Minister's Office, 1998). However, the image has been replaced with a similar pressure from authors who condemn young singles continuing to live with their parents even after they become adults. Although this trend can be explained in terms of both cultural and economic factors, Yamada (2000) called this group of 20- to 34-year-olds *parasaito shinguru* ("parasite" singles), claiming that they lack independent spirit and are unwilling to work.

Women still encounter pressure from coworkers and bosses to marry, although such pressure is declining (Lieberman, 1999). Yet many men who want to marry cannot find partners because fewer women want to marry and also because women with economic independence are exercising their options. In addition, more than 80% of unmarried women live with their parents, generally with their mothers available to cook for them. When a woman marries, she typically leaves her family for the groom's family, so if she is not marrying, there is no reason to leave her family and forgo its help and comfort. Today, men are more likely than women to view marriage as desirable, for after marriage men remain a part of their families of origin. Among those who do marry, the divorce rate is increasing, and divorce may seem to be a more preferable option for women than for men. When a woman divorces, she comes back to her family of origin, where she again has a place to live, someone to cook for her, and family support. Although parents generally do not encourage divorce, with their divorced daughter returned to the parental home, parents may feel comfortable knowing that as they age she will be there to care for them, whereas if their daughter were still married she would more likely be caring for her spouse's parents. For a married man, it may be harder to make clear choices about divorce. Because a married man would have never left the family home, he has no place to "return."

One factor that can increase the pressure to marry today is an unplanned pregnancy. In the past, a woman was likely to either have an abortion or not discuss it with her male partner so that he was unaware of the pregnancy. It is not clear whether premarital pregnancy rates in the past were specifically related to couples being less sexually active or more careful given that sexual activity did not carry the same level of prohibition as it did in Western countries. Today, with few other pressures to marry and many disincentives for leaving the home of one's parents, pregnancy is one of the few factors that add pressure to marry. A young man and woman may wonder why they should marry when the woman is not pregnant, they both have jobs, and life is already good the way it is.

One area that seems slower to change is the society's discomfort with dating or marriage to non-Japanese (Piper, 1997). In 1965, more than 99% of marriages were among couples where both were Japanese; by 1999, that percentage had declined only slightly to 95% (National Institute of Population and Social Security Research, 2000). Most of those are Japanese husbands with non-Japanese wives. The non-Japanese spouse is most likely to be Korean given that there are many Koreans living in Japan. Other non-Japanese spouses are likely to be Chinese or originally from the United States (National Institute of Population and Social Security Research, 2000). It is difficult for some Japanese to accept the idea of heterogeneity as an acceptable national characteristic. Although acceptability differs in relation to race and ethnicity of the non-Japanese spouse, about 20% of Japanese people openly express discriminatory attitudes toward marriages where one of the partners is a Japanese resident of Korean descent, Burakumin (Japanese from a stigmatized cultural background and area), or non-Japanese (Noguchi, 2002).

With many Japanese women attending universities in other countries, one may wonder about their dating experiences when they return to Japan. In addition, would they face prejudice for having dated non-Japanese men while abroad? A qualitative study of 20 women who had attended universities in the United States before returning to Japan may shed some light on these issues (Murray, Kimura, & Peters, 2000). Respondents were equally divided as to whether they thought dating while they were students in the United States resulted in Japanese men now seeing them as more or less desirable dating partners. Those who thought it made them more desirable indicated that Japanese men thought they were "bicultural," bilingual, and/or more interesting. Those who thought it made them less desirable happened to be more likely to have dated African, African American, or Middle Eastern men while they were in the United States. They also indicated that men thought they were more independent than other women in Japan, that men did not like the idea that they had dated many men in the past, and/or that men were jealous. Many of the women dealt with this issue by not letting Japanese people know who they had dated in the United States. About half of the women indicated that they had dated only Japanese men since they returned, whereas a fourth of the women indicated that they had dated mostly non-Japanese men—typically Anglo-American men. Only 20% of the women said that they had made changes in their behavior, used coping skills, and done something to make themselves more desirable so as to fit in with the dating situation in Japan. All women in the study said that they were experiencing some pressure from their families to marry. This pressure usually came from their mothers but also came from grandparents, siblings, and nieces. Their fathers were not named by any of the women as pressuring them to marry. About a quarter of the women felt substantial pressure from their coworkers. All of those respondents over 28 years of age were currently looking for marriage partners, and many indicated that they had experienced the "marriage drought."

Partner Selection Process

There are four patterns of couple formation in Japan today: love marriage with dating and relationship development (most common), arranged marriage with relationship development through serious dating, arranged marriage with ritualistic relationship development, and arranged marriage without dating or relationship development (least common). The practice of dating became popular during the mid-1960s. Many people think that dating and marriage are quite different; therefore, they distinguish between two types of dating: deto and otsukiai. One can deto casually, pick someone who is fun, and date many people. Marriage is viewed as having more specific purposes and financial security. Therefore, dating with the expectation that it will lead to marriage is primarily a process of getting to know each other in a serious way (otsukiai).

Deto can include going out with friends for fun. Sexual activity is not expected to happen on a first date, but people are not shocked if it does. Typically, an adult is discreet and will not discuss dates openly with family or coworkers if he or she is not in a serious relationship. It may be only the friends with whom the adult spends much time (not necessarily his or her closest friends) who are aware of the dating partner. High school students can have deto without thinking of marriage. This may be the first generation of teens to show affection in public such as kissing on the train; those who are in their 20s or 30s typically do not show such affection in public. It is unclear yet whether this change will carry on into adulthood or whether the teens will stop such public displays as they age, realizing that they are not appreciated by the society.

Japan's leading role in the development of technology has also influenced the dating situation by creating other methods of introducing people.

A growing number of couples first got acquainted through Internet user groups, whose participants share common interests in music, sports, or culture and establish their relationships by e-mail or Web-enabled cell phone contact. Others have been meeting through the more than 550 Web sites for Japanese dating services (the online equivalent to "lonely hearts clubs"). Such dating services have become increasingly popular but have also been used by criminals who rob, rape, or kill their dating partners when they finally meet face-to-face. There are also numerous groups, such as alumni associations of universities and senior high schools, that may arrange introductions of potential marriage partners. Singles also can seek partners through "blind date parties" at nightclubs.

When men or women believe that they are ready to marry (because they are the right age or feel pressure to marry), they quit "dating around" and decide to find someone who is looking for marriage. Japanese people often acknowledge their shyness, and help in locating a partner has often been sought. A man or woman may find that person at work or through coworkers, siblings, or friends by announcing, "I'm thinking of marrying. Do you know someone who is interested?" When friends or others reply that they know someone who is also looking, they may arrange for the man and woman to meet. This meeting then begins with another purpose, that is, the possibility of beginning otsukiai or getting to know each other in a serious way. During this meeting, either partner can decide not to pursue the relationship. One may have many introductions before both partners agree to develop a serious relationship, and there is generally an expectation that there will be some exclusivity before an engagement takes place.

Descriptions of characteristics viewed as common in Japanese culture and communication styles would be expected to be reflected in the "first date" experience of a couple. Thus, authors have speculated that there would be wide differences in the behaviors of men and women (with men being self-directed and women being reactive) as well as less of a verbal orientation, that is, more indirect and hesitant expressions of ideas and feelings. Although there are gender-related differences in that women have a much more developed "schemata" of dating, university students report that there is an active exchange of personal information. Couples use interrogation and self-disclosure as part of uncertainty reduction processes to find a common ground (Nakanishi, 1998).

What do Japanese adults look for in a mate? Are there differences between the attributes that would encourage one to enter into a dating relationship and those that would lead to development and intensification of a relationship? Reports from open-ended questions posed to unmarried university students indicate that they value a combination of traditional

Japanese attributes and some more materialistic characteristics. For males, the major characteristics sought in someone to begin dating (as well as in the ideal mate) were (in descending order) physical attractiveness, good cook, kindness, youth, love, and honesty. For females, these attributes were (in descending order) love, wealth, fun to be with, honesty, sportsman, employment, kindness, and happiness. It is interesting that these students did not perceive marriage as different enough from engagement to list them as separate stages in the couple formation process (Nicotera, 1997). Other studies from the 1980s and 1990s suggest that women have much higher expectations than do men. They seek men who are taller than 5 feet 7 inches, have a high salary and high level of education, will help with child care and housework, will tolerate a wife's career ambitions, and are not the eldest or only child (the latter bring greater responsibilities for taking care of their aging parents or may require the wife to move in with his extended family).

Arranged marriages (formally called *omiai kekkon* or, more commonly, miai), said to account for only 10% to 15% of new marriages today, have moved away from the traditional idea of uniting two families and toward helping two people to find each other. Miai marriages range from a marriage where the parents try to persuade the daughter or son to marry the one they have picked out to a marriage where parents, relatives, and friends of the family just provide introductions to eligible men and women. College students who want to have arranged marriages say that they do not have confidence in love marriages and that they can meet more suitable partners with better qualifications with arranged marriages (Hirano et al., 2000). Typically, an acceptable mate from the proper category of individuals is found within the set of relations that is known to another person in one's family or local network. Appropriateness is defined in terms of *iegara* or *kakushiki* (primarily their family attributes and, to some extent, personal traits) such as level of education, income, occupation, social standing, physical appearance, lineage, reputation, mental health background, and etiquette (Applbaum, 1995, p. 38). This partner can be viewed as a "knowable stranger" such as someone who an aunt, an uncle, or a neighbor may know. Locating this stranger has depended on the use of a go-between who has higher social standing or is older than the couple.

That assistance may come from either a family member or a nakodo. A nakodo is someone with many connections who is well respected and sought after for advice and assistance. In 1990, more than 86% of couples indicated that they used a nakodo; in 1999, only 20% indicated that they used one. The nakodo not only has the responsibility of bringing two acceptable people and their families together but also traditionally plays a role in the engagement party, wedding, and reception in addition to serving as a source of advice during the years following the wedding. Whether a nakodo is used or a relative suggests a suitable partner, photos and biographical statements are exchanged. If each partner is agreeable, there is a meeting of the man and woman and their families for introductions. The meeting usually takes place in a restaurant, hotel, or theater. There is no obligation for either party to agree to get married. Family members of either prospective marriage partner can decide against beginning the relationship by politely indicating that the other party is "too good" for their child. If they feel inclined, the man and woman may start otsukiai dating. It is not uncommon to have 10 to 30 introductions before finding a partner to marry, allowing one to meet many individuals without wasting a lot of time in between. The miai process has become more informal and is sometimes compared to the "blind date" in the United States, although the meetings are arranged by someone of higher status rather than one's peers. Although people often appoint a *tanomare* nakodo who is involved in the wedding rituals, among the young there is some stigma attached to using a nakodo as a matchmaker in the process of choosing a marriage partner.

With urban migration, as well as with social and geographic mobility, it is more difficult today for adults to find desirable marriage partners. In response, a category of professional go-between services has developed, modeled somewhat after the nakodo of the arranged marriage and for the purpose of arranging marriages. Applbaum (1995) called them *puro nakodo* or *pro nakodo*. They generally have not been a part of the couple's or families' networks before these procedures, and they are part of a two-person team (one pro nakodo for each side of the families). Their services are advertised, and they have less to do with the couple after the marriage than does the traditional nakodo.

Engagement

Couples date an average of 6 to 7 months before arranged marriages and an average of 2 years before love marriages. It is usually the man who makes the marriage proposal, but today some women are also proposing. It is not uncommon for a woman who is ready to marry to indicate to her partner that it is time for marriage or that she will begin dating others. With Japan's long history, it is difficult to identify just what is a "traditional" engagement activity. Typically, when the Japanese discuss a traditional practice, it refers to one that is expensive, grand, and similar to those used by many others; nontraditional refers to events that are simple and unique to a specific couple. In 1990, 84% of marrying couples had traditional engagement parties; in 1999, only 39% had these kinds of parties (Maramatsu, 2001); and in 2000, it was estimated that 52% had traditional engagement parties (Abe, 2001). The decrease and fluctuation have been due largely to economic problems in Japan and the desire of couples to have something unique and Western.

A *yuino* or *uinou* is a formal meeting, gathering, or ceremony that makes the engagement official. It is a ritual that came from China around 1700 CE. The families of the prospective bride and groom meet over food and drink, exchange gifts, and celebrate the upcoming union. Customs still differ by region, but generally the man's family brings money in fancy envelopes (averaging $7,000 to $10,000) and asks for permission for the man to marry the woman. They may also bring "good luck" tokens such as abalone (symbolizing the desire for a long life) and kombu seaweed (representing prosperity of future generations). The parents of the woman accept the gifts and agree to the marriage. The man and woman make a promise to marry (*kon'yaku*) and announce it to family, friends, and coworkers. However, the ceremony is often just a formality; all of the decisions are made behind the scenes beforehand. The purpose of the money is to help the woman prepare for the wedding and as compensation for being cut off from her family of origin after the marriage. She often uses the money to buy a dresser and bureau for her clothes and things and for bringing them with her after the wedding when she moves into her husband's family home.

Increasingly, instead of the yuino ceremony, the man gives the woman an engagement ring, a practice borrowed from Western cultures. If a ring is given, it is typically a diamond and, according to Japanese advertisements, should be equal in cost to 3 months of the man's earnings. In return, the woman may give the man a present, usually something like a writing pen.

Formalization of Partner Choice

The preferred time for Japanese weddings is the spring or fall. Traditionally, the *koyomi* (astrological calendar) may be consulted for choosing such special days. Weddings are most often held on a Sunday (a day off from work for most people) or a national holiday, but many young couples today are ignoring these traditionally preferred days. There are four styles of wedding ceremonies currently practiced in Japan. In 2000, approximately 67% of weddings were Western or Christian style, 20% were Shinto style, 10% were "marrying in the presence of people," and less than 2% were Buddhist style. As mentioned earlier, one's personal religion

The Bride and Groom and Their Guests, Including (in front row) Groom's Employer (and his wife) and Couple's Parents

and choice of religious ceremony do not need to be consistent. In addition, many couples are choosing to forgo wedding ceremonies and just file the legal documents themselves. In 2000, 41% of weddings were held at hotels, 26% at wedding ceremony buildings, 9% at churches in Japan, 5% at churches overseas, 3% at public community halls, 3% at Shinto shrines, and 3% at restaurants (Abe, 2001). This is possible because many hotels and wedding halls have church chambers where either Shinto or Christian ceremonies can be held. Japan has two magazines that are devoted to helping couples make decisions in planning their weddings.

Christian or Western weddings are fashionable. They are often conducted at a church, performed by a minister or priest, and include biblical passages that the bride and groom believe add to the atmosphere (although they do not agree with all that is in the Bible). The bride and groom affirm their marriage vows to the guests rather than to God. Buddhist weddings are officiated by a priest, and the bride and groom announce their marriage and make their wedding vows to Buddha. "Marrying in front of people"

Bride and Groom in Traditional Japanese Attire Cutting Wedding Cake

weddings can be conducted at any site but are largely for getting the approval and support of family, friends, and community. Shinto weddings, common until the early 1990s, are held in front of a shrine. Only close family (including aunts, uncles, and grandparents) and the tanomare nakodo attend. The two families face each other, with the couple and the nakodo in the middle. Rituals include the couple drinking *sake* (rice wine) from a bowl passed back and forth and parents also drinking sake. In each of these four types of weddings, the couple may have two tanomare nakodos, a respected married couple (e.g., one's boss and his wife), who may either take an active role as models for the couple or just attend as a matter of formality (to fill the designated seat in the wedding ceremony).

During the ceremony, the bride usually wears a traditional white robe or kimono and headdress (which are usually rented), and the groom usually wears a long black or gray *haorihakama* (a man's formal gown comparable to a woman's kimono). The bride and groom give presents (*hikide-mono*) to those attending the wedding, often chosen individually for each guest. Today, wedding rings are often exchanged and cost approximately $4,000 each. However, these rings are Western traditions. There is no current symbol of marriage that is uniquely Japanese. This lack of a symbol to identify one's marital status is not an important concern because the assumption is that all of the relevant people around a person will already know his or her marital status.

Typically, a wedding is followed by a reception party. This occasion is a chance to celebrate, publicly announce the marriage, and show support for the couple. The newlyweds and their parents greet the guests at the entrance to the reception hall. Guests bring *oshugi* (money in decorative envelopes). When congratulating the couple, they avoid words such as "cut," "separate," and "send back" and instead focus on words related to happiness. The reception begins very formally with the couple's entrance. The nakodos generally give a speech; however, if they feel uncomfortable with public speaking, a hired nakodo specialist can be brought in to give the presentation. A *kanpai* (toast) comes next and signals the start of the banquet, during which the guests can eat, drink, relax, and talk. At this point, the bride will leave the hall for her first *oironaoshi*, that is, a change into a second rented kimono or dress, usually red and white. She may wear a headdress or have her hair tied up in a traditional manner in the *bunkin takashimada* style. This signifies that the bride has returned to the everyday world and is preparing to begin a new life with her husband. The groom does not change clothing during this part of the reception. The bride's change of costume also signals the change from the formal reception to the informal reception. Guests may give congratulatory speeches, do karaoke, and give dance performances. At some point (during either the formal or informal reception), the bride and groom may engage in activities such as cutting the large Western-style wedding cake, symbolizing one of their first acts as a married couple. Guests respond with loud applause, wishing them a long and happy married life. Later, the newlyweds may leave the reception again, with both returning in rented Western-style wedding costumes. They may engage in the shared lighting of candles. During any of these three stages of dress, commemorative photographs of the two families may be taken. Usually the bride and groom (who are not commonly smiling), their two nakodos, and their parents sit in the front row. The bride's family members stand behind her, and the groom's family members stand behind him.

During the wedding and reception, the bride's father often shows his sadness in public, including crying. Fathers in Japan typically spend more time with a daughter than with a son as the child grows up, in anticipation of her marrying and leaving his family. At the close of the reception, the newlyweds may present their parents with bouquets of flowers, including the bride giving one to her father to show her sense of appreciation and the sense of accomplishment that brought her family to this point. At the end of the reception, the groom or his father thanks the guests for attending.

Bride and Groom Conducting Candle-Lighting Ceremony to Show Their Unity After Changing Into Western-Style Wedding Attire

Announcement cards are sent after the wedding with a photo of the newlyweds and other details, including their new address.

After the wedding festivities have ended, the only visible sign that one is married may be a change in a woman's appearance. Some women begin to dress more conservatively, with longer skirts, shorter hair, and lighter makeup. In other words, they do not dress as nicely as before because their husbands may wonder whether they are trying to impress other men. No comparable change in appearance has been noted among men.

A major issue for some couples is the legal requirement that, when they marry, they both must adopt one of their family names and register themselves as a married couple under that same last name. Typically, a woman will join her husband's family, take his name, and care for his parents (especially if he is an oldest or only son). Her name would be removed in the governmental registry from her family of origin and moved to that of her husband's family, showing that her first line of obligation is to his family. However, a wife will probably continue to ask her own mother for help, such as with child care, because she is more comfortable asking for help from her own parents. She also will remain emotionally attached to her parents and will give tangible help to them. Particularly in urban areas, couples are likely to do what feels most comfortable rather than follow customs. Although in some rural areas daughters may provide the primary source of help to their in-laws, in cities not many couples live with the husband's parents. The newlyweds are more likely to have a small apartment nearby, although in some cases parents have built a new house with two separate entrances (one for the young couple and another for the already existing family members).

With family sizes now averaging fewer than two children, an aging population, economic uncertainty, and high real estate prices, daughters may be feeling pressure to preserve their own family names and to care for their own parents. Grooms adopting their wives' family names was an ancient Japanese custom that has faded. Although it is uncommon, some men are living with their wives' families, assuming the burden of caring for their wives' aging parents, and maintaining their wives' family grave sites in exchange for the wives accepting their husbands' names. This compromise situation is more likely when the man has a brother who can help with his own parents, but it still results in competition between the two sets of parents. Legislative changes have been proposed to repeal the family name registry law, but these proposals have been tabled so far in the Diet, the Japanese governing body.

Most of what has been written about dating and couple formation is about women, was written by women researchers who have a liberal point of view, and used samples of university students. At this point, it is unclear whether such writing reflects the ordinary woman's point of view. Take, for example, this issue of women not wanting to change their last names after marriage. Articles have reported stories of individual women, or surveys of cohabiting couples, who indicate that this family name registry law is a major reason why they choose not to marry. However, it is not known whether this law is an issue for ordinary women.

Conclusion

Japanese couple formation may take many forms, each with differing amounts of emphasis on individualization and connectedness to others. Values and practices common in Western countries coexist with those viewed as more traditional. In actuality, the practices are not necessarily just Western but also represent a resurgence of Japanese practices from earlier eras. Whether marriages are arranged or based on romantic love and free choice, they involve complex processes with multiple dimensions that may appear inconsistent from a Western viewpoint. Changes in gender expectations and women's work roles, as well as national social and economic situations, urbanization, and growth of Web-based technology for communication, all have affected relationship development practices and values. As the world continues to evolve, Japan, with its historical and cultural pool of many couple formation practices, will be poised to meet new challenges to relationship development.

References

Abe, T. (2001). *Konyaku to kettsukonn no techou* (Notebook on engagement and marriage). Tokyo: Shougattsukan.

Applbaum, K. D. (1995). Marriage with the proper stranger: Arranged marriage in metropolitan Japan. *Ethnology, 34*, 37–51.

Conover, K. A., & Gaouette, N. (1997, October 15). Giving Cupid a nudge. *Christian Science Monitor*, pp. 1, 6.

Doi, T. (1986). *The anatomy of self: The individual versus society*. New York: Kodansha.

Goldman, N. (1993). Perils of single life in contemporary Japan. *Journal of Marriage and the Family, 55*, 191–204.

Hatfield, E., & Sprecher, S. (1995). Men's and women's preferences in marital partners in the United States, Russia, and Japan. *Journal of Cross-Cultural Psychology, 26*, 728–750.

Hirano, J., Sodei, T., & Kin, K. (2000). Attitude toward marriage and mate selection among Japanese and Korean college students. *Journal of Social Sciences and Family Studies, 7*, 25–39.

Institute of Population Problems. (1994). *Single youths' views on marriage and childbirth* (second report of the 10th basic survey on birth trends, Ministry of Health and Welfare). Tokyo: Public Relations Office.

Iwao, S. (1993). *The Japanese woman: Traditional image and changing reality*. New York: Free Press.

Kaku, K. (1999). *Otoko to onnano monogatari nohonshi* (Men and women's stories in Japanese history). Tokyo: Koudansha.

Kimura, N., & Murray, C. I. (1998). Cultural archetypes of adolescent females in human relationships in teen magazines in Japan and the United States. *Journal of Selected Papers in Asian Studies, 1*, 153–160.

Kitayama, S. (2000). Collective construction of the self and social relationships: A rejoinder and some extensions. *Child Development, 71*, 1143–1146.

Kumagai, F. (1995). Families in Japan: Beliefs and realities. *Journal of Comparative and Family Studies, 18*, 135–163.

Lebra, T. (1994). Self in Japanese culture. In N. Rosenberger (Ed.), *Japanese sense of self* (pp. 105–120). Cambridge, UK: Cambridge University Press.

Lester, D. (1996). The impact of unemployment on marriage and divorce. *Journal of Divorce and Remarriage, 25,* 151–153.

Lieberman, L. (1999, December 31). I want to be a princess: Japanese women in the workplace. *Off Our Backs: A Women's Newsjournal,* p. 13.

Maramatsu, K. (2001). *Endan kara shinseikatu made: Yuinou, kekkon joushiki jiten* (From partner search/marriage proposal to newly married life: Encyclopedia of common sense about engagement and wedding). Tokyo: Shufu no tomo.

Murray, C. I., Kimura, N., & Peters, D. (2000, November). *Japanese women's experiences with dating and marriage desirability after higher education in the United States.* Paper presented at the annual meeting of the National Council on Family Relations, Minneapolis, MN.

Nakanishi, M. (1998). Gender enactment on first date: A Japanese sample. *Women & Language, 21,* 10–17.

National Institute of Population and Social Security Research. (2000). *Population census* (Ministry of Health and Welfare). Tokyo: Public Relations Office.

Nicotera, A. M. (1997). Japan. In A. M. Nicotera, *The mate relationship: Cross-cultural applications of a rules theory* (pp. 77–92). New York: State University of New York Press.

Noguchi, M. (2002). *Kettsukon sabetsu ni eikyou wo ataeru youinn ni tsuite* (Factors that influence marriage discrimination). *Buraku Kaihou Kennkyu, 144,* 14–26.

Notter, D. (2000). Intimacy encoded: The "love marriage" in historical and comparative perspectives. *Kyouiku, shakai, bunnkakenkyuukiyou* (Bulletin of Research on Education, Society, Culture), *7,* 73–95.

Piper, N. (1997). International marriage in Japan: "Race" and "gender" perspectives. *Gender, Place, and Culture, 4,* 321–338.

Prime Minister's Office. (1999). *Opinion survey on social consciousness.* Tokyo: Public Relations Office.

Prime Minister's Office. (1998). *Public opinion survey on issues concerning women.* Tokyo: Public Relations Office.

Raymo, J. M. (1998). Later marriages or fewer? Changes in the marital behavior of Japanese women. *Journal of Marriage and the Family, 60,* 1023–1034.

Rothbaum, F., Pott, M., Azuma, H., Miyake, K., & Weisz, J. (2000). The development of close relationships in Japan and the United States: Paths to symbiotic harmony and generative tension. *Child Development, 71,* 1121–1142.

Sougou joseishi kenkyuukai (General Women's Studies Research Group). (1992). *Nihon josei no rekishi: Sei iai kazoku* (History of Japanese women: Sexuality, love, and family). Tokyo: Tokyo University Press.

Sugiyama, T. (2001). Toukei ni miru kettsukon, rikon, hikon (Statistical data on marriage, divorce, non-marriage). In R. Kohiyama & R. Kokujou (Eds.), *Kettsukon no hikakubunnka* (Cultural comparisons on marriage) (pp. 3–31). Tokyo: Keisou Shoubou.

Takahashi, K., Ohara, N., Antonucci, T. C., & Akiyama, H. (2002). Commonalities and differences in close relationships among the Americans and Japanese: A comparison by the individualism/collectivism concept. *International Journal of Behavioral Development, 26,* 453–465.

Takeishi, E. (1998). Gendai ni okeru kettsukon no imi (Meaning of today's marriage). *Nissei Basic Research Report, 17,* 19–24.

Yamada, M. (1999). *Parasaito shinguru no jidai* (The age of "parasite" singles). Tokyo: Chikuma Shinsho.

Yamada, M. (2000). Kekkon no genzaiteki imi (Current meaning of marriage). In K. Yoshizumi (Ed.), *Kekkon to paatonaa kankei* (Marriage and partner relationships) (pp. 56–80). Kyoto, Japan: Mimreruvashhobou.

Yamazaki, M. (1994). *Individualism and the Japanese: An alternative approach to cultural comparison.* Tokyo: Japan Echo.

Yoshizumi, K. (1994). The presence of nonmarital couples. *Municipal Problems, 85*(8), 23–37.

Author Index

Subject Index

About the Editors

Raeann R. Hamon is Professor of Family Science and Gerontology in the Department of Human Development and Family Science at Messiah College. She currently holds one of two Scholar Chair Awards at Messiah College. She received her Ph.D. in family and child development and her graduate certificate in gerontology from Virginia Polytechnic Institute and State University. She has numerous publications and presentations on topics such as filial responsibility, family relationships during later life, parents' experience of adult children's divorce, intergenerational service learning, Bahamian folklore, and Bahamian family life. A certified family life educator, she is an enthusiastic teacher of courses such as Marital Relationships, Dynamics of Family Interaction, Sociology of Aging, and Foundations of Marriage and Family. She is currently president of the Association of Councils and is a member of the executive board of the National Council on Family Relations, where she is also an active member in the International section.

Bron B. Ingoldsby is Associate Professor in the School of Family Life at Brigham Young University. He received his Ph.D. in child and family development from the University of Georgia. A leader in the area of cross-cultural family research, he is the author of numerous professional publications, including (with Suzanna Smith) *Families in Multicultural Perspective*. His current work focuses on family change among the Hutterian Brethren and marriage in Latin America. He is a popular teacher of courses such as Marriage Preparation, Family Theories, and Family and Culture. He was honored as the 2002 recipient of the Jan Trost Award for Outstanding Contributions to Comparative Family Studies by the National Council on Family Relations (NCFR). He has served twice on the NCFR board as the chair of the International and Religion sections.

About the Contributors

Nuran Hortaçsu is Professor of Psychology at the Middle East Technical University, Ankara, Turkey. She received her Ph.D. in psychology from the University of Massachusetts, Amherst, in 1973. Her research interests include family, interpersonal relationships, culture and relationships, intergroup relations, and developmental social cognition.

Naoko Kimura is a doctoral candidate in counseling and educational psychology at the University of Nevada, Reno. Her academic emphasis is on multicultural counseling and college student development. Her research interests include using relational-cultural models in the study of international adolescents, college students, and women. She holds an M.S. in human development and family studies from the University of Nevada, Reno.

Nilufer P. Medora is Professor of Family Studies in the Department of Family and Consumer Sciences at California State University, Long Beach. She has a master's degree in life span human development and family studies from Maharaja Sayajirao University, Baroda, India. She also has a master's degree in child development and family studies from the University of Arkansas, Fayetteville, and a Ph.D. in family studies from the University of Nebraska, Lincoln. She teaches a variety of courses in family studies, including Family and Personal Development, Family Life Education, Child and Family in the Community, and International Families: Families in Cross-Cultural Perspectives. She is also the coordinator of the Family Life Education certificate program. Her research expertise and interests are in the areas of cross-cultural studies, criteria for mate selection, attitudes toward love and romanticism, family strengths, and teenage pregnancy.

Colleen I. Murray is Associate Professor of Human Development and Family Studies and the Interdisciplinary Ph.D. Program in Social Psychology at the University of Nevada, Reno. Her research interests focus on adolescent women's relationships and development within the context of the social construction of meaning across cultures, grief and families (including media reporting across cultures of mass tragedies involving children or adolescents), and theoretical and methodological issues in the study of families. In addition to teaching courses on theory, methods, and relationships, she has developed Web-based courses in the areas of adolescent development, grief, and loss. She received her Ph.D. from the Ohio State University.

Lucy W. Ngige is Senior Lecturer and Chair of the Department of Family and Consumer Sciences at Kenyatta University, Nairobi, Kenya. She holds M.A. and Ph.D. degrees in family and child ecology from Michigan State University. She also has taught at Manchester Metropolitan University, Manchester, United Kingdom. She has served as UNICEF research consultant for early childhood, women, and family development in Kenya and Sudan; as national vice chairperson of the Child Welfare Society of Kenya; as national treasurer of the Kenya Home Economics Association; and as a member of the Home Economics Association for Africa.

J. Roberto Reyes is Associate Professor of Family Science and Director of the Latino Partnership Program at Messiah College. Prior to his move to Pennsylvania in 1996, he resided in Southern California, where he taught part-time at Azusa Pacific University and worked as coordinator of mental health services for the Family Preservation Program at Foothill Community Mental Health Center. He received his Ph.D. in marital and family studies (1995) and master of divinity in marital and family ministries (1992) from Fuller Theological Seminary. He is a certified family life educator with the National Council on Family Relations and a clinical member of the American Association of Marriage and Family Therapy. With extensive clinical experience working with Latino families, he has also conducted parenting education classes for both Latino immigrant parents and their adolescents. He is originally from San Juan, Puerto Rico.

Shulamit N. Ritblatt is Associate Professor in the Department of Child and Family Development at San Diego State University. She received her Ph.D. in family relations and child development from Florida State University in 1993. Her work experience ranges from working with families and children from diverse cultural backgrounds in educational settings, psychotherapy, and interventions programs to teaching a wide range of undergraduate and graduate classes. Her research focuses on parent-child interactions across the life span, images of elderly and grandparents in children's literature (cross-cultural comparison), theory of mind and emotional development in young children, transitions, and the home-school relationship.

Paul L. Schvaneveldt is Assistant Professor in the Department of Child and Family Studies at Weber State University. He completed his Ph.D. in human development and family studies at the University of North Carolina at Greensboro in 1999. His research focuses on Latin American families and youth. He has served as executive director of the Idaho/Ecuador Partners of the Americas.

Winston Seegobin is Associate Professor of Psychology at Messiah College, where he is also a psychotherapist with students of color and international students at the Messiah College Counseling Center. He has a Psy.D. in clinical psychology from Central Michigan University. He is a member of the American Psychological Association. A national of Trinidad and Tobago, he has written and presented on marriage and is currently conducting research on legal and common law marriages in Trinidad and Tobago.

Bahira Sherif-Trask is Associate Professor of Individual and Family Studies at the University of Delaware. She received her undergraduate degree in political science from Yale University and her Ph.D. in cultural anthropology from the University of Pennsylvania. Her research centers around the intersection of work and gender in ethnically diverse and international families.

Baffour K. Takyi is Assistant Professor of Sociology at the University of Akron. Originally from Ghana, he obtained his B.A. from the University of Ghana, Legon, and his M.A. and Ph.D. from the University at Albany, State University of New York. His research interests include household and family processes in Africa, reproductive health behavior, and African immigrants.

Kristen M. Tarquin is a graduate student in the doctoral program in counseling psychology at the University of Buffalo. She is currently working as a graduate assistant in the Department of Counseling and Educational Psychology.

Linda J. Trollinger is a doctoral student and research assistant in the Department of Family Studies at the University of Kentucky. Her research focuses on family dynamics within Appalachian, Kenyan, and Native American families. Her work emphasizes informal family support, couple formation, social and cultural competency, and elder life experiences.

Manfred H. M. van Dulmen is Research Associate and Instructor in the Institute of Child Development at the University of Minnesota. He received his M.A. degree in clinical child and adolescent psychology from the Free

University of Amsterdam and his Ph.D. in family social science from the University of Minnesota. His current research interests include the investigation of individual and relationship processes underlying the development of adaptive social behavior during adolescence and young adulthood, integrating cross-cultural perspectives on social development.

Stephan M. Wilson is Professor and Chair of the Department of Human Development and Family Studies at the University of Nevada, Reno. His general areas of research and scholarly expertise are adolescent development within the context of families and parent-child relationships. He has examined family contributors to adolescent social competence, autonomy and conformity to parents by adolescents, the status attainment of adolescents and young adults, and family influences on young adult outcomes (e.g., relationship development, marriage readiness) among youth and families in the United States, China, and Kenya. He received his Ph.D. from the University of Tennessee, Knoxville.

Yan R. Xia is Assistant Professor of the Department of Family and Consumer Sciences at the University of Nebraska–Lincoln. Prior to that, she worked at the Girls and Boys Town National Research Institute for Children and Family Studies. A Chinese native, she received her master's degree in marriage and family therapy and her Ph.D. in family science at the University of Nebraska–Lincoln. Her current research focuses on immigrant youth and parents, substance abuse issues, and Chinese marriage and family.

Zhi G. Zhou is Honorary Professor of Hebei University, Baoding, China, and is currently working as a senior statistician for First Data Resources. He earned a B.A. in English at Hebei University and an M.A. in English at Jinan University, Guangdong, China. He went to the University of Nebraska–Lincoln to study family sciences in 1993 and got his Ph.D. in 2000. His research interest has been in early childhood education.